CIVICS, DYNAMICS, & THE MIND

THE COMPLETE SOCIAL PSYCHOLOGY
WRITINGS OF ARLAND DEYETT WEEKS

Compiled and Edited by Ken Lefebvre

CINCINNATI

IMPRIMERIE VILLE DE PAPIER

2021

ISBN 978-1-7370610-3-8

Library of Congress Control Number
2021920215

Printed in the United States of America.
October 2021
First Edition

INTRODUCTION

In the last century, technocracy has assumed many forms in our daily lives. A century ago, a college dean, Arland Deyett Weeks, described many of the mechanisms that would come to determine concepts like "nudge theory" and "libertarian paternalism" in the 21st century. While finding these writings prescient, I do find myself disagreeing with Weeks's outlook, that they were tools for social betterment, rather than too often tactics for enslavement. Particularly of note, his notion of progress behind the suppression of "archaic ideas", as he describes them, is eerily cold and calls to mind the ideas of the "Cultural Revolution", and the social media-driven consumerist-capitalism we see reshaping our society today. However, the verities written in these works offer the opportunity as well to identify the weaponization of the human psyche in civic discourse in the past century, often by moneyed interests.

Such statements, laid bare still offer wisdom in the age where social media has succeeded the arenas of old. Though he describes himself as a conservative in other passages, Weeks is not averse to the pooling of capital internationally. He is a starry-eyed internationalist, stating at one point that the "world is my country". He spends great time discussing the minutia of national civics, but neglected the social mechanisms that would balance any authority of global proportions. In *Social Antagonisms* Weeks describes the psychology of social engineering and discusses how governments may appease the needs of man. However in this modern age, in "appeasing" them, I would argue we have in some circles extinguished our discontent in a stupor that does not remove desire, but coddles and cultivates it in the basest sense. Such instant gratification of creature comforts is contemporary with the later definition given to it by Huxley in his works.

Other key observations portend modern heuristic control methods, such as one passage in *The Control of the Social Mind* where Weeks discusses the notion that, when "a person is told not to do a thing, he is given a suggestion of doing it coupled with a suggestion of not doing it... It is better to say, 'Sit up straight,' than to say 'Do not sit bent over.'" Such psychological imprinting can be seen in advertising from the mid-20th century through today, and recalls to mind a specific ad campaign for children in the United Kingdom that once used the dubious slogan— "Never say yes to a cigarette."

Form your own opinions about the outlook that Professor Weeks offers. If you watch modern media closely today after reading this book, you too might notice some of the principles he describes here being used in real time. Whether that is to our benefit as a society or its detriment, I leave to you, dear reader.

Ken Lefebvre
September 5, 2021

TABLE OF CONTENTS

Books

The Control of the Social Mind (1923)
Part I

Part II

Articles

Index

The Psychology of Citizenship

ORIGINALLY EDITED BY
Dr. Frank L. McVey, LL.D.
President of the University of North Dakota

FIRST PUBLISHED IN 1917
BY A.C. McCLURG & CO. OF CHICAGO
AS PART OF "THE NATIONAL SOCIAL
SCIENCE SERIES"

CHAPTER I
CIVIC DEMANDS UPON INTELLIGENCE

O NE of the most used words is "problem." There are the problems of city government, of taxation, of immigration, of pure food, of education, of the liquor traffic, of the judiciary, of direct legislation, and many others. Modern civilization presents a snarl of problems.

1. Social Problems Complex

There must have been plenty of problems of old, but people did not always define them. Many issues have been hatched by modern conditions, such as changes in industry and transportation and growth of population. Moreover, with greater general enlightenment society has become self-conscious, for intelligence has a revealing power. The discovery is made that social relationships are not all they should be, and reform is undertaken.

Making the world over is new business and difficult. We can scarcely say that people are prepared for it, for a large part of the development of society has heretofore been as free from foresight and conscious direction as has the evolution of the society of bees and beavers. Much of our present order has been brought about by mere force of circumstances, by an impromptu unwinding of events which men have barely understood, let alone directed. There has been little anticipation of social outcomes or attempt to substitute planning in place of evolution. Society has arrived at its present organization largely without knowing why or electing aims; it has gone forward in some such way as the individual grows up, his vital processes taking place in the absence of intention or understanding.

14

But this is changing. Society consciously seeks social ends as truly as the individual seeks personal ends. Conditions have so changed that the individual, in order to get what he wants, must combine his efforts with those of others. A revolution in economic, industrial, and commercial relationships compels the individual to make common cause with others, leads him to look at life from a social viewpoint, and causes social questions to demand the expenditure of more and more mental energy.

The social machine is complex. Physical force will not operate it. The man who got along in the twelfth century by using his fists now has to use his head. Thought rules, and it is only by study that social ideals may be realized or that individuals or groups may protect themselves in a noiseless warfare in which the most dangerous enemies and devouring opponents may be as invisible as germs.

To accomplish ends through social machinery is a real intellectual feat. Political and social science as a branch of learning is not easy to grasp. There is perhaps no kind of subject-matter which taxes the mind more severely. A high degree of culture is required to enable one to understand the movements and issues of the times. The intellectual requirements for capable citizenship, for ideal citizenship, are exacting.

Now the mind which is available for the conscious direction of society was shaped under a different set of conditions from those prevailing in the modern world. Hence we find individuals who would be highly effective in a physical struggle or in contesting with nature for subsistence but who are at a loss in an environment so new to the race. Everywhere there is evidence of a bewilderment. There is little agreement among specialists in political science. Social engineering tests the capabilities of the human intellect. A singular confession of weakness is that represented by the action of the Senate at Washington in voting to reject the annual contribution of $250,000 from the Rockefeller General Education Board, which had been used for farm demonstration work and the extermination of the boll weevil. A senator declared that the money was covered with "the blood of women and children shot down in the Colorado strike." This incident brings out in strong relief the shortcomings of legislation, for it should have been possible long ago to curtail centralized wealth to which such abuses are ascribed. Legislators appear strangely limp in dealing with conditions whose evil results are denounced on every hand. Of thirty-two acts of parliament, Herbert Spencer found that twenty-nine produced effects opposite from those intended. The utterly diverse views of public men indicate that social administration is a problem outtopping the average of ability.

2. Limits of Reasoning Ability

In the last analysis the reasoning capacity of the individual is called in question. Ours is not a race of supermen, and mental limitations enhance the difficulty of making headway. Consider the fact that we have to "study" to understand. If a novice could sit down with Euclid and in an evening know geometry! It takes weeks and months of painful concentration to master a branch of learning represented by books which could be read through in a few days, so narrow is the gateway to understanding. Man is a reasoning animal, so it is said, though in discussions regarding the power of animals to reason some scientists hold that not only do animals not reason but that very few human beings reason. Men reason not from choice but from necessity. Reasoning occurs when a situation cannot be successfully dealt with in some other way, as by imitation, habit, or memory, or by getting someone else to do it. But oftentimes the pinch of a situation, instead of evoking reasoning, will call forth a futile deluge of emotion, and the citizen will swear. We hate to think; we avoid it if possible; we think only under pressure, and not always then.

The reasoning faculty in its fulness develops late in the individual, and on the other hand may disintegrate in the closing years of life; it is first to be disturbed by alcohol, sickness, or fatigue. The freshest hours of the day are required for work that involves the nice balance of logic. We hesitate to attack problems, and gladly defer consideration to the next day of those matters that call for vigor of thought. Frequently people will exhaust every means of dealing with a difficulty except that of reasoning, and persistently try to flank a situation that might be resolved by direct mental exertion. The tendency is to rely upon the lower mental processes.

Concepts and principles, with which reason deals, are products for which the mind has less affinity than for objects. The vastly greater appeal of the objective is attested by a thousand evidences. The concrete is popular, while the abstract is synonymous with dryness and difficulty. A speculative exposition or a dissertation on principles repels all but a few, while satiating and repetitious concreteness attracts a multitude. But it is the concept and the principle that are of chief significance, for they represent meanings. Thinkers are characterized by grip of abstractions and the ability to pursue a generalization, undisturbed by the swollen floods of concreteness. In reasoning, meanings rather than images engage consciousness and for it Plato held that but few were fitted by nature.

3. Civic Issues Require Imagination

A good imagination is the basis of reasoning and a trait of infinite significance for social betterment. But what of its prevalence? The mere restoration of a past experience is common enough; vivid recollection of something actually experienced is indeed characteristic of children, and "narrative old age" employs the almost photographic images of earlier years, but a constructive, original, penetrating, and interpreting turn of mind is a different matter. Otherwise it would not take a third of a century to secure even partial realization of the trust issue or of the meaning of watered stock.

Many evidences of the failure to see the significance of facts will occur to one: the young married woman who laughs at the spectacle of a drunken man on the street; the teacher who uses uncomplainingly a textbook containing a picture of a rooster on a cannon; the working-class mother who is pleased when her son joins the national guard; the farmer who does not distinguish between his labor income and the income derived from his money investment, who "buys a job"; or the young English woman who expects to tour the United States in three days, not thinking it so "frightfully large." And is it not usually the case that one is much more concerned about the loss of a shirt stud than of a hundred dollars abstracted from the family income by invisible but real tentacles?

The absence of ideal conditions is little noted if the familiar is found in place. If the man lower down had the gift of vision would there not be new chapters in history? Here and there are those who image the advantages of other status or penetrate mentally into the monstrous mushroomism of privilege or follow with the mind's eye the play of social and economic forces, but can it be assumed that actual realization

of harmful conditions is at all usual? Is not invisible evil
effectually protected by lack of vision? It is still vastly more
heinous, because more objective, to steal a horse than to steal
a franchise. The fact that the mind tends to adhere to objects
of direct acquaintance, making a little world out of the
materials within the sweep of the eye and less frequently
rising to a stage from which the larger world may be
surveyed, is fateful with reference to the rational ordering of a
better civilization. Constituents are proudly triumphant when
their representatives force through a bill compelling railroads
to bulletin the time of arrival and departure of trains, but are
not particularly curious as to the relation of freight rates to
the cost of living; women highly, if not well, educated oppose
suffrage from inability to represent to themselves the various
situations in which a voter's power affects their interests;
politicians find that temporizing often wins over
statesmanship; omission and inefficiency make far less
impression than the unimportant overt act ; a scientific
management and the avoidance of waste are long delayed.
Ever the tangible reality of the moment rather than the
greater reality of the ideal moves men.

4. Study of Civic Problems Necessary

Indisposition to think and the circumscribed field of
imagination are significant, for in social administration the
power of generalization and logical sequence is much
engaged. The usual sciences are actually more simple than
the knowledge with which the voter, ballot in hand, is
presumed to be acquainted, the science and philosophy of
society. In fact the belated development of sociology and
allied subjects may be taken to mean that social phenomena
are reduced to system only with unusual difficulty.
Anthropology, social psychology, civic theory, and economics

deal with elusive and thought-taxing materials. Governmental issues cannot be wisely dealt with on the spur of the moment.

To know the nature of the task of imposing intelligence upon the social order is to recognize the need of I a more intensive study than is common. Serious discussion, one subject by this group, club, or coterie, and another topic by others, is needed, each to arrive at a degree of expertness, each to contribute to a common fund of thought? The absence of insistent inquiry and discussion among the people is a source of political weakness, for men elected to office reflect the common attitude and are circumscribed by prevailing conditions of insight and interest. The average voter needs to be convinced that unless he studies issues he will be unprepared to deal with them; he needs to study his lesson. Government is a matter requiring downright application on the part of citizens. Political questions must be framed for discussion, terms defined, and time devoted to the study of principles. Civic welfare cannot be achieved with a general avoidance of strenuous mental effort, and with a spatter of attention and a lust for amusement to fill every free hour.

The faulty management of public business raises a question in some minds as to the possibility of successful collective enterprise. It is doubted whether the people are capable of sustaining consciously a far higher social organization. When one tyranny is overthrown, it is argued, another will rise in its place. There is implied in many quarters the view that the people collectively are inadequate for perfect self-government and for achieving a genuine community welfare. "Things will not be any better than they were before" is the melancholy comment on programs of reform.

5. New Type of Education for Citizenship

The answer is education, an education that centers on thinking. And as one cannot think unless he has materials with which to think, it is important that there be provided specific thought-materials bearing upon the evolution of the state. There is need of a subject-matter compounded of biological, historical, scientific, and evolutionary data the upshot of which would be a grasp of underlying social principles. More need an acquaintance with the kind of material found, for example, in the works of Spencer, John Fiske, David Starr Jordan, Metchnikoff, Haeckel, Karl Marx, Darwin, Alfred Russel Wallace, Henry George, Lester F. Ward, and Prince Kropotkin.

The culture required for social ends receives too little attention, owing in part to the prevailing enthusiasm for training for salaried employments. As a result there are engineers and chemical experts who are not interested in politics. Technological preparation is often a mechanizing process which in adapting for a necessary function widely deflects consciousness from social issues.

Nor is the student of ancient history and literature, of the time-honored classics, necessarily well equipped for the coming nation. He possesses, indeed, the advantage of contact with the best minds of the past; he has associated, not with groundlings and slaves, but with masters Caesar, Xenophon, Marcus Aurelius. A certain aristocracy of associations is thus established, and it is not to be wondered at that the early American clergyman, lawyer, and public man approached life from a high plane and carried a dignity derived from the stately and poised spirit of classical letters, essays, and orations.

Horace and Cicero were good consumers, and slavishness did not infect the underfed and impecunious student of early Dartmouth or Amherst. Fresh from the uppercaste associations of Virgil or Lysias, the early American college student was keyed high and was notably rich in historical ideals, though perhaps walking the streets of cities in poverty without the collateral of skill.

But the very fascinations of the classics lead to a certain disqualification; the view is backward, and the enthusiasm of youth becomes attached to a gloried past. And the mind nourished on prescientific literature cannot take quick offense against pseudo-science. Not that the Apollo myth or the prowess of Beowulf are really credited, but there exists a haze not conducive to realism. The classical scholar tends to be but partially scientific, from the permeating influence of ancient misconceptions. The need of instruction actually clarifying mental processes even the need of educating the educated may be inferred from the fact that "sucker lists" are compiled from college catalogs.[1]

---

[1] The following clipping from the *Chicago Record-Herald*, of February 11, 1913, speaks for itself:

"SUCKERS" ALL COLLEGE MEN
Hawthorne Case Witness Tells Where He Got 700,000 Names

NEW YORK, February 10 — The so-called "sucker list" of mining companies promoted by Julian Hawthorn, Josiah Quincy, Albert Freeman, and Dr. William J. Morton, who are on trial for alleged fraudulent use of the mails, was compiled from 400 college catalogues and contained 700,000 names.

Freeman so testified today under cross-examination by government counsel. He identified a check for $20,000.00 as one of his own and said it was drawn to cover the expense of making the list of names of persons to whom literature was sent.

Testifying as to the cost of printing circular letters sent out, Freeman said: "I did not care how much I paid if the letter was perfect. But the trouble was to get the different names put into the letters in such a way as to make those who received them think they were personal letters from Hawthorne and not mere circulars. I sent out fully 700,000 of those letters."

A type of education which would avoid the dubious qualities in classical subject-matter and the isolating and mechanizing effects of occupational instruction is needed. The ideal society cannot be formed of men whose interests are no wider than money-making, nor of men whose instruction has incorporated into their outlook a mythological squint which exposes them to the patent medicine vendor or causes them to look upon nations as big personalities, rather than, as Chancellor Jordan remarks, jurisdictions. What tendencies to exaggerate, to hope unduly, to misread evidence, to exalt intuition, to obtrude emotions, to idealize animals, and to personify property or cities are not bound up with an intellectual nurture based on the age of fable! When the small boy says that the luck has gone out of a trinket which he carries about with him, and when in a single day in Chicago 25,000 people gather about a miraculous shin bone, the need of intellectual reorganization is evident.

Clarifying and disillusioning instruction is needed with regard to social organization. Undue veneration for constitutions implies a misguided study of history; for the men who framed constitutions, so far as not merely responsive to special interests, were attempting no more than the people of today attempt in dealing to the best of ability with the problems of the hour, and that any particular authority attended the deliberations of early publicists, in excess of that attributable to the latest session of a legislature, is no more credible than that the impressions of today should be imposed on the public of a century hence.

The educational system suffers an underdevelopment, for it is responsive rather than dominating. Institutions of learning tend to conform rather than to form, and the seal of approval is placed on unregenerate ambitions and the ethics of disorderly competition. Young men who should be in a spiritual kindergarten, whose conversations are crude and gossipy, and whose reactions to quality are wonderingly skeptical, are released at graduation certificated if not refined. The vices of the street— "clamorous, insincere advertisement, push, and adulteration"— may possess the graduate as well as the entrant, and the aim of a department may be colored to the purpose of the crafty student who would equip himself to make "a heap of money" by overcapitalizing electric-lighting plants in small towns which should be taught how to manage their own public utilities.

Within the total body of knowledge there exists an enormous quantity of material which is inert or irrelevant. It is a serious dissipation of energy that youth should devote years to a relatively inconsequential learning. The good general repute of knowledge has thrown the mantle of approval over types of learning which, considered from the point of view of a dynamic society, represent a deadening load upon the factors making for progress. Often one hears it said that a given person or a certain class is "well educated," there being no distinction made between highly educated and well educated; whereas there is all the difference in the world between the two conditions. Many great scholars have been very highly, and at the same time very poorly, educated, when regard is had to mental content. Certainly no very extensive improvement in brain capacity has occurred since the Middle Ages or the days of Diocletian, and whatever of human weal has been achieved for the present as against former periods is to be referred to mental content rather than to increase of brain cells and spread of cortex. Too much emphasis can hardly be placed upon the actual character of the information which society permits to circulate or deliberately diffuses through agencies under state control. The substitution of valid materials for those not meeting the most searching tests of value must occupy the foreground of effort for social betterment.

If there is a wide range of values in real knowledge,

how significant becomes the toleration of pseudo-science. Error obtains widely, and indeed a certain conventional respectability attaches to quantities of traditional material which any scientist knows could not bear scrutiny. Much of this is so knit up with emotion that scholars plow around it rather than risk the consequences which a too fearless opposition would entail. Hence it is that verified knowledge and pseudoscience may achieve a considerable circulation in the same community, the one to a degree undoing the work of the other, but with no joining of issue and thorough enlightenment. There is an immense circulation of worthless reading matter, ranging from dream-books and drugstore almanacs to pulpy fiction. The church would do well to inspect closely the materials which are placed before millions, often as their almost sole mental food, and should not be unaware of the possibility of benumbing intelligence by forever dealing with points of doctrine or the minutiae of Jewish history. One may listen attentively yet unprofitably.

The practice of systematically misinforming children cannot be too strongly condemned. Parents allow their children to be taught matter known to be misleading. The presentation of myths and attractive falsifications befogs the child's mind and contributes to the permanence of a public expecting to meet with the fountain of youth in the decoction sold for "a dollar a bottle." The strange case of mythology and actual science in the same mind may be due to the duplicity of the make-believe literature on which children are nourished far into the age of reasoning.

A great gain will have been made when there is a more general realization of the importance of building up an effective civic mind. The social outcomes of various types of cultural material and of training deserve consideration. Especially is it important that there should be convictions regarding the scientific character of social questions. A function logically requiring the highest devotion and insight— government— is too often given over to men who are not grounded in appropriate learning, and the citizen himself too often lightly dismisses civic obligations which should set him to burning midnight oil.

CHAPTER II
SOCIAL INERTIA

PROGRESSIVE movements are held severely in check by habits and customs. As one grows older he becomes, unless under unusual conditions, firmly set in feelings and views. Habits tend to grow into the very constitution, and represent a force whose power is experienced whenever a new idea is introduced in the world. Repetition of movements and of thoughts results in fixed arrangements of the brain cells. The grooves of thought become deeply worn, and the mind comes at last to resemble in definiteness of character and permanence of structure the physical body which supports it. It is the exceptional person who keeps green at the top, and who remains in sympathy with dynamic phases of society.

1. Environment Affects Views

The paths of thought are greatly influenced by one's surroundings. Not without cause do we wish to know where the individual came from, who his parents were, where he went to school, and what his occupation is, and our curiosity extends to his wife and children. The ethical atmosphere which one has known, combining elements from many sources, essentially determines interests, outlook, and opinions. The individual is to a great extent a composite of the ideas which environment has forced upon his attention. Differences in native ability are apparently less determinative than those resulting from the complex of suggestions associated with one's place of residence, acquaintanceship, and social contacts. The to us strangely inverted views and practices of alien peoples, ancient or modern, are none other than we ourselves, transferred to other environment, would have approved. The culture materials of the Kentucky mountains and those of a northern city are respectively instrumental in creating most diverse types. One cannot escape the pressure of environment. Even the greatest minds are a reflex of their age, sharing in contemporary attitudes and errors: Pascal believed in French miracles and Sir Matthew Hale in witches.

Especially do first impressions last. The importance of a fifty-cent jackknife to a boy sinks deep into the emotional nature, and men of means will flinch at the expense of a new pocketknife in unconscious revival of emotions of childhood. Stamped with the forms of religion, language, or manners, as a child, one can never be fully freed from either their good or bad features. The Negro who was invited to sit with his white employer at a dinner in the South, but at the table trembled with fear, gave evidence that legal emancipation did not carry with it emancipation from the psychology of slavery. Pronounced radicals exhibit on occasion the awe which undemocratic centuries have bred into the emotional life. One brought up to refrain from gladness on Sunday may convince himself of the acceptability of tennis on that day, but may experience difficulty in bringing his feelings into accord. Not readily do sentiments and prejudices, reverences and submissions disappear. How rare it is for a community to change its feelings to correspond with the development of one of its gifted sons or daughters; hence a prophet is given scant honor at home. For which reason discerning youths go to new parts where there is exemption from the levity of reminiscence.

2. Habit and Custom

The persistence of habit and the inertia of custom are everywhere to be discerned. Sudden transformations are rare. Though terms change, realities abide, as witness pagan gods succeeded by saints as numerous, feudalism transferred to industry, and the fetishism of the elk tooth. Writing of the Incas, James Bryce notes that the Spaniards abolished human sacrifices— and burned heretics.

Without special efforts to change habits, or the supplying of conditions which enforce new ways, the probability of considerable changes in social orderings is slight. People will go on in the same old ways, and it is the next generation that is the principal hope of those who strive for change. Laws influence society but slowly; they are rather the reflex of states of mind than actually agencies of social transformation, and it is to educative factors that attention should especially be given in reform. A weakness of the older socialism was its disregard of the persistence of habit, showing in the ten thousand enmeshing sentiments of the static multitude. Writers still imply the possibility of a sudden redirection suggestive of the "conversion" of the religious revival, which itself is far from being a comprehensive change. Inertia is an outstanding trait of primitive peoples, whose characteristics obtain in no small portion of modern society, and a trait, as well, to be reckoned with in individuals more advanced.

The threat of revolution can never be more than partly executed, for in the greater number of relations the individual will continue to be as he was before. Those who have been servile will continue to be servile. Under the older system of family discipline the youth looked forward to becoming of age, only to find when he arrived at that time that both docility and authority persisted. In fact, the only social revolution which seems possible in view of the tenacity of habit is one which slowly proceeds under the pressure of conditions and is directed by strong leadership. There was never yet a revolution or emancipation which was true to the full vigor of the term. For sharp social advances, shock and surprise and the dislocation of environment are required. If psychology has a message for progress it is that efforts must be focused upon the disorganization of old and, in turn, the establishment of new habits.

Actual contentment under unfair conditions may exist through the spell of environment. One becomes so used to things as they are that the prospect of change is unpleasant. The farmer's mortgage becomes part of his cosmos. Conditions which would appear most singular from a fresh point of view come under the principle of habituation and scarcely attract attention. Improvement means change and confusion, the rupture of accustomed ways and adjustment to a new order, and it is bewildering to face new conditions, even if theoretically better; hence the inevitable reaction which follows a mood of reform and the slight immediate response made by the mass of mankind to idealistic appeals. Privilege and exploitation, parasitism and humbug, are relatively safe when rooted in the old order. To look at such in a new light would be their extermination, but it is not usual to look at things in a new light.

3. Servile Emotions

A popular weakness is susceptibility to undemocratic emotional attitudes. It is a well-known fact that one's reason and emotions may not agree perfectly, and that feelings are likely to be the deciding factor. Our feelings have been gathering force since early childhood, while our arguments may be of recent acquisition. A substantial fund of emotion comes down to us by tradition from far absolutist regimes; we are early infiltrated with archaic sentiments from a thousand points of cultural contact. As a result democratic attitudes are less prevalent than democratic opinions.

"And your petitioners will forever pray..." these words appearing at the close of a legal paper are redolent of history. While phrases of courtesy have a place not to be lightly surrendered, this form points to a former social order in which power did not flow from the people to officials but on the contrary favors were from the rulers "vouchsafed unto us." The awe which does hedge about "his honor" is perhaps not so much an expression of respect for the law— for laws are abstractions— nor deference to one's self, the voter who elects judges and builds courthouses, but more likely a mood which comes to us by relayed example from the days when civic humility worshiped at the feet of kings. We believe that our officials derive their powers from the consent of the governed—help thou our unbelief! For while we believe we may yet feel otherwise. One dictates to a stenographer a letter to his servant, the congressman, and finds that the dictated formal close, "Yours very truly," has come under the pervasive influence of inherited deference to office and reads instead "Very respectfully," which is indeed better than "Your obedient servant." Of course it is the congressman who should address the voter, by whose consent he exists, with the prostration of phrase which creeps into the voter's letter to him. Men of toil come upon the campus of a state university, their institution by right of taxes, hat in hand, instead of in the consciousness of owning the place. Truly, for lack of what meat does the citizen remain so small!

The timidity of the public in pressing claims against corporations seems to be founded on traditions of servility. It seems almost like interfering with the course of the planets to compel a railroad company to stop a long train at a mere county seat, and when a citizen tells the president of the road a few human facts staid residents get their heads together in a certain consternation. Walt Whitman in a memorable poem justifies man to the bigness of material things, like great machinery and buildings, trampling them under foot of a forced accession of self-respect. But it requires no little temerity to lay the ghost of mere bigness, and the lowly spirit of the peasant uncovered before authority still lives to a degree.

Yet men desire to be as good as other men— or a little better— and if defeated and humbled by others' huge success, resort may be had to the theory of compensation. So-and-so is rich, but his home is childless; he visits Europe, but he has arteriosclerosis; he has a beautiful residence, but he is not happy. Social evolution would move more swiftly if once for all the supposed compensations of misfortune were subjected to actual observation, and the fact frankly recognized that some conditions of life are better, immeasurably better, than others. A fatalistic doctrine of compensation disposes one to bear those ills which under a different philosophy he would flee or fight. When one secures a benefit he does not thereby release the lever of a correlated misfortune.

Possibly the conventional doctrine of compensation is related to limitations of experience. Habituated to salt and potatoes, the individual denies the advantage of mutton chops. The benefits of travel come to be seen obliquely, because travel cannot be afforded. The grin-and-bear-it attitude becomes confirmed into a religious devotion to hardship. Misfortunes thus undergo an apotheosis into blessings, and happiness is expected not to last; there are "terrors of cloudless noon." Moreover, the great mass of mankind have had meager experience as consumers, and therefore the upper ranges of life are seen in false perspective, which fact gives color to compensation. The development of suitable wants throughout populations is accordingly preliminary to democracy. In fact, not until mere maintenance ceases to absorb the major portion of one's efforts may the possibilities of human nature be realized. At the very basis of social inequality is an ancient cringing spirit and a time-honored glorification of suffering.

A vast kingdom of inherited fears and deferences, of shadowy evasiveness yet substantial reality, prevails, especially in older societies. The error of not "knowing one's place" thus becomes obnoxious, and the particular merit of the great English public schools, regarded from the aristocratic point of view, has been that through "fagging" the boy was taught to know his place, a subtle social system of distinctions thus being fortified by training. The shocking nakedness of communication in the western states implies by contrast the traditional deference which exists in older communities for academic, political, or economic status. Prevailing sentiments of deference are very often inappropriate, and a rational skepticism of conventional attitudes is warranted. Lack of intelligent unrest and challenge lies at the basis of backward conditions. As one measures himself so is it meted out to him. Development toward democracy requires a stimulation of personality and the charging of individuals with ideals of larger attainments. To preserve fairly even conditions in a population requires watchfulness against an invidious conventionality.

Oftentimes conventional attitudes are singularly at war with what facts warrant. Consider the social prejudice against basic productional occupations. The honor accorded arms is something of an anachronism when the world is held back from peace only by false ideals. The most toilsome and necessary labor is not recognized as meriting special approbation, while predaceous wealth is never without distinction. All degrees of respectability prevail in modern employments, to a large extent based upon inappropriate considerations. All necessary forms of work should be held alike worthy, and the performance of disagreeable and dangerous tasks deserves special commendation.

Traditional conceptions as to who deserve credit for wealth production, coupled with a certain obtuseness with reference to the fact that society overtly or tacitly fixes incomes, give rise to astounding overpayment and underpayment, to a most unscientific scale of remuneration. A degree of imagination is required to see things in their true light, in default of which nothing appears surprising. Social conditions are so largely a reflex of prevailing states of consciousness that to change conditions is first to change minds. The cherishing of economic tradition by those who would most profit by a new outlook, the possession of the "capitalist mind" by the expropriated, is a singular obstruction, only to be accounted for by the static condition of intelligence which prevails when not guarded against the domination of custom and an excess of habit.

4. The Law of Shock

A consideration of the force of environment gives a clue to the extreme significance of new surroundings; change of environment provides a multitude of suggestions resulting in new methods and ideals, but is especially important in compelling, through the rupture of habit, the reasoning reaction. Men's minds tend to conform to their immediate surroundings as truly as the color of the fur of a prairie dog to the dun expanse of its semiarid habitat; there is thus an underlying quality in the intellectual processes which relates *homo sapiens* to the birds in the tree and the imitatively colored larvae which coat its leaves. As the inherited powers and instincts of man are in a large way the reflex of the requirements made upon him through unmeasured prehistoric time, so the thought of the individual of today is in direct response to the features of his environment. If environment is easy, little mental effort will be exerted, but if the individual is placed under exacting conditions whose demands cannot be met by memory, habit, or impulse, then activity is forced upon the reasoning powers.

To supply the conditions which compel development new environment is effective. One is rarely acquainted with his own capabilities until he is thrown upon his own resources through some dislocation of his habitual setting. We are full of surprises to ourselves, the tug of effort to effect a new adjustment being the prerequisite of disclosure. One may believe that he is making the most of himself in a given place in the world, but upon being subjected to fresh demands he may feel with the character in Mark Twain's *A Double-Barreled Detective Story*: "Duffers like us don't know what real thought is." To suitably precipitate upon one thought-provoking requirements, the importing of new elements into one's daily order, or the bodily transference of the individual to different surroundings, is necessary.

Evidence of the part played by change of surroundings in stimulating intelligence may be gathered from various historical occurrences. The England of Shakespeare was convulsed with the realization of a new world— imagine what would be our reaction if communication were established with a race on another planet! Under the law of shock new intellectual manifestations appeared in the Age of Elizabeth, of which an invigorated drama and an unwonted buoyancy of phrase were a normal expression. Unfortunate the age that has no new worlds to discover or no thrilling vision to provoke the creative spirit.

The shock of the frontier resulted, in the case of the

American people, in a remarkable burst of initiative, resourcefulness, and idealism. The patent office at Washington, which bears witness to an inventiveness unique in the history of the race, is evidence of the stimulating effects of a new environment. In New Zealand, likewise, where within memory the cannibal Maori feasted on "long pig," the response to new demands is to be read in laws which are wisely imitated in older countries.

It is ever the emergency-meeting race or individual that generates progress; static conditions tend to reduce mankind to a set of fixed reactions, whose insidious approach may be noted in the unprogressiveness of old communities where the leading citizens have hung their hats on the same hooks for forty years. Likewise in the iron environment of cities, where, especially among clerical and commercial employees, may be found signal provincialism, there is ample illustration of the dangers of routine. To one who has not the means to travel, to occupy the same house or apartment for a long time is unfortunate, and occupations which have a migratory character contribute in no small way to the yeast of civilization. The automatism of fixed conditions and the approach to a moribund zone were unwittingly illustrated in the reply of a denizen of a torpid village when asked if he expected to be buried in the local cemetery; he replied, "Yes, if I live" ! The tendrils of sentiment twine more closely indeed about the familiar, and there is a tragic note in the snapping of ties, but the law of human evolution reads that only by the advent of the strange may welfare be won, and the pains of readjustment are less to be feared than the corruption of habit. Any Utopia which left no channels free for the forces which break habit and thrust upon society the urgent need of solving new problems would, after the first fruits of system were garnered, tend toward stagnation. With the passing of frontiers and the rapid filling in of the inhabitable empty areas of the earth, with the question of habitability still pending as regards the enormous and fertile *selvas* of Brazil, and parts of Africa, the problem of environment takes the form of other means to insure the individual such thought-taxing situations as will result in progressive mentality. In some phases of modern life there seems to be a letting down of insistent requirements. It should not be necessary to return to the primitive in order to stimulate initiative and circumspection. It should be permissible to turn a tap rather than wade through snow to a pump for water, but unless there be requirements which fairly equate with the pricking rigors of a less conventionalized life we need have no doubt as to the results— degeneracy will appear.

Notwithstanding the complexity of life today it is doubtful if it represents, so far as the separate individual is concerned, the complexity of demand of earlier conditions. The total social mass is complex, but the individual may— indeed, typically does— find that his daily requirements, especially in urban employments, entail but slight resort to constructive ideas. "All you have to do" in many positions consists of a narrow range of mechanized tasks apportioned under a business system which makes independence impertinent. The great mass of employees today are following orders, with not enough participation in the problems of the occupation to provoke thought. It is a misfortune to be connected with an enterprise where the individual is not weighted with all the perplexities necessary to tax the association centers of his cerebrum. A single day of camping out will perhaps raise more problems than months of routine occupation.

In individual cases the transforming effects of a change of place or occupation are often to be observed. An elderly east Tennessee farmer moves his family to western Washington and takes up a different type of agriculture, with the result that by a decade later he has "renewed his youth," gained an evident adaptability, and multiplied his interests. The arrival of the first baby of middle-aged parents results in a rejuvenation and development directly traceable to dealing with the enigmatical creature. If the Supreme Court were never to hold two sessions in the same room, a more modern atmosphere would no doubt attach to its deliberations. Even a change of clothes has its developmental aspects.

The misfortune of failing of a shift in associations is to be noted in the cosmic quality of views and feelings characteristic of classes that but slightly change environment, being rooted to place, as in the case, historically, of the peasants of the Old World. In the recent revolution in Portugal, from which ancient kingdom the late monarch left "without leaving his address," it was the agricultural classes that opposed the change. And indeed in America, among the stationary farming class, there has been at times the political apathy which is likely to appear wherever movement and new surroundings are least experienced.

The equivalent of the stimulating effects of new scenes may largely be duplicated by importing into one's usual environment new elements. The progress of recent years has coincided with the growth of reading habits and the break-up of static local conditions; at first, to considerable degree, by the advent of the bicycle, and later by the trolley, rural free delivery of mail, and the automobile. A steady influence making for adaptability is represented in the social center in both city and country, where an exchange of ideas results in the formation of fresh opinions. Education, reading, conversation, the theater, marriage, and sickness are meaningful variations of environment.

But especially among the agencies to which we must look for establishing adaptability and resourcefulness are those which bring about change of residence. Travel has an important function to this end. The traveled person is tolerant. Race hatred grew up in the days of the pack mule and the ox cart and of the watertight compartments of mountainous regions where every peak meant a different language. An American public man, it is said, once begged that he be not introduced to an enemy, for he said he could not hate anybody with whom he became acquainted. The flood of ideas which is brought against preconceptions through travel represents a thought-compelling situation of the greatest significance. The acceleration of progress which this age witnesses is in no small degree the outcome of the fact that of late, for the first time since history dawned, men have been able freely to visit new scenes and far countries. Individual travel should by all means be made universally possible through the widest opening of the gates of transportation.

CHAPTER III
THE LIMITS OF ATTENTION

PSYCHOLOGISTS have demonstrated the fact, which anyone may verify, that attention may be focused upon a given point for but a few seconds. Let the mind be directed to a given object, and it is found that actual attention plays over a multitude of minor aspects or darts away to remote considerations, to return perhaps in a twinkling; but at no time does attention really stick to a given phase of the object for more than a few seconds. When we say that we give perfect attention for an hour, it is not to be inferred that our attention has been unvarying, but it is rather the case that our thoughts have been directed to one large subject with its associated details.

1. Inheritance of Type of Attention

Why we possess a nerve apparatus which functions in this type of attention is evident upon a moment's consideration. In the ceaseless war of the lower world the animal that was not alert to every significant stimulus was likely to lose its life. The eye became trained to flit to every point from which danger might arise, and mind followed the eye. Attention is a mental trait whose character is derived from the nature of the surroundings which have pressed upon the organism during the clockless depths of time. Every quivering leaf in heated jungles now converted into coal, every prowling beast stirring the reeds, every dancing gnat, every rush of wings tended to break into bits the consciousness of our prehuman forbears, and through inheritance to give the average mind a power of attention somewhere between the inconsequential zigzag of the phrase talker and the philosopher's stuck-fast consciousness, miscalled absent-mindedness, but on the whole a distinctly unstable type of attention.

Now the fact that the power of human attention, even in its highest development, is selective, partial, variable, and hopelessly and forever short of that simultaneous and comprehensive consciousness of all events present and past which has been imputed only to deity, has a multitude of bearings upon the affairs of civilized society and especially must be reckoned with in laying the foundations for achieving social welfare. How frail a remedy, for example, against the "malefactors of great wealth" would be the proposed remedy of publicity taking the form of social ostracism. Attention flags, and our grievances are short-lived. Even the drama has retired the delayed-retribution motive and no longer asks the audience to follow a character who bides his time for a quarter of a century and brings his enmity rank to the tragedy just before the curtain falls. Attention shifted so rapidly at the close of the Civil War that the wind went out of the sails of revenge.

2. Need of Effective Publicity

In the first place we simply cannot give our attention to a wide range of matters, past or present, and any exhortation to the public to give its attention beyond the normal stretch is futile. Governmental complexities soon must pass beyond the unaided attention of the great majority of citizens; if a vast deal more attention must be given by the citizen to details of government while engrossed in his personal affairs, then we have come to about the end of the rope. The limitations of memory and attention must be acknowledged with scientific frankness and efforts to prod our millions into an abnormal attitude of mental strain abandoned, and in their place must be substituted schemes by which the rational ordering of society for general betterment may be brought about in conformity with the laws of the human mind. When aroused by flagrant abuses or shocking imposition the citizen and the reformer feel that such will never occur again; the affair is burning-white in the center of aroused attention, but, as it is said, the people soon "go to sleep," which, indeed, is perfectly natural. And within a month the gas company is again selling air, and the food manufacturer, while perhaps removing benzoate of soda, puts his goods in smaller containers at a higher price. The public cannot give its attention in detail to all its public affairs, and plans of social improvement that rest on such assumption simply delay the sort of progress that rests on human factors. We have seen public attention swing ponderously in recent years from one issue to another, and while one evil was under attack others were escaping.

The public, like the individual, frequently thinks it is giving its attention more fully than is really the case. Let one try to recall what he had for dinner yesterday or try to list his expenses for the past week; the events that one does remember give a fallacious sense of the fulness of recollection, but upon close investigation it is found that thousands and thousands of items and incidents have gone down with scarce a bubble on the surface. Indeed the normal feeling is that one who is consistently attentive, as to the single tax or the physical valuation of railroads, is a crank— he is a person of "one idea."

The popular mind shows the same kind of variability exhibited in the individual who is absorbed in one topic this week and in another the next. Today it is the Dayton flood or a Billy Sunday revival and tomorrow oil wells or the Poughkeepsie regatta, but always a singularly piecemeal consciousness. Even a three-ring circus is too much for any one patron. When one's business expands one is sure to neglect some part of it. The press reflects the fickleness of attention. For a period a piece of big news throws its shadow across many columns, then to be succeeded by another equally engrossing subject. The influential criminal wins delays, and when his case is finally disposed of the echoes of the former outcry have died away. Congress attacks its problems *seriatim*. Immigration, the parcel post, rate regulation, rural credits, the trust question, all have their day and cease to be ; one waits on another, and all wait on the tariff— the tariff has been a colossal sponge licking up the consciousness of the public for a third of a century while hundreds of issues have waited to be heard. There are cases where issues have been raised to divert the public mind on the principle enunciated by Josh Billings: "Tight boots make a man forget all his other troubles."

In appraising, then, the mental factors which must be employed in social reconstruction, it is well to recognize these limits. In private affairs the individual is likely to develop a system for jogging his memory; he may tie a string in a buttonhole, or place a pencil in his left shoe the night before; he knows his frailty, and perhaps thinks other people are not so but they are. There is need of a system of memory-jogging for the public with reference to public business. At any rate let note be taken of the limits of attention as a fact to be considered when public welfare is sought to be promoted. This feature of mentality should be recognized in a far more effective system of publicity for governmental affairs and the utilization of special agencies by which the variable consciousness of the public may be brought back again and again to matters of import.

A flitting attention has its chief function in bearing to consciousness information needed to keep one in adjustment to physical surroundings. One must notice a drop in temperature, the smell of escaping gas, and a thousand stimuli which are significant for personal safety. But the inherited and confirmed tendency rapidly to shift the mental eye is a fundamental disqualification for concentrating thought upon abstruse problems, while the completeness with which one idea dispossesses another and one topic forces another out of mind suggests that special methods of publicity be employed for marshaling thought for civic ends.

CHAPTER IV
FORMS OF DISTRACTION

A FACT which has a bearing upon the improvability of society is that the individual has only a certain amount of energy and that if this is drained for physical purposes there is a shortage for mental processes. Mental and motor activity are, of course, closely joined; without motor expression mentality is not clearly defined; thought is generated and quickened by demands upon the muscles, and physical and mental training have much in common. But nevertheless the balance between typically physical and mental activities is easily disturbed, and the outlook for a higher civilization is in no slight measure concerned with the extent to which motor expression unnecessarily obtrudes and consumes energies otherwise more effectively employed.

1. Brain Work vs. Physical Labor

That there is a conflict between intellectual and physical employments is evident. The housewife, busy with a wide range of manual activities, not only often does not find time to read, but even when time is found discovers that her mental grasp is disappointing. Days of toil in the field dispose rather to torpor and slumber than to thought. At Brook Farm the author of *The Blithedale Romance* learned that there is an inconsistency between meditation and hoeing corn. So protected must be the easily blown-out flame of attention and thought that, with many, mere sense stimulations, as a rattling window, a fly buzzing in the pane, the infrequent beating of a distant door, or street sounds quite interrupt these processes; for which considerations, perhaps, philosophers are associated with the desert and divers authors "take to the woods." The splendor of the intellectual life of England has been ascribed to the existence of a leisure class. The leisure represented by the school is the very foundation of civilization.

The evolution away from big bodies and small brains, of the age of the Dinotherium and the mammoth, is presumably paralleled in mankind by an evolution away from mere muscle and toward rational attainments. Accordingly, the shortening of hours of labor, the providing of vacations universally, the substitution of machinery, and the guarding of the years of youth and of leisure in maturity are of the utmost meaning for progress. Under slave and factory conditions the absorption of energy in motor uses is often so complete that mentality can hardly appear, and even in the intelligent farming class interminable hours of work and "chores" so sop up the nervous forces that few in this occupation have been found with the mental activity required for the leadership of country life. We properly distinguish between brain work and other work, and only by holding down physical labor to a moderate maximum may there exist generally throughout society the alert mentality which the social vision requires. The great majority of people do not regularly find time to read and think, and so when an unexpected leisure occurs there is little preparation for making the most of it. As a result the physical laborer is likely to spend his odd hours sharpening his pocketknife or wandering aimlessly about in the woods or fields, subject only to the minimum stimulations of raw nature.

The political sagacity of a people who in the majority spend nearly all their time in physical activities is sure to be disappointing. The slave-owner of the South opposed the teaching of slaves to read, realizing its stimulating effects. But "free" labor may be so arduous that the benefits of reading are but slightly realized. Probably the immense majority of adults in the United States do not read a book a year, and many who take papers do not find time to read them. Included in the non-reading public are five and one-half million persons in the United States, over ten years of age, who are illiterates.

> In double line of march, at intervals of three feet, these 5,516,163 illiterate persons would extend over a distance of 1,567 miles. Marching at the rate of twenty-five miles a day, it would require more than two months for them to pass a given point.[1]

It is indeed a wonder that political progress is making so rapidly when so few have opportunity for intellectual development and the obtaining of appropriate information. The factory hand who reaches home tired late in the day is in no condition to weigh political theories or follow the lines of thought in the more profitable articles of the day. A more just division of time between physical and intellectual exercises must be attained. Democracy implies a reasonable universal leisure.

2. Energy Given to Sports

But leisure does not insure against a disproportionate devotion of energy to the physical. While health, recreation, and valuable social training are promoted by participation in sports and games, athletic activities may become an obsession and displace other important interests. Athletic training finds its warrant in developing a good body as a basis for moral and intellectual possibilities. Knobby muscles and Herculean physique are unwisely exalted when standards are set up which in effect discriminate against mentality in favor of

---

[1] *U. S. Bureau of Education, Bulletin No. 20, 1913.*

"beef." It is indeed a confession of the impotence of the intellectual appeal of universities when it is argued that without militant football the energies of the student body would turn to vice, for which the pigskin is a prophylactic.

The absorption of energy in motor interests takes a peculiarly degenerate turn in the riotous abandon of enthusiasm displayed on the "bleachers," where neither the benefit of actual exercise nor the stimulus of mental effort is experienced. The significant term, "rooting," represents a phase of American life of more than passing importance. When 30,000 people "go wild" at a ball game which settles no issues and involves no uplift, and when "fannism" is the principal avocation of multitudes of voters whose vocations are in many cases those of office routine or are narrowly mechanical, it is to be doubted whether commercialized sports are an unmixed blessing. Divided thus between vocation and avocation, is it any wonder that it has taken the people of the United States a quarter of a century to secure a pure-food law, and that the people's Congress is styled by H. G. Wells as the "feeblest, least accessible, and most inefficient central government of any civilized nation west of Russia."

Any interest may acquire an abnormal development, and physical expression not rarely passes moderate bounds, and consumes nerve forces which would otherwise be available for grappling with the problems of the age. Attention may be deflected from social issues by athletic propaganda, as witness the promotion by the Russian government of sports and games with a view to counteracting radical tendencies among young people. One cannot attend to several things at the same time, and if a youth is "baseball crazy" he is not likely to worry over the evils of absolutism. One has only to listen to conversation to be convinced that the procession of athletic topics throughout the year, chronicled in acres of print, has a tremendous diverting effect upon public intelligence. The reader will be able to call to mind cases of individuals whose mentality is perpetually dissipated through attention to this ever-recurring sensationalism.

3. Excess Sex Interests

Passing to a different phase of life, the dominance of the sex interest must be recognized. Of all the innate interests sex is the dominant one, radiating through the whole social structure the heat and light of a primal force. The aim of life, biologically, is reproduction. There is a sex element, accordingly, in all activities and relationships. Mating-psychology looms large in human nature and is an element to be reckoned with in appraising the forces available for the improvement of society. Robert Burns wrote many songs, but the socially reconstructive "A man's a man for a' that" stands alone; more characteristic is,

> Oh, my luve's like a red, red rose
> That's newly sprung in June.

The mating instinct influences the rate of progress, especially as it may acquire abnormal recognition and represent an undue absorption of attention. While it would not be well to join too heartily in deploring with the poet "the time I've lost in wooing," yet one is impressed with the immense deflection of thought from social issues which artificially stimulated sex interests entail. It is only under ideals of gossipy sensationalism and by means of modern facilities for diffusing ideas that the attention of millions could be almost exclusively fixed upon an unsavory criminal action or centered upon newspaper discussions of a dubious picture. If unsupplied with suitable culture materials and exposed to protean suggestions, the individual may attain a sensuality of outlook probably unparalleled in savagery. Society in its collective wisdom may well concern itself with the character of the channels through which mentality finds expression. What ideas enter the mind is of radical significance, for interests may be caused to grow or to wither. It is accordingly a vital question whether public attention is excessively directed to sex.

While the drama of human life extends vastly beyond early love affairs or the maladjustments of marriage, nevertheless mating is ingeniously exploited and made the central subject of popular literature, as the "best sellers" bear witness. Despite the fact that millions of people have suitably adjusted their connubial relations, the printing presses are clogged with the literature of mating, and heads of families who venture betimes to the theater are regaled with eroticism. It is demonstrable that the post-adolescent years abound in an exhaustless supply of materials for novel and drama, but that themes from this fruition period of experience are effectually displaced is evident.

Possibly the delayed age of marriage has much to do with the preponderant attractiveness of the mating theme and its consequent financial exploitation. Be this as it may, the problems of the years that follow the heyday of youth should not be unceremoniously put to rout, nor should the forces which might energize social betterment be dissipated in a promoted and protracted absorption in sex themes. If the edge of revolution may be turned by the inspired circulation of pornographic literature, it is evident that there is loss in the obtrusion of sex sentimentalism into thought-currents. The attention of thousands is consumed at popular entertainments where whole evenings are devoted to "numbers," musical or otherwise, in which the mating theme is worn to shreds, and not the slightest impulse is given to creative thought in any direction. Time thus spent may be absolutely crossed off the records so far as progress is concerned.

The biological impulsions to mating would hardly of themselves excresce into obstructions to progress were efforts not inspired by commercial motives to play upon sex inclination. Advertising seizes upon this interest, even to the distraction of thought from the merits of goods advertised. For example, a men's clothing advertisement on a billboard represented a young woman dressed in a man's suit; eight young men, the number interrogated, testified that they did not notice the brand of clothes advertised, their attention being given solely to the illustration. Society is familiar with the idea of commercialized vice, but there is also, from the viewpoint of energizing progress, a problem arising from the unrestrained commercial exploitation of sex interest through a multitude of appeals in advertisements of travel, personal belongings, beer, and cigarettes. An obsession of sex interest is readily developed, abetted by trade, the sentimental song, the problem play, and sensational journalism.

4. *Woman and Dress*

A feature of mating whose social significance can hardly be exaggerated is dress. The burden placed upon woman, rather than upon man, of attracting the other sex— in the lower animals a burden borne by the male— is deplored by Mrs. C. P. Gilman.[2] In any case woman has largely assumed the load of sex ornament, and it is a heavy one. Not only during the mating age proper does the "sex vanity" of dress nearly monopolize attention, but as well quite commonly for a longer period, either because mating is not a

---

[2] *The Man-made World.* The Charlton Co., New York.

closed incident or because of the vitality of a strong interest, transferred to rivalry in jewels, equipage, and pursuit of fashion. The volume of interest and intelligence thus prevented from being directly available, not only for the improvement of the status of woman, but for general social betterment, is enormous. Observe the thought-currents of the chance feminine group or of the tense Easter assemblage, and note how often hardly a rill of intellectuality flows out toward the world's wider movements. Great amounts of "crystallized labor," which is capital, are Moloched to fashion, and vast energies are thus lost to constructive social effort.

An acceleration of progressive movements would doubtless follow the adoption of more uniform dress, while such economic readjustments as would permit marriage at an earlier age in certain classes would tend to enlist interests in the larger social issues. Surely commercialized suggestion merits disapproval. To build the ideal future requires the conservation of suitable ideas and a reasonable exaltation of other than sex topics.

5. Other Interests

Whatever occupies the public mind to the undue exclusion of public affairs may be set down as retarding the solution of the issues which lie at the threshold of rational civilization. Historically, the focusing of attention upon a future world, in which the evils of the present would disappear without human effort, proved an unwitting ally of temporal injustice. The expectation that the world would come to an end in the year 1000 had a paralyzing effect upon the energies of Europe. Wherever injustice has been passively endured because of faith, injustice has become more firmly rooted. Hence the vast importance of the newer viewpoint which assumes that one is his brother's keeper and that the highest ideals of religion are to be exemplified in current human relationships. In the new drift of religious thought there is the promise of unprecedented social betterment, for an immense volume of feeling and will, at one time not so active a reform force, now supplies motive power for progress.

The intellectual capital of the world consists largely of people's interests; and these are subject to modification; they may be enlarged or diminished, and new interests may be developed. It is highly important, this, what people are interested in, because there is no doubt but that people may readily become interested in the best things. While there is a substratum of permanent tendencies, one is nevertheless susceptible to extensive redirection.

The interests which characterize the public today are often criticized as trivial and unworthy. A writer ventures the following as a truthful list of the great "interests" which make up American life: (1) the ticker; (2) female apparel; (3) baseball bulletin; (4) the "movies"; (5) bridge whist; (6) turkey trotting; (7) yellow journal headlines and "funny" pages; (8) the prize fight. And the estimate is made that 100,000 Americans are genuinely interested in the foregoing matters to every 5,000 who are interested in politics and to every 1,000 who are interested in education.[3]

This list is not a highly creditable one, and it is not one that speaks hopefully of the ability of the people to inject intelligence into the social process and achieve reforms of government. As long as such interests dominate there can be but an imperfect base for democracy. But it may be that these interests are receiving a hothouse culture or that they represent but frivolous moods. There are solider elements in

---

[3] *The Independent*, April 17, 1913.

human nature, to which appeal may not be made in vain.

CHAPTER V
THE EFFECT OF MACHINERY UPON THE MIND

THE most obvious aspect of the use of machinery is that it frees muscle and shifts a tremendous burden from flesh and bone. An immense amount of heavy, grinding work has been transferred to inanimate forces and nerveless matter. This is a great gain; in the first place because of the increase of production. The average man today, through the use of machinery, produces twenty times as much as was produced by the average man 250 years ago.

1. Leisure Possible

When farmers cradled their wheat, bound it by hand, and threshed with flails, the operation required for one bushel of wheat the labor of one man for an average time of 183 minutes. With labor-saving machinery, the modern farmer can do the same work in 10 minutes. Seventy-five years ago, 66 hours of labor were expended on an acre of oats, whereas the labor time is now but 7.1 hours. Modern civilization rests upon an increase of wealth traceable to the industrial revolution and a machine era. Libraries, universities, assemblies, the press, and other agencies of enlightenment rest squarely upon the machine, which enables mankind to realize a higher culture. The educated and leisured classes owe their emancipation to an easier production of wealth.

Time and energy are afforded for intellectual pursuits. Heavy physical labor is incompatible with mental exercise. A long working day leaves small energy for brain activity. When to feed, clothe, and provide shelter for the world required unceasing toil, the masses could not be expected to develop a thought-life. A certain amount of physical activity conduces to mental development, but there is ample evidence that motor employments have an arresting effect. Larger and larger numbers enjoy the possibility of exemption from the deadening effects of severe physical toil, a fact which throws a most favorable light upon a machine age. There is a mental bondage where there is muscle bondage. The long-continued existence of a near-slave status on the part of women finds a partial explanation in the fact that household labor has been hand labor and that it has been excessive.

2. Machinery May Stimulate Thought

Not only is energy released for mental development, but efforts to provide new devices and improvements are distinctly stimulating, and a remarkable intelligence appears in a limited class. Here is a field which has furnished large incentives for active intelligence; not only in mechanical invention, but in repair and regulation, is a resourceful mind called for. A considerable body of men are employed in thus dealing intelligently with motor vehicles, power machinery, typesetting machines, and the like, and in the installation and regulation of all sorts of manufacturing equipment.

This sort of activity stimulates intelligence, though it must be conceded in all fairness that the mechanical genius or the expert repair man may be unlearned in philosophy, ignorant of political science, unacquainted with history, and destitute of an appreciation of poetry; but for all that, his intelligence is quickened and all he now needs is concrete instruction along other than mechanical lines. He has undergone cerebral stimulation; he has learned how to think and to adapt himself; he can seize upon a problem. A dull person could not install dynamos or repair microscopes. The skilled mechanician may have his limitations in liberal culture and sociological insight, but he has real problems to face and he meets them successfully. The plumber who is called in consultation upon an inadequate heating system is quite as professional for the time as the physician called to deal with sudden illness. The farmer who buys a new windmill, a wild-oats separator, or a milking machine is made to take a learning attitude. A piece of machinery that will not work may nearly if not quite duplicate the unparalleled educational situation represented by a balky horse. No people can remain entirely uncivilized if visited by salesmen of modern appliances, subjected to the instruction of innumerable advertisements, circulars, and pamphlets, and impelled by the necessity of knowing how to operate the contrivance when once it has been purchased.

Under certain conditions machinery has a stimulating effect upon intelligence. It presents problems to be solved; it necessitates a concentration of attention; it constitutes a new world for mankind and represents a complexity which compels thought. To keep in proper adjustment to this mechanical environment requires a degree of mental alertness. There has been upreared on the earth an artificial environment which taxes attention and thought in a way no less real than in the case of nature. It is not to be inferred, however, that such effect of machinery is to educate for civic or social relations. In estimating the general culture of the individual, it is quite fitting to look principally to his preparation for comprehensive social relationships, and while the skilled workman is often a highly intelligent citizen and voter, or perhaps a philosophizing socialist, yet various phases of intellectual life are doubtless but indirectly if at all favorably affected by mechanical training.

3. How Machinery Affects Operatives

But to turn to a very different class of people, a very large class, compared to whom the creative mechanicians are but a drop in the bucket— the operatives— we find that machinery has its bad effects. The operative who performs but a mere repetition of movements is subjected to about the worst possible influence from the standpoint of mental development. It is true, of course, that motor activity, as in manual training, has a stimulating effect, but just as soon as movements become habitual, mental development therefrom ceases. It is educative to learn to drive a nail, but when the driving of a nail is performed automatically as the result of practice it ceases to be thought-provoking. Manual training is an important adjunct of the educational system, viewed simply from the point of view of mental development; but when the exercises are fully learned the individual must pass on to new situations or suffer arrest of development.

Machine production tends toward a minute division of labor and a specialization inconsistent with the mental welfare of the operative. There are over four hundred and fifty operations in making of the upper of a shoe and each of these is performed by a different man in a well-run shop. Such division of labor results in an intense monotony on the part of the workman. The whole manufacturing world is adjusted to such specialization, the peculiar value of which is that it tends toward increased production. No one has ever argued that the individual was benefited by doing work under the conditions of intense specialization and rigid routine. President Hibben, of Princeton, says:

When mind becomes mechanical it is departing radically from its essential source as a living organism. It depends wholly upon the manner in which we treat the mind whether it retains its vital character or becomes a mere machine.

Employers and employed unite in the view that routine is undesirable from the individual standpoint. Long subjected to unvarying employment, the individual loses initiative, spirit, and will-power. His work is planned for him by someone else and a limited range of physical movements engrosses attention. Such conditions are inevitably stupefying. The operative becomes a mere adjunct to his machine. All except the most elementary forms of reasoning are dispensed with. Consciousness sinks to a low level and the lower centers govern responses. Especially are the results harmful when there is speeding up and the individual is left with no surplus energy.

Frederick W. Taylor, author of works on scientific management, made the following statement before a special committee of the House of Representatives:

> I think this tendency of training toward specializing the work is true of all managements, for the reason that a man becomes more productive when working at his specialty, and while it is deplorable in certain ways (there is no question about it, there are various elements in this specialization that are deplorable), still the prosperity of the world and the development of the world— the fact that the average workman in this day lives as well as kings lived 250 years ago— that fact is due to a certain extent to just this very specialization.

This statement by the high priest of scientific management indicates that production, instead of the welfare of the workman, proceeds from mechanical specialization.

A recent magazine interview with Henry Ford, of the Ford Motor Company, runs as follows:

> "You put the man at a machine, teach him to control it, and he stands there weeks and months and years mechanically producing one trifling thing. How does that affect him temperamentally?"
> "It drives him crazy," said Ford, positively, as he had said

everything else. "But we see to it that a man does not do one thing too long. We keep him moving through the shop."

The effect which Ford deliberately seeks to avoid is one which prevails almost universally. The state of the machine-tender is authoritatively described by Samuel Gompers, president of the American Federation of Labor. Gompers says: -

Wage-workers in factory occupations tend machines, and by tending of such machines do not have the opportunity of making or completing any part of the whole, but only perform a minute and infinitesimal part of a part. As a consequence, the people who gain their livelihood by tending such machines become automata. They become part of a machine— thoughtless and spiritless to such a degree that they are unable to do the slightest thing, or perform in any way to their own advantage, or to the advantage of their employer, unless they have a prompter at their side in the shape of a planning master, a foreman, or a boss of some other title.

It is the most pronounced in the textile industries— silk, wool, cotton, cordage, jute, etc.— the novelty industries— watch making, furniture manufacture, paper making, and many other of our basic industries.

Some American employers have commenced to see what a dilemma they are facing for men and women capable of directing their departments and divisions of departments. They have brought down upon their own heads the alarming situation of working for profit to such an extent that they have neglected to train men and women to take responsible official positions of administrative capacity in their own factories, and such manufacturers have at last commenced to appreciate the foresight of the American Federation of Labor in its efforts to establish vocational education and national trade training schools by federal aid in all of the states.

It stands to reason that, if men and women are reduced by force of circumstances, and through the folly of certain so-called efficiency systems promulgated in recent years by fanatics on that subject, like Messrs. Taylor, Gant, Emerson, Harrington, and others, the workers in our industries will be deprived of all opportunities to develop mentally or physically, because when the aspirations of men and women are submerged and stunted they become dependent upon the whim, the will, the direction of a superior, and there is nothing left to them but merely to become docile, obedient, willing servants. Such a situation is not only degrading to the individual, but is a menace to society.

Machine production is characterized not only by specialization and monotony, but by the centralization of intelligence in officers and overseers. There is a division of labor as between the physical and mental aspects of industry. The board of directors, the superintendent, and the boss largely monopolize the function of direction, while the employee takes orders and follows rules. The logical result of this is the creation of intellectual classes. The worker loses his power to initiate and to think, while on the side of the management there is a signal development of ability. A parallel case is that of officers and men in the army. It is the officer who undergoes mental development; it is the private who becomes a machine. Military obedience results in physical and in mental traits which are to a high degree mechanical. It is only too true that the well-drilled company or regiment is a machine; that is a peculiar condemnation of a military system.

> Theirs not to reason why,
> Theirs but to do and die.

It may be a good investment from the standpoint of production that the superintendent should do the thinking, but looking at it from the social point of view, it is disastrous. Especially in a democracy is the importance of widely diffused ability to solve problems to be emphasized. The increasing automatism of modern industry has in itself a power to create castes based upon intellectual traits.

Routine-afflicted operatives are dumb driven cattle

before the political trickster and the domineering employer. The fact that after a century of factory conditions the successive generations of workers have been unable effectively to propose political and economic remedies for appalling industrial conditions and must still employ the often self-defeating and shortsighted strike method is convincing evidence of a mental arrest which a factory dispensation encourages

It is possible, of course, that the workman may be so privileged, as in the case of the Ford system, that the full force of a deadening routine is avoided. The shortening of hours of labor, provision for recreation, avoidance of fatigue, and stimulating experiences outside of working hours might successfully be employed as an offset.

But too often such humane considerations enter but slightly into the wage relation in manufacturing enterprises. Not rarely employers have desired workmen to be content under an injurious monotony. They have desired employees who were tractable and mechanized. An eastern manufacturer complained to President Harvey, of the Stout School at Menominee, Wisconsin, that his experience with the graduates of certain industrial schools had been unsatisfactory. He said that boys whom he had employed from the schools were not contented when doing the kind of work he wanted done; as soon as the boys mastered certain processes they were anxious to go to something else and to rise, whereas he wanted workmen to "stay put." President Harvey replied that it was not the purpose of his institution to train boys who would "stay put." Along with the enormous social justification for trade schools, there is without any doubt, in certain quarters, a desire to use these as a tail to a dividend kite. The importance of vocational education is indeed great, but it should be guarded from the designs of employers who are interested in the workman only as a producer.

The boy educated as a workman should also be educated for rising in his calling, and receive instruction, which would make him capable of expressing himself effectively through government and of sharing in the fund of modern thought and culture.

There is evidence that less and less intelligence is called for in certain industrial positions, and that the demand is for many unskilled or narrowly skilled and for only a few really intelligent workers. Glass making at one time required skill and intelligence; but machinery is being introduced which dispenses with these qualities. With the introduction of improved machinery, a lower grade of labor is utilized in steel making and in mining. The very perfection of machinery tends to lessen the importance of really capable workmen. It is an urgent problem of society to utilize to the full the vast benefits of machinery and to minimize the deadening effects of industrial service. In industry as now ordered mental welfare is unthought of. Personal development remains to be promoted through labor-autonomy, the rotation of processes, and the recognition at every point of psychological factors.

4. Routine Employments General

The effect of machinery, however, is not limited to its influence upon the factory employee, but has a bearing upon occupations in general. The machine era has resulted in the development of a very large number of employments which are in a high degree mechanized. A division of labor originating in factory conditions and based upon industrial concepts is carried out into practically all fields of enterprise. There result many occupations or jobs which are essentially as monotonous as that of watching a loom or pasting labels.

Routine characterizes an increasing number of employments. Take, for example, the work of a railway postal clerk. On certain runs the names of as many as eight or nine thousand post-offices must be borne in mind, together with forenoon and afternoon connections. Constant diligence is required to maintain efficiency; as a result, the postal clerk is thoroughly mechanized. An intelligent man who recently left the service contributes some interesting information on the effects of the system upon the individual. He testifies that the service narrowly limits the range of one's mental activities. The subjects discussed in off-hours are likely to pertain only to the technicalities of mail distribution. Conversation is confined to the details of the business. "Probably a man would know who was president of the United States," said he, "but that is about all." This occupation is merely typical; in many others similar tendencies are discernible.

The sufficiency of one's intelligence comes to be popularly judged by its sufficiency in a routine employment. One feels no humiliation in confessing ignorance in regard to a multitude of matters if they are not in his line. There is a possibility that such modesty may become altogether too widespread and confirmed. One who aspires to general information is old-fashioned. One may safely blink ignorantly at thousands of marvels provided he has the requisite information pertaining to a specialty. It requires a syndicate to deal with any project having a variety of aspects. We insist upon having most of our thinking done by somebody else.

The possible future development of this peculiarity of modern life constitutes a fascinating appeal to the imagination. Are we destined to evolve a society in which the individual will, first, be limited in range of information and in mental activity, and, secondly, become destitute of the power of self-direction and, like the fully automatized bee, as described by Maeterlinck, be absorbed in the spirit of the hive, whose organization and nature are far beyond conscious intelligence? Is the complexity of our industrial and social structure passing beyond the possibilities of the individual mind? The field of information which is occupied by all in common is narrowing and the apportionment of the intellectual world becomes more and more definite and minute.

5. The Fool-Proof Machine

An interesting phase of modern environment is that represented by the fool-proof machine. A multitude of such appliances are put on the market. Consider, for example, the automobile. Most of these machines are run by people whose ideas of the essential parts are about as clear as they are of darkest Africa or of the nervous system of a starfish. A public official in a western state who had run a machine for years, upon seeing the chassis of a car in an engineering laboratory, was full of wonder and admitted that he knew nothing about how his machine was made. People ride in street cars who have but the most airy conception of a trolley system. How many cooks have an adequate understanding of the principles of the modern range ? The office-building elevator is accepted with that lack of wonder which Carlyle described in connection with a second rising of the sun. A modern city, with its telephone lines, its water supply, its sewer system, its electrical distribution, and its subways, is seen in its mechanical wonderfulness only by a discerning few. Those who plan and organize profit by an intellectual stimulation; but those whose only interest is convenience, those out of respect for whom fool-proofing is done, go scot free of even the slightest cerebral excitement. A coffee percolator turns out a uniform product for one who can watch a clock; even the flame will be shut off at the proper time so that the user need exert himself only to the extent of stirring in the sugar. Prosperous young people and often their elders, too, for that matter, exhibit an innocent composure apparently never disturbed by any disposition to resolve the problems of their mechanical environment or to go behind a luxurious adjustment to perfected conveniences.

One may be made inquisitive, inventive, or indifferent, dulled, and conventional, by environment. The level of intelligence in society may be greatly raised or lowered according to culture conditions and of these conditions machinery represents one of the most potent. If in large sections of the population there is a dementalizing, this fact becomes of great importance, for the need of initiative and self-dependence is great. The social order should lend itself to the development and availability of the highest possible intelligence. While the production of wealth is of fundamental importance, it is less important than the preservation of conditions favorable to the development of every individual, and indeed in the long run even the production of wealth must be guaranteed by preserving the most favorable conditions of individual development. Society does not profit most by people who are routine slaves, dulled, regimented, and automatized. Democracy requires the development of the average man. Skilled craftsmanship or drudging labor may alike be divorced from general ability and vital knowledge and from those mental traits and habits which are necessary for the good of a people, while the spread of routine throughout all sorts of occupations and the slight demand for intelligence in the operation of perfected devices alike constitute a dementalizing circumstance.

CHAPTER VI
THE SPIRIT OF LABOR

INTELLIGENCE may be judged by the conditions with which one is content. One may labor under conditions known to be unsatisfactory but over which one has little if any control. But if the conditions under which large numbers work are unjust the fact is an indictment of the collective intelligence which functions in government, for government determines, actively or passively, all social conditions not chargeable to nature itself. Are prevailing conditions of labor rational and acceptable?

In a multitude of situations today the spirit of joyful accomplishment is absent. Freight cars are slammed together— they belong to the "company." Workmen loiter, and the comings and goings of the boss are noted with extreme interest. The ticket agent who "damns" the railroad upon opening his envelope, containing in fact a slight advance in wages, reveals a state of mind. What of the inner strain and depression of employees in factories when they—

look upon their employer as an aristocrat, their foreman as a slave driver, their machine as a treadmill, and the world at large as against them [and when] their faces are frozen in a perpetual grouch?

1. Recognition of the Worker's Interests

Of all wastes that of untapped or improperly tapped reservoirs of human energy should receive first consideration. To align occupations with the currents of nerve force deserves the attention of science, not alone for increase of production, but especially out of regard for the increase of the sum total of happiness, for the whole world labors and too rarely happily. Differences in zest are not entirely peculiar to the individual; the eager employer and the lagging crew are fundamentally alike, as would be shown upon exchange of places. If the wheels of the world's work turn slowly, or if, when they turn, they revolve with the friction of joyless effort, it is no fault of original nature, for that nature is a dynamo of nerves and muscles whose very joy is exertion. Of course the world's work, at least some of it, gets done; but how?

A large part of modern employment is an evident maladjustment to the worker. Due to technicalities and abnormalities of land ownership or transportation or profits, the factory worker too often suffers a wearing outrage of instincts by being confined in a species of artificial inferno. The division of labor has committed the toiler to a monotony of task which is absolutely without warrant in his psychological economy, for a natural environment affords a range of experiences and draws upon all parts of the organism rather than overtaxes a nerve center or set of muscles. The forced production represented by slave labor and the difficulty of getting people to work with spirit suggest that there has been historically and is today an almost complete neglect of the organization of industry with reference to natural incentives. People cannot be kept from working, provided employment corresponds to nervous organization. Need there be so complete a divorce between spontaneity, preference, and play, and the job?

It might seem difficult to introduce into a system of production a distinct recognition of the natural tendencies of experimentation, curiosity, sociability, leadership, and the like, but only by more fully conforming to natural interests may drudging labor be transformed into joyful effort. For example, why should not employees occasionally travel, even if more goods could be made and sold by keeping for a lifetime one man on the road and another stationary? A larger recognition of natural interests and capacities in industrial organization would involve many changes, but it is beyond dispute that the dementalizing of employees by monotony and the development of a sizzling animosity, the everywhere observed discord between occupation and interest, the hating of the job, bode no good. The short answer, "Quit your kicking or get out," is hardly an appropriate one to the problem of irritating conditions.

2. Motivation in the Factory

It is in connection with the sense of utility and remuneration that the problem of motivation becomes most acute. Not that the employee of a swollen trust sees no use in making window glass or steel billets; the social use of manufactured goods must appeal even to resentful labor— barring commodities of worthless or shoddy character— but of what use is it to one to sow that another may reap? To the factory hand it is a sobering thought that for his cents others take dollars. "I should think your employees would strike," said an unsophisticated western lawyer to an old-time friend, the manager of a textile factory in New England, on being told that the profits of the concern were over 300 per cent the previous year. "They *would*, if they knew it," was the reply. A recent writer of conventional point of view naively remarks: "The size of the profit per unit of output is not generally known to the mechanical departments."[1]

When compensation is limited, bearing no equitable relation to production of the worker, there is not the slightest incentive to labor with enthusiasm; on the contrary, to a

---

[1] Hartness, James, *The Human Factor in Works Management*. McGraw-Hill Book Co., New York.

thinking person, there are strong motives not to. With emulation planted deep in the nature of man, implying an eternal struggle for equality, it can scarcely be expected that the process of shaking the bough for someone else to get the apple can be lastingly typical of production. The only peace in the industrial world that may exist under the wage system depends upon not letting the employees know what the profits are; hence the popularity of watered stock and the secrecy of business details. The suddenness of modern wealth-making has concurred with a miracle of inertia on the part of the general public to postpone the day of reckoning, and the preposterous abortion of the present distribution of wealth is only recently producing its effects upon emotions.

The current disposition to identify religion with the affairs of the day results in disinclination to rely upon the righting of the balance in the hereafter through the difficulty with which the rich man enters heaven as compared with the welcome to the expropriated. The employee is willing to take his share of the world's goods now, and suffer the consequences, though the idea that poverty is a blessing has a longevity which is but slowly affected by actual evidence of its devastating character, as shown in the operating rooms of hospitals, in stagnant farm homes, in the aged faces of child labor, in jaws made toothless from lack of a dentist's services, and in the dulness and bigotry of isolation and absence of books. The impecunious religious enthusiast of old looked forward to golden streets, in the meantime being disdainful of his neighbor's higher economic status, but the theoretical ulterior advantages of poverty are depreciated when the vital functioning of wealth for welfare appears at every turn. Indeed even not yet fully laid is the poor-student myth; that anyone should believe that an undernourished youth dividing his daily energy between hard labor and studies should thus make sure of laurels is about as reasonable as to expect a horse from a laundry wagon to reach the wire ahead of a racer in the pink of condition.

There should be proper and sufficient motivation in industry. To work because one fears to lose a position is a low condition, and the dread of the displeasure of the boss reduces one to the status of dumb driven cattle. Even to spend a lifetime in labor for the sake of anticipating funeral expenses does not strike one as adequate motivation. There must be sizable returns or explicit approval; there must be the feeling that one is getting somewhere, that he is getting something out of his work for himself, and that every stroke tells. To exhort one to love his work when he gets nothing out of it is unseemly. Our systemless compensation leaves the great bulk of population without effective incentive. True, the occasional person sees an opportunity for a "killing," and his community is afforded the spectacle of a man really in earnest, but the average workman, and, under present conditions, in many cases the governmental or civil service employee as well, suffers from lack of motive. The proprietor of a clothing store shows a real interest in selling goods; but his clerks, especially in his absence, may greet the incomer with a look of glazed indifference; yet such will "yell their heads off" when the home baseball team scores.

An argument for motivation may be drawn from the case of the small farmer. He directs his own labor and feeling that he is free is really little concerned with the measure of gain; he is "independent," and the fact, which should be disconcerting, that he often throws in his labor to obtain such a return on his capital as, otherwise invested, he might secure with little or no labor, impresses him but slightly— he is his own boss. Indeed, the hope of securing liberty with a few acres inspires a great many people in cities. Now to clamp a person into a position where he neither knows how much he produces, but is sure that his compensation will in any event be a minimum one, nor has a voice in the management of his employment, seems a peculiarly obnoxious affront to personality, and "industrial war" is a logical result. It is a scientific wonder that the gear of industry does not clog hopelessly under these conditions. Industry must sooner or later answer to each man his question, Of what use is it to *me*? To substantial, rational, and satisfying rewards, not complicated with gross advantage to others, the productional system must move forward, presumably through occupational autonomy, but in any case in conformity with the psychology of motive.

Where there is a feeling of injustice in economic relations, where there is imperfect motivation for effort, a spirit of indifference and protest develops which results in a kind of sabotage. Sabotage is not new; it is as old as the hills, if by it be meant injury to the quantity as well as the quality of the product. The difference in zeal between the man who has a stake in the outcome of an enterprise and one who believes he has none is so wide as not to have escaped attention the world over. Soldiering and inefficiency are characteristic of millions today, who under a different industrial organization would be energetic and optimistic. A subtle sabotage may be discovered in a thousand quarters— the waste of materials, neglect of tools and equipment, and manifold unwillingness to take pains. But how idle to expect the employee to take the same degree of interest as the employer, if the latter reaps preponderant benefits.

3. Pleasure in Work

It is a question of much importance whether real pleasure is taken in work. The actual mental attitudes prevailing among people working for wages and salaries are, if among the more elusive, yet among the most important conditions of society. If there is chronic discord between the man and his job, something is fundamentally wrong. Even in cases where irritation does not take the shape of open complaint, a seated sense of injustice deeply influences happiness on earth. Young men set out in high hopes, to become soured and careless upon being inoculated with the suspicion that a square deal in the economic system is out of the question. They see great rewards going to questionable beneficiaries; they see the industrious exploited; they come to fear that everything worth going after has been gobbled up by the representatives of privilege and corporate influence. They ask if it is worth while to try to get ahead; they believe the cards are stacked against them. The rewards which society should place before the individual should in one respect be like the penalties for crime— they should be certain.

The loosened moral fiber of great numbers, the flabby attack on difficulties, the disposition to go with the current, and the apparent passing away of a certain Spartan quality of perseverance are associated with a growing skepticism in regard to certainty of reward.

There are a multitude of the so-called shiftless. The labor market is full of men who lack incentive; is it solely their fault? But shiftlessness is bound to increase with intelligence if there seems a lessening chance of success. Is the spirit of play, of adventure, of exploration, of wager, if you please, lacking in those who make up the army of the unemployed and of those who merely mark time? Tenant farmers— and three-fifths of the farms of Illinois are operated by tenants— are notoriously shiftless. Shiftlessness would lessen if they owned the land and did not expect to be robbed in the market. The tenant who is thought to make too much money for the landlord may lose caste. It is less a wonder that so many people do so ill than that in the absence of appeal to effective motives so many do so well.

It may be argued that conditions are no worse than in the past; but it is really not by the past that the sufficiency of motivation should be judged. It is rather by the possibility of releasing energy and joy in work under more ideal conditions. Work has been a "curse," and even now the great majority, barring, among others, artists, Chautauqua lecturers, mothers, and dray drivers, who often seem to be enjoying life, seek their pleasures apart from the employments in which their lives are spent. It is commonly accepted that there is to be little happiness during working hours; some fleeting digression from occupation is looked forward to as the justification for industry, and vain amusements feebly fill a want which would better be supplied by pleasure in one's tasks.

4. Fear as Motive

Fear is still a dominant motive; fear of discharge, of disgrace, of the gun man and the militia, of starvation. The masses are not really inspirited to labor; they are driven and compelled under a fear system so rooted as to be respectable. Insufficiency and uncertainty of reward are coupled with a lagging which only the threat of suffering may overcome. But fear is blasting in its effects, even if men are so wonted as not to be acutely conscious of it. The stimulation to effort is often a push instead of a pull, but the ideal incentives are those which enlist the individual gladly for the sake of an objective clearly seen and hopefully sought. Greater openness of opportunity to all comers; less privilege and exploitation; a fairer field and fewer favors; more certainty of that social approval which consists of adequate income; better adjustment between desert and remuneration— such conditions would put spirit and joy into occupations and would advance enterprise; such conditions would be a sufficient answer to time-honored complaints in regard to the lack of interest on the part of labor. If only the world's work sprang from its hopes and ideals rather than from its fears!

In view of the actual nature of people— the springs of action— one can hardly deny that modern industrialism represents maladjustment between work and the man. Occasional employers pride themselves upon taking into account the welfare of employees, but our social and industrial standards are strangely inverted when the happiness of the worker is an afterthought.

It is possible for an employee to labor efficiently for years without knowing for a certainty that his work is appreciated. What a state of affairs, when the very breath of our nostrils is praise. Consider the lack of honor for those who do dangerous and severe work; indifference if not contempt is often their portion.

5. Self-Government in Industry

One of the requirements for a satisfying life is to have a voice in management. To have a voice in government is not more important than to have a voice in the business with which one is connected. But the autocratic principle prevails in industry. Democracy is yet to be extended to productive enterprises. The boss, the superintendent, and the proprietor have the same sort of relation to employees as autocrats to their subjects. The principle of self-government is as desirable in a factory as in a state.

As great as is the unrest of labor it is far less than autocracized industry warrants. Those who protest are still in the minority. There are still numbers like Daudet's peasants and the simple British workingmen whose psychology is so clearly described by Robert Tressall.[2] There must be a wider dissatisfaction before economic democracy may be attained, and after dissatisfaction there are problems of reorganization fully as onerous and complex as those of political democracy now in process of solution.

---

[2] *The Ragged-trousered Philanthropists.* F. A. Stokes Co., New York.

CHAPTER VII
THE CONTROL OF SUGGESTION

PROGRESS is determined largely by the thought-materials which are brought to one's attention or which, imbedded in environment, press upon the individual and insensibly shape his outlook. If we could once get away from all that is undesirable in the thought-world and move over into a world affording only the best suggestions and ideals, civilization would leap forward.

1. Inheritance of Ideas

Ideas govern action, even putting a clamp on the strongest inherited tendencies, as witness the vows of religious orders. If the modern world could be released from archaic ideas and false notions, and in their place installed the best thought and finest ideals, society would undergo swift transformation. The trouble is in clearing the decks and giving the newer thought a full opportunity. Explore the mind of the man on the seat by your side, and you will perhaps discover a flinty prejudice which could be traced back through centuries— a possession drawn out of that large fund of atavistic consciousness which science in all its pride has as yet but slightly overcome.

This control by the past is through thought-materials which come down to us in unbroken succession. Early in life one becomes saturated with sentiments and opinions from former generations. These adopted ideas govern conduct and establish types of citizenship; they determine attitude with reference to industry, science, and the state ; they create deference for ancient institutions, and sanctify imposition and caste. To secure a fresh civilization— radically to change conventional ways— would be to break with former systems of thought and sets of concepts.

The kind of ideas determines the kind of man. The reactionary is a reflex of a system of ideas dominant at an earlier period; he, for example, looks at woman suffrage in the light of former periods and applies obsolescent concepts to international differences; his concepts are stationary while society is dynamic; if the world could be turned back he would feel at home; terms like *labor, capital, patriotism, thrift, business*, and *woman* have each a different meaning to reactionary and progressive.

The basic method of changing conditions is to change ideas. The best views are often of recent origin, for the older thought was a reflex of an older social order; a new social order implies new thought.

It is not easy to shake off tradition. As population has flowed down the ages, there has been a laying on of hands upon the young in more senses than one. The old order is forever indoctrinating the young with old sets of ideas. Fortunately, youthful perversity leads to differences of opinion; cloyed with imitation, the child does the opposite of his instructions just to see how it will seem. A certain development of new thought is inevitable.

A slow-moving transformation of ideas takes place, but it would be well if tradition might be more effectually blocked and if progress-favoring ideas might be sent coursing through all the channels of intelligence. The controlling of ideas is the battle of progress the world over. Social reconstruction involves displacing certain ideas with others.

It would be idle to expect to secure always quietly and peacefully a substitution of the new for the old, for personal advantage is derived from tradition. The man who is drawing dividends from the ignorance of others is not likely to be enthusiastic for enlightenment. Privilege on the part of the few requires a corresponding education to servility on the

part of many. So in the case of various matters in dispute
agreement is hopeless; only force or the threat of it can
prevail. But outside the lines of economic warfare there may
be general agreement to oppose pernicious and encourage
salutary suggestion.

In cases where what seems evil to some seems good to others
social quarantine can hardly be attempted, and a multitude of
differences of opinion appear in relation to values; but
assuming a real concurrence among the majority of thinking
people with reference to thought-materials, the protection of
society against undesirable suggestions is as logical as the
isolation of smallpox. It is well known, for example, that the
cheap novel which exploits the crudeness and crimes of
desperadoes is, in the hands of boys, a most pernicious
influence. Not infrequently astonishing crimes are directly
traceable to the reading of accounts of brigandage, and the
glorification of lawless adventurers. Society is warranted in
defending itself against ideas that have notoriously
unwholesome effects.

2. Influence of Literature

The very reservoir of ideas inimical to an ideal
civilization is literature. Writers of former generations lend
themselves unwittingly to the defeat of the visions of the
hour. Poems are frequently a source of suggestions out of
keeping with modern aims. "The Charge of the Light
Brigade" is an example. War is irresistibly sanctified by a type
of literature which, false and misleading through omissions
of circumstances, tends to attach the highest sentiments to a
brutalizing folly. More consistent with the aims of peace are
Walt Whitman's "A Night Battle," and the Matthew Brady
photographs of the Civil War.

The influence of the monarch-revering and laborer-despising Elizabethan play is a real force making for the persistence of states of mind not conducive to modern welfare. Early literature and history are so impregnated with socially atavistic suggestions that a new literature must batter a way for truer democracy. The more impressive pre-modern literature is to one, the more unlikely is he to be found sympathetic with hopes of the hour. It is usual to side with the "lord of the vineyard" against the workers who objected to paying out of scale. It is important that the reactions of the youthful reader be carefully observed when perusing material which consorts ill with fairness to the Jew or implies the unworthiness of those who do physical work.

In many cases the reader seems to react but slightly to such early thought-materials and would hardly admit that he was to any extent controlled by the suggestions received. But if not affected by prescientific ideas of the universe, debased conceptions of womankind, the theory of human depravity, the sanction of slavery, and race prejudice, is one affected by any other kind of suggestion? All suggestions rest upon the same psychological basis. The idea that is centered in consciousness exerts its thrust in the direction of action and modifies the emotional life. At an earlier period vivid representations of future torment gave strength to the arm of persecution and resulted in peculiar horrors. If the body be thought of as, in the words of John Knox, a "wicked carcase," and if "every prospect pleases and only man is vile," why should there be any particular attention to sanitation? The immense and cherished literature of sacred song and story includes in its conglomerate a mass of materials strictly characteristic of the mental advancement of the peoples and times of their origin, and a process of sublimation and restatement, like that represented in the new prayers of Walter Rauschenbusch, is needed. Upon the extent to which outworn social concepts are supplanted in popular thought depends the rate of progress. Thus the shutting of the gates against a flood of undesirable tradition assumes large importance. English courts did not permit butchers to sit on juries in capital cases; but the slaughterhouse is not the only source of suggestions tending to indurate sympathies and degrade conceptions of human nature.

In this connection may be noted the activities of scholars who exploit the past or reconstruct former historical periods. That certain events have happened is not sufficient reason for calling universal attention to them. The world may very well forget a great deal that has occurred; we progress as we shift attention to forward-looking matters. Devotion to history, unless inspired by the desire to illuminate modern life, has but limited social value. The historical student sees objections to reforms which less informed men accomplish through unscholarly optimism. The predominance of historical elements in one's thought is of the nature of a disqualification for the attainment of newer ideals. If one reads the memoirs of a general of the Civil War one's mind will be given a reactionary set. Mark Twain believed that the South was greatly harmed by its admiration of the works of Sir Walter Scott.

3. Advertising Good Examples

There is much of a positive character to be attempted in the utilizing of the force of suggestion. The best practices and the most significant steps taken for progress in any part of the world might well be systematically called to the attention of the public. This type of constructive suggestion is illustrated in the practice of the United States Bureau of Education of sending out almost daily reports of educational progress from all parts of the nation and from abroad. The best ideas in effect anywhere are thus directed to points of possible application, and an imitation instituted which may shorten the period required for a measure of advancement. Similar efforts in other fields would tend to do away with delays in the attainment of better conditions. The advertising of good examples and the diffusing of constructive ideas should be carried on effectively through system.

The diffusion of constructive civic ideas is fundamental to social betterment. Limited reasoning and lack of creative imagination, so far as they exist, make it necessary that means be provided to reach the intelligence which do not imply mental powers above the average. Social reform requires successful appeal to the millions in whose hands rest the ballot and the ratification of programs. Everywhere arises the problem of making people understand; at this point reforms stumble and confusion begins. Kropotkin declared that the Russian peasant was capable of understanding any social principle or natural law, provided he was addressed in words of his vocabulary and the person making the explanation really knew what he was talking about. This testimony of revolutionist and scholar is indeed significant. However, it is common experience to meet with discouragement in attempts to promote measures or to popularize unfamiliar topics, and a real association of ideas is not easily brought about. Booker T. Washington tells of a Negro who was convinced in conversation of the need of substituting other crops for cotton, but when finally asked what crop he would plant answered, "Cotton." Principles agreed upon by all who give them careful and disinterested thought are slow in finding popular acceptance. Ignorance and prejudice long hold their ground. Either there are many who are unequal to taking an intelligent part in social direction or means are yet to be devised by which latent intelligence may be generously set free for such purposes. The state of civilization reflects popular intelligence, but the full power of this rarely, if ever, is evoked.

4. Use of Pictures

To secure popular response with the least expenditure of energy is a desideratum. The most open avenues of influence are to be found and used, the lines of least resistance followed. The prominence of vision among the senses offers a suggestion for directness of persuasion. The clinching evidence is that one "saw it with his own eyes." Now it is evident that the voter may not see with his own eyes the elusive brigandage of monopoly or witness the progress of a ten-million-dollar battleship from the tax collector's office to the junk heap, but by a far greater resort to pictorial methods a convincing knowledge can be imparted. Literature with its roundabout symbolism is quite inferior for various purposes to the picture-writing which historically preceded it. Illustrations make a strong appeal.

Could a more extensive educational *picturature* be developed as a substitute for verbal symbolism the response of the average mind would be greater. Many intelligent people do not care for books, never having acquired the racially recent taste for looking at queer marks on a page and trying to make out what they are all about. Where such callousness is encountered the resort to the picture would be the most effective alternative in default of oral speech, to which likewise the picture is often superior. A picture of a case of "phossy jaw" arouses a larger response than any amount of verbal statement. The public will react to a suitable stimulus— it cannot help it— but the stimulus must be one which conforms to mental laws. It would be well to photograph every social maladjustment by way of argument. Unfortunately, from some points of view, there are more authors than artists, and cameras cost more than pens and ink. A rogues' gallery of modern evils, supplemented by constructive suggestions pictorially represented, would have possibilities. Indeed, extensive use is made of the pictorial, but a larger and more convenient presentation of this kind of material is feasible.

There are limits to the effectiveness of pictures for social education, but it would appear that their possibilities have been overshadowed by the use of print. The picture method is vastly more elemental and forceful, and might be adapted to evoke popular responses for which the symbolism of type is ineffectual. True, no elaboration of the pictorial could ever carry the subtle and the associational so successfully as words, but the distinction between the eye-minded and the thinker in abstractions and principles may well be taken into account. In fact, a stage may be reached where the illustration becomes even a slight impertinence, the statement of a principle carrying the highest degree of conviction; but under the conditions of the day there is need of presenting truths in such telling form that efforts for social welfare be based as broadly as may be upon the consciousness of a public differing widely in mental content and capacity. The formal treatise and the philosophical exposition have their peculiar value, but the limited market for books that are "dry" is evidence of a rather permanent division in the interests of the reading public, while to the non-reading public the specific case and the visual argument are the principal recourse. The instant response of millions to the moving picture creates a suspicion that reform has quite too fully relied upon a relatively unpopular method— that of printed or spoken arguments. The same forces of perception and emotion which now so often go to waste in attention given to distressingly weak subject-matter at the cheap-show place might, if applied to social ends, work in brief time advancement which otherwise would require centuries. A

very extensive redirection of human forces, which so richly
abound and which so often flow aimlessly to waste, is
practicable. One is frequently surprised at the quickness with
which a desirable thought will take effect. Control images,
and civilization may be made to approximate any ideal.

5. The Slogan

After the actual picture is the word-picture. The
economy of brief statement and striking phrase is recognized
in advertising, and the joy of discovering a suitable slogan is
known to campaign managers. Brevity and imagery
characterize the statement on which reliance is placed to
secure results in dividends and votes. The spurty nature of
the commercial and political war cry, while, like the
"tiresome paradox," no source of lasting enjoyment, is
adapted to a flickering attention and to the piecemeal and
discontinuous character of consciousness in modern life.
Brevity is forceful, and headline logic must play an important
role in social reconstruction. For example, "Idle lands for idle
hands" perhaps could hardly be improved upon as
crystallizing the arguments against the present land tenure in
England, and "Votes for women" has a telling effect.

To be sure, the slogan is not without its drawbacks;
for every slogan there may be a counter-slogan, and the
reasoning process is by no means obviated; however, the
succinct presentation of issues conduces to their profitable
consideration, and indeed when a position is not susceptible
of direct and simple statement it is possibly untenable. A
claim to privilege which might be made to seem reputable if
glossed in two hours of oratory may be routed by a single
"bombshell" of rejoinder or a clarifying characterization. The
art of divesting an issue of irrelevancies and of presenting

truth naked and unashamed is one of real respectability.

There is economy in appealing in familiar terms. To bring about improvement by novel proposals is difficult, but when the new comes in familiar guise resistance is greatly lessened. The tendency is to adapt rather than invent, to modify rather than change abruptly. Merchants retain goodwill by leaving up their predecessors' signboard or incorporating under a dead man's name. Labels must be satisfactory. Political leaders know the advantage of adapting old names to new organizations. New journeys must be made by seeming to follow old routes where familiar guide boards stand. It would be easier to arrive at federal banking through the postal savings bank than by a more direct route. To do away with private express companies by the gradual expansion of the parcel post would be more practicable than to seek this result at a step. The free feeding of school children could hardly come before the free supplying of mental pabulum in the form of community-owned textbooks, and before that the community-paid instructor. The advance toward the ideal social state is a matter of slow campaigns. The thoroughgoing theorist cannot convince the public, for progress is made by short, tentative steps which do not require a high degree of vision, and by seeming to follow familiar paths.

CHAPTER VIII
CIVIC PUBLICITY AND THE VOTER

OPPOSITION to experimentation and change in the social order has a cause in a suspicion that things might be worse. The citizen often has little confidence, distrusting his own knowledge and that of others with regard to the social machine. Civic ignorance breeds a diffidence and a willingness to leave matters as they are. The fullest confidence is not reposed in public agents because so much of their work is not generally known. A better attitude would be established through civic publicity.

1. Reports upon Public Affairs

Civic administration is work for the expert, but with the transfer of power to individuals there is the danger of the unobserved abuse of that power, and it becomes necessary to develop agencies which will have the effect of placing public servants on a platform of observation and in a light which leaves nothing to the darkness which evil loves. Such transparency of office can be secured by developing official publicity far beyond its present stage. True, we have the reports of officials, as treasurers, commissioners, and boards, though, for example, the services of a congressman are not formally reported. Probably ninety-nine constituents out of a hundred have but the faintest ideas of what their representatives actually do. This is due less to the incapacity of constituents to understand language than to the absence of authentic, skilful, and ample reporting.

Moreover, the governmental report is often unduly difficult to comprehend, and, while its bulk may assure the citizen that his interests are amply protected, its obscure recesses discourage even the specialist. The art of reporting official acts to the general public is not much developed. Men are needed to tell of the work of the various offices, and thus lay a foundation for an understanding of plans of improvement and of an appreciation of exemplary service.

Even the laws are largely unknown by the public. While every citizen is presumed to know the law, no one believes that the citizen has more than an inkling of the laws under which he lives. To learn whether a city has a given ordinance may entail a visit to the city hall and exploration of a poorly arranged mass of legislation. Legislatures adjourn after sending statutes to the public printer, with little concern as to making known to the citizen what laws have been enacted. The voting public is a board of directors, but could it be imagined that a successful private corporation would be so uninformed in regard to the activities of its agents as is the voting public? Every significant detail of social administration should be flashed upon the public mind through the perfection of agencies of civic publicity, and the limitations of attention should be recognized in ingenuity of reporting. It is idle to expect the citizen to be himself a competent collector of that information which he must possess in order to vote and legislate properly at the polls. The miscarriage of modern politics is probably due more to lack of civic publicity than to lack of mentality or character. Of special interest are the attempts at civic publicity represented by the municipal journals of Baltimore, Los Angeles, San Francisco, Denver, New York, and Tacoma. The voters' pamphlet in Oregon, and the project of a state journal of governmental information in that commonwealth show an awakening to the need of agencies of civic communication in excess of those represented by the private newspaper, whose aims and interests render it not the most useful or perfect medium of political intelligence. The universities should train men and women in the technique and ideals of civic journalism. Probably most voters need only to know the sensible thing to do it, and only from lack of information vote incompetents into office or respond to disingenuous appeals which result in legislation deviously contradicting their most cherished interests.

2. The Uninformed Voter

Much is said first or last— or left unsaid— in regard to the ignorant voter. With over five million illiterates in the United States, there is a vast amount of ignorance in regard to general subjects and an amount of ignorance in regard to civic matters which should be alarming. But the essential consideration is whether ignorance represents mental incapacity in many cases or merely lack of information. It is probable that the general and civic ignorance of the illiterate and the civic ignorance prevailing among literates are but rarely due to lack of ordinary capacity. The average citizen would be found able to reach up to the point where the functions of the civic expert should begin. It is important that the special knowledge which functions in good citizenship be widely diffused and that there be actual preparation for civic responsibilities.

The idea that ballots should be weighed rather than counted is likely to occur to one when instances of civic ignorance come under observation. It is not pleasant to realize that the most judicious exercise of the ballot may be neutralized by the vote of the individual who would not appear at the polls except for the diversion of a free ride. The value of some ballots is vastly greater than of others; there are the widest differences in the actual qualifications of voters to make intelligent decisions. There are differences in age, experience, traditions, mentality, and specific information.

Statutory equality by no means implies equivalence of fitness, and in fact the exclusion from the ballot of all below twenty-one years of age and of women would indicate that prevailing tests of fitness are far from exact. Who should vote? What qualifies a person to vote?

Evidently one should know the subject-matter of elections— issues, candidates, measures, political conditions, and the trend of society. One should have a preparation comparable to that which would warrant expressing an opinion on architecture, sanitation, engineering, agriculture, or poetry. If issues have been reduced to simplicity and there is a leadership in which confidence may justly be reposed, a minimum of social science may serve, by making use of the analytical powers of others. A person who would fail in every test of specific information might vote right from intuition or by accident, but the test of information is one which is relied upon in judging the qualifications of physicians, pilots, chemists, and postal clerks, and it evidently should have exceptional weight in ascertaining fitness to fill the position of voting citizen.

But how could a mental test be applied? While there is a sentiment in favor of educational tests for voters, and in at least one state (North Dakota) the constitution enjoins upon the legislature the duty of establishing educational tests, practical difficulties interpose. Yet no one can question the need of distinguishing between fitness and unfitness. With constitutional amendments and measures in detail coming before the electorate, especially under direct legislation, it is reasonable that the civic board of directors, which is the collective body of voters, should be admitted to the exercise of their function only upon proof of competence.

3. Is an Educational Test Feasible?

Fortunately an effectual educational test is within easy reach and indeed is in process of realization. The submission of specific measures 1 as under the initiative and referendum, tends to make voting difficult, requiring not only interest but attention and reasoning. Heretofore voting has required the barest minimum of information. But with a ballot containing matter which must be read with attention to be understood, and with the relegation of partisan and personal considerations, voting becomes a feat of slight appeal to any who are not conscious of the nature of public questions. A weeding out in the electorate accordingly results, as witness the diminishing vote of Wisconsin under direct primaries and direct legislation. The relatively small vote usually cast upon constitutional amendments and city charters when submitted to the electorate is evidently not due to their unimportance but rather to the absence of an interest derived from knowledge. There is an inevitable mental test when measures are submitted to voters, and a diminished vote may be construed as meaning that a stimulus is being applied which should result in citizens studying more. The person who knows nothing about the merits of a proposal on his ballot will naturally not vote on it, thus becoming automatically disqualified by ignorance. Mechanical voting, even for candidates, should be rendered unlikely or impossible.

While perhaps sufficient difficulties are inherent in direct legislation, surely no predigestion of subject-matter should be attempted in behalf of those, no matter how large their numbers among rich or poor, male or female, who are indolent, careless, illiterate, or incompetent. The intelligent and thoughtful should rule, and civic incompetence should not be afforded an opportunity to vote by means of a ballot so designed as to allow voting to be an unthinking process. Voting has been much too easy. The man who conscientiously follows political questions should not have his vote counteracted by that of one indifferent to public affairs. The inequitable character of easy balloting is evident, for the person who takes pains to inform himself is not rewarded by a larger measure of participation. With the ballot itself so devised as to be an educational test every citizen fitted to vote has the privilege, and disqualification may be removed by effort. Voting should necessitate reading and understanding whatever might appear as an educational test upon the ballot.

Inasmuch as one's interest in a subject is closely related to his knowledge of it, the actual number of those voting upon a measure would approximate the number of voters really prepared to vote, and the smallness of the number of votes cast should not be at all disconcerting. Such provision of law, as that of the constitution of the state of Minnesota, which requires that a high percentage of the electorate must ballot upon proposed constitutional amendments for a valid decision, are of doubtful wisdom, especially if adequate provision is made for publicity with reference to pending measures. When once freely informed of issues, the individual who does not vote may wisely in most cases be thought to be lacking in those qualities which should count for most in elections, and the smallness of the number balloting be regarded as good evidence of its select character. Surely the right to vote should be contingent upon the correlated duty of knowing upon what one is voting; it is a common rule that one should know what he is doing.

No educational test would work properly in the absence of stringent enforcement of corrupt-practices acts. The citizen who has so little interest and information as not to go to the polls of his own volition should not be solicited. That one should have to be urged to vote indicates that his ballot might safely be dispensed with. Improper solicitation of votes should be made impossible, and the few worthy citizens who forget election days if not sent for might well be a sacrifice to the general cause. Under the foregoing conditions balloting would take on a character of distinction, and the seriousness of an examination for the credentials of the profession would to a degree appear.

The questions of Negro and woman suffrage would easily be resolved under the principle of mental fitness. Such Negroes and such women, and, as well, such present voters, as whose capacity and information qualified them to vote, would realize the right. The line of separation between voters and non-voters would not be artificially drawn, but would nearly coincide with actual fitness. Thus there would be every incentive to qualify, and no one would be excluded from voting except for reasons under his control.

The submission of propositions under direct legislation stimulates civic intelligence. If balloting be merely upon names, perhaps followed by party symbols to guide the uninformed, as in Massachusetts and New York, there is less incentive to study civic questions. Voting upon definite proposals encourages a study of government. The submission of question after question to the electorate, perhaps with greater frequency of votings during the year, would connect public opinion directly with government and result in a far higher level of civic intelligence. Incalculable stimulus would result from balloting upon propositions for representatives to carry out rather than merely for representatives. To be limited to voting for candidates when there are scores of issues upon which many voters would like to express themselves dulls interest in public affairs.

CHAPTER IX
THE LEGAL MIND

THE psychology of the bench and bar is especially important because of the large part played by the courts in shaping civilization. The United States is in a sense under a commission form of government, the commission consisting of the federal Supreme Court, with its power over legislation. The power of the judiciary is immense and determinative. And when we group bar with bench the character of prevailing mental states becomes a matter of great importance. Attorneys are of a type with judges, and the legal mind has marked characteristics.

1. The Rule of Precedent

Law represents a continuity with the past like that of few other occupations. The lawyer's training harks back to early English and Roman law. Of much influence is the study of cases, of varying antiquity or recency, from which points of view are derived and bearings established, and by which the mind is shaped into conformity with legalistic ideals. The full force of legal tradition is brought to bear, both in schools of law and through association with the elders, upon the naked natures of young men and a distinct mentality results, characterized by logical structure, subtlety, and conservatism.

Compare, for example, the training of the student of science with that of the law student. The former is led to believe that experimentation is the key to truth, and the older a textbook the less authoritative is it regarded. Ideas are discarded with actual fervor, and stiff orthodoxy is impossible. In scientific learning the spirit is that of progressive adjustment; in law this spirit is not dominant—

quite the reverse. Indeed, the weight of tradition in the law gives the legal mind a quality which tends to freeze society into static conditions. Emphasis upon the application of rules to social problems does not accord with forward-looking tendencies. The role of remembering how things have been done and of striving to apply possibly inappropriate rules to current affairs limits outlook.

What is perfectly possible may be legally impossible, and what is legal may to the layman appear unreasonable. Rules of evidence have wandered so far from rationality that young attorneys are advised not to try to see the reason for some of them but to remember them as they are. One must renounce the world as he knows it in order to attain the legal cosmos. The real world and the judicial world conflict the moment one brings social and moral ideals into the atmosphere of the law; a professor of law once remarked to his students, "You are here not to learn what the law ought to be but to find out what the law is."

Possibly the root of such opposition of law to progress is in the attempt to reduce to settled concepts a social flux. The notion that law is a science— in the sense in which physics or chemistry is a science— is misleading, and to apply the word science to a subject-matter consisting, under progressive conditions in society, of transient expedients and adjustments and halfway places introduces error. Hydrogen, two parts, and oxygen, one part, form water; but rage and a knife do not equate perfectly with fourteen years in a penitentiary. Seeming inconsistency is not incompatible with justice. Rules are properly subordinate to discrimination. But it is objected that with discretion enthroned no one would know the law; who knows it now?

The fixedness of the law is its undoing. It is not from an earlier social order that we should seek guidance for present relationships; moreover, various legal positions and doctrines have the dubious ancestry of privilege. Only such former

decisions as are approved by modern thought have any
authority and these merely through the accident of
concurrence. Cases should be subjected to fresh thought and
their disposition be made to square with present standards.
The law is not more reputable than the circumstances of its
origin, reflecting, it may be, the unjust power of lords of
manors, holders of royal patents, owners of sailing vessels,
masters of servants and apprentices, and husbands. The
discord between ethics and "what the law allows" is
notorious. Even the ideal of one law for the poor and the rich
is open to criticism. What fairness, for example, in applying
the same anti-trust law to grimy and poverty-stricken coal
miners and to a billion-dollar monopoly? Worthy judges are
not rare; but to the extent of their excellence they dare
excursions into the world of today and tomorrow.

2. Lawyers and Society

The type of learning most needed in the
administration of justice is that represented by the social
sciences, especially those applications of sociology which deal
with actual conditions among laborers, wives, children, and
other classes. The recent recommendation of the American
Bar Association that law students be required to pursue the
study of psychology indicates an awakening; for the
examination of witnesses is a matter rather for a
psychological clinic than for denunciation and oratory. In
fact, oratory and tradition have conspired to render the legal
profession, with its nearness to legislation, especially in the
United States, an obstacle to public welfare. The striking
progress in government in New Zealand has been explained
as being due in part to the almost total absence of lawyers
from the parliament of that country. A fresh view of human

possibilities is a high qualification for service in a legislature. To serve at important points in the administration of justice, would it not be well to seek men and women who should follow the advice of former Judge Gaynor to throw away law books for the reading of Browning? The presence of "lay judges"— to represent the non-legal point of view— provided such were to consist of eminent publicists, sociologists, educators, journalists, and social workers, men and women, would prove a corrective.

Moreover, conditions prevailing in courts do not lend themselves happily to actual justice. Litigants are aggressive, and attorneys are not engaged to report after the manner of the scientific investigator. When ingenious and hardened advocates are fabulously financed to circumvent justice when necessary for private advantage, and when successful subterfuge reacts to the fame of the advocate, there is real confusion. Not thus are scientific issues resolved. The attorney should be a real officer or agent of court, paid by society. The pronounced forwardness on the part of retained attorneys is an impertinence. The German system of people's courts without lawyers represents a triumph of method, and the recently established lawyerless courts of Kansas afford profitable suggestions.

Prejudiced advocacy, characteristic of the bar, is not confined to the courts, but in part through legal example perverts behavior elsewhere. Thus the college debating team elects as its aim, not the impartial revealing of the merits of an issue, but rather the adroit presentation of "one side" of a question, and to beat the opposing group of advocates is the prime consideration. In the course of such partisan strife the truth may be forced out— recently established lawyerless courts of Kansas afford profitable suggestions.

Prejudiced advocacy, characteristic of the bar, is not confined to the courts, but in part through legal example perverts behavior elsewhere. Thus the college debating team elects as its aim, not the impartial revealing of the merits of an issue, but rather the adroit presentation of "one side" of a question, and to beat the opposing group of advocates is the prime consideration. In the course of such partisan strife the truth may be forced out ultimate influence upon legislation and social welfare, or on the other hand a system of training judges and attorneys might be installed which would modify the obstructionistic nature of the law, doing away with antiquated concepts, sacred rituals, and deteriorated wisdom. The socializing of the lawyer's functions as in the public law office of New Zealand, where the citizen may secure legal advice from a state-paid official, is desirable. Today, under the system of fee-taking, the average citizen is not quite sure whether the lawyer is a curse or a blessing. The bulwarks of privilege and social atavism represented by the legal mind deny the modern spirit free expression. The diversion and unworthy devotion of talents appearing in the retaining of a swarm of the keenest minds in the service of predatory wealth— essentially in a battle against the poor— represents an impressive miscarriage of a mentality which should be harnessed to social welfare, and creates a condition against which the more idealistic of the legal profession must rebel. Lawyers need a thoroughly modern education, which means that they should not study too much law. They need to get the biological or evolutionary point of view, to conceive of society as on the way to being different. The authoritative solemnity of the legalist needs to be mitigated; justice does not reside in the breasts of judges unless judges look upon life unfettered by tradition. There is a better intelligence than that represented by the law. There is a valid idealism which is everywhere blocked by legalism. It is unfair to measure the intelligence of a people by their institutions provided a tradition-revering type is in a position to apply a stranglehold on new thought through power to interpret and to pass on the constitutionality of laws. With government thus subject to the legal mind, popular intelligence cannot function happily.

3. Experimental Legislation

The legal point of view is seen in the citizen who opposes experimental legislation. To experiment in affairs of state is regarded as objectionable, and to style a measure an experiment is intended as an argument in opposition. From a scientific point of view this aversion is an anomaly. Why should there not be experimentation in social administration? There is a suspicion that objection is often from fear lest novelty should prove a success, to the abatement of privilege; but quite aside from selfish strategy there is no doubt a real opposition or indifference with reference to the adoption of laboratory methods in civic affairs.

To be sure, the subject-matter of society is less amenable to convenient experimental treatment than are acid soils or guinea pigs; even so it should be possible to study social reactions under experimental conditions. Whenever an opportunity presents itself gratuitously for a study in government, be it the recall of judges in Arizona or the single tax in cities of the Canadian northwest, let the most be made of it. Indeed, let it be urged as a reason for proposals that they are experiments. That the light of the past should be the only guide is a confession which in the field of science would discredit the proclaimer; the light of theory and trial is also a strong light.

A desire for repose and a settled order no doubt contributes to the feeling that there should be no tinkering with laws. New measures are adopted with hesitation, and a common attitude of mind is that a measure, once accepted, should remain unchanged. The proposal to limit legislative sessions to rare intervals seems quite opposed to the spirit of experiment.

A vast amount of futile talk would be displaced by the simple expedient of trying proposals for improvements in civic administration; there would be less occasion to "view with alarm" if it were commonly accepted that in case an experiment turned out poorly there should be a return to practice. Does the abolition of capital punishment in one state increase murder therein as against another state in like circumstances? Let an experiment be tried to find out. It is better that a homicide should live than that doubt should exist. Is the commission form of government applicable to states? We should rejoice if a given state has the seeming temerity to try it. An experiment could not be less undesirable than uncertainty. Would votes for women "ruin the home"? Observation should decide, not speculation. Is a two-cent rate on railroads impossible, or even a lower rate? The answer is, try it. Would the country go to the dogs if life insurance were offered by a commonwealth? We should indeed be appreciative of the spirit which gains for Oregon, Wisconsin, and New Zealand the reputation of being experiment stations in government. It would be better that Congress should guarantee against want the owners of the steel trust than that doubt should remain as to the necessity of a duty to protect its products. Let us gather the facts even as truth is sought in the laboratories of the chemist and the bacteriologist. It is to be expected that when benzoate of soda, under a pure-food law, becomes a political rather than a chemical term, self-interest will oppose and confuse; but there is no good reason why a few should be allowed to block attempts to find the best ways of doing things. Possibly the great advances in natural and physical science have come about so readily because of the negligibility of the cross fire to which scientists have been subjected.

In case of governmental experimentation, however,

there is present the bad boy of big business to break the microscopes and spill the cultures of tentative reform. But the inductive method is a rock and refuge.

The device of permissive laws is useful in introducing novelty. Let the people of a civil division be at liberty to experiment. The terms of a law may be made to apply at the discretion of those concerned.

The spirit of experimentation characterizes some occupations rather than others, and the advantage of having legislation, so far as it is conducted by chosen bodies, directed by men and women of known progressiveness occurs to one. The dead hand of tradition holds reins which should be held by individuals accustomed to methods of investigation and discovery and familiar with hypothesis. Indeed, a bureau of social engineers might well be established to make novel proposals, which, upon popular ratification, would promote welfare by demonstration. Experimentation should be utilized in the field of social developments, for it is one of the strongest aids of mind. The scientific method may well be applied to government, and the spirit of the scientist and the seeker after truth be made to supplant the widely diffused mild horror of social experimentation.

CHAPTER X
VIEWS OF PROPERTY

THE relation of wealth to welfare is so close that almost every social issue leads to a consideration of the distribution of wealth, which rests upon certain mental traits and states of opinion.

1. Exclusive Ownership

In dealing with property psychology we meet first of all with the idea of exclusive possession, an idea that is fully as instinctive as rational, for in a multitude of cases the personal ownership of a utility is not important for its enjoyment. A concrete walk in front of one's house is of no more utility to the owner than is his neighbor's walk over which he passes; of course as such walk would raise the value of his property and would therefore have an exchange value, there would be advantage in ownership. But for practical enjoyment a multitude of objects are perhaps even best owned by someone else. It was Thoreau who visited various farms, talked with their owners in regard to his purchase of them, and went away without buying, having absorbed, so he wrote, the real value in them from having clambered over their picturesque acres. He left to the farmer the burden of ownership while he stole away with the principal delights. Even the Great Man who talks for a dollar admission fee may deign to say a few words to the group at the railroad station, and anyhow his likeness is in the discarded magazine, and his remarks, even perhaps more inclusive than those actually made by him, may be found in a newspaper from the waste-paper basket. So many values become uncorked that the veriest hobo is not to be denied his share in a free wealth of society. Here and there are individuals who say they cannot really enjoy unless they own, but what difference does ownership make provided one has the use of a thing? It is only for use that ownership rests at all in reason rather than solely upon the acquisitive instinct.

Uses can be enjoyed increasingly in common, and to this extent private ownership is growing to be an anachronism. Not by any means that great wealth has become more than faintly reduced to common uses, but the tendency is manifest. The number of utilities in whose use the public may readily share is growing. Why should a man having boys buy them sets of tools when the city school has its equipment of hammers and saws? Few private collections of books can equal those of a modest public library, and one's home may well be used for other purposes than the storage of books not in active use. Free lectures are as inspiring as if paid for dearly, and they are numerous. The counsel of an expert of the United States Department of Agriculture is as valid as if he took fees for advice and one were to give him two-thirds of the first year's crop upon the contingency of a good yield. The public school returns one's child in as good condition as if from the ministrations of a tutor, and the postman who delivers one's letters would not be complimented to be told that he has all the faithfulness of the expressman.

But, to be sure, we all own a share in these governmental agencies— we own them, but not as private owners. Joint ownership thus is not exclusive, and it carries with it a distinctly higher social sense. And this sense of common ownership is most desirable. Property sentiments may be transferred to public-owned utilities. The feeling in favor of exclusive ownership is mostly pride and prejudice. Really only a few things need be privately owned, these being utilities whose use could not be shared; but in an increasing number of cases joint enjoyment is possible and tolerable.

The things one would not share with others belong especially to the sphere of food, clothes, physical maintenance, and immediate surroundings. The fruitlessness of the holding of wealth by the overrich is revealed by willingness to part with it for a slight consideration of repute, and the inability to make other than social use of great wealth is evident. The development of common wealth stores will follow the conviction that one need not own in exclusion in order to enjoy.

With social ownership the sense of possession would simply be transferred to social types of property, and what is "mine" would include an undivided share in what society owns. One requires wealth only for its actual consumption or for the assurance of future income; accordingly the primal instinct of self-preservation, which appears as the desire for possession, would be amply recognized in the common ownership of social utilities, which are legion, and especially in the guaranty by the state of an adequate income, resting upon individual contribution to the total production of society.

2. Ownership and Social Viewpoint

The effect of social ownership upon the outlook of the citizen would be far-reaching. The government would be his business. The interest of the man of independent means is now often solely that there be no interference with his income; he rarely feels a common cause. A social point of view can scarcely develop under dominant private ownership. Common ownership affords a basis for a brotherhood preached but not practiced. The antagonism between ethics and business will continue until economic causes are removed.

Not only may culture establish a sense of public

property, but definite gratification may be developed with regard to the participation of others in all those utilities which might be made accessible through social ownership. Narrowly instinctive possession is accompanied by callousness with reference to the privations of others. At the present stage in the evolution of social sentiments striking indifference to the extent of others' deprivations unfortunately appears.

The dealer in pianos is indifferent as to whether he sells one piano at a profit of a hundred dollars or two at a profit of fifty dollars each. In numberless cases a far wider use of commodities would be made if the principle of maximum use were substituted for an indifference as to the number making purchases provided the profits are the same with a large or small number of sales. If the success of a railroad were judged by the number of persons or tons of freight transported for a given annual net profit, rather than by profits alone, public welfare would be immensely furthered. Under social ownership the opening wide of the gates of transportation would be an ideal and the actual extent to which the public used railroads would be the test of efficient management. The extent of consumption is the most acceptable criterion. The management of the telegraph should be judged by frequency of use. Today when a citizen of the United States receives a telegram he fears someone has died. The public librarian counts success by the number of volumes drawn for use. Consumption, not profit, is the true measure.

Through the ownership of the means through which labor operates to produce wealth, namely, capital and tools, a few are enabled to exclude the many from utilities which might be caused to exist, and indeed bring it about that in a world where endless productivity is possible, with resulting welfare, the securing of a job, at modest compensation, becomes a goal of intense rivalry, to obtain which laborers not

infrequently break one another's heads. The exclusion of
people from work is, upon consideration, a remarkable fact;
but as work is merely a means to a living, the real fact
illustrated is the exclusion of people, sometimes in great
numbers, from the privilege of securing goods whereby to
live. When the producer creates more wealth than he can buy
back with his wages he contributes to his own downfall, and
is even denied the opportunity of further employment, for
"overproduction" occurs and men are thrown out of work.
Ownership results in the exclusion of would-be producers
from tilling idle lands, and occasionally from working more
than half-time at factories which turn out commodities
which the public would be very pleased to consume if they
had the money with which to buy. Joblessness is a strange
feature of a system of production. Of all economic mysteries
that of exclusion from productive labor is the most
outstanding. It is possible so to order industry that
production would not need to back-pedal lest there should be
too much produced of things people really want.

3. Thrift

A phase of privation to which even some honor is
accorded is that of self-exclusion from enjoying the utilities
which one actually succeeds in securing the means to pay for.
Thrift, so far as it inures to increased production, evidently
has merits, but, so far as it implies a pinching of life, is
distinctly opposed to a higher civilization. The effort to save
up enough money with which to pay one's self a pension
during old age often results in a life of meagerness, and a
legacy. The recipient of a two-thousand-dollar income who
saves half of it is a thousand-dollar man in the meantime,
with the limits of experience and outlook which go with such

expenditure. One must spend to grow; hence the doubtful virtue of strict economy. And such economy most often falls hardest upon the wife; is this a reason why woman has been so long retarded in civic and intellectual development? The world is really relieved from the possibility of a desperate stagnation by the person who spends money. Were saving governed by discretion as to choice among ways of spending money, an immense acceleration of progress would ensue from the development of new wants and a consequent broadening of experience and mentality. To save money so as to be able to buy desirable goods or services, resulting in personal development, is one thing; but to save to accumulate a fund the interest from which will support one in old age, in the meantime paring down life to meagerness, may be necessary under present conditions but should not be mistaken for an absolute virtue.

Very likely the instinct to own would not appear in so extreme a form if it were not for the ever-present fear of not being well taken care of in old age. Impelled by this fear many find less than possible enjoyment in life year by year, and an unworthy obsession drives them to accumulate more and more. When actual happiness comes to be given due consideration in the social economy the abolition of unnecessary concern about support in old age will receive attention. The net result of this fear is to subtract from daily joy, without supplying the best set of motives for conduct and enterprise. The greed of property and the disputatiousness of bargaining rest to a large degree upon considerations of personal safety which might be more happily recognized in social assurance of care in disability and old age. Even the possession of large means does not dispel such fear, for one's property may be lost.

4. Great Expectations

The tendency to private rather than social ownership arises partly from great expectations. The individual dreams of the golden fleece, of a lucky strike, of great good luck. A much-advertised success fires with the hope of individual aggrandizement and puts the virus of non-cooperative selfishness into the blood. With every man expecting that he will be the one to "strike oil," the prosaic certainty of fairly uniform meagerness of income has little chance of credence. To face the truth that under existing conditions the fate of the great majority is to remain below a certain economic level, and that personal ambition can rarely avail if system is opposed, is less agreeable than to indulge hopes of special providence. The most stupefying social inequalities therefore pass without challenge— for tomorrow I may also be of the chosen. Under exceptional conditions, as in the industry and trade of pioneer communities, based on limitless natural resources, self-sufficiency has a degree of justification, but under more usual conditions the expectation of individual wealth lacks support. One of the first steps for economic democracy is to convince the individual of the fact that no bank has more than one president, and that the wealth of the world would not suffice to make every clerk a man of millions; upon which considerations a bristling assurance of not being as others are would suffer a certain eclipse. There is a kind of hope which delays the arrival of a rationally ordered economic society. The billions of organized wealth in a few hands rest largely upon the obsession of money adventure which afflicts the miracle-loving and luck-expectant mind.

5. Attitude Toward Taxes

A state of mind which constitutes a real obstacle to progress is opposition to paying taxes. The dislike may be partly due to fear lest one should pay more than his share, but presumably is rather because the services and utilities which the state affords are not so clearly realized as are those bought individually. To the extent to which public money is raised inequitably or expended improperly the citizen may well resist, but only through civic nearsightedness could the collective purchasing by society of schools, medical attendance, expert service, fire protection, parks, and transportation be opposed. A common playground renders it unnecessary for every family to own a private playground. One may see the ocean and reflect upon barnacle-incrusted rocks as fruitfully in the public park of a seaport town as from any other vantage point, and one's contribution to the social purchase of utilities should be made with downright satisfaction. Far from grumbling upon payment to the state, the citizen should cultivate a satisfaction in social ownership. By contributing to the purchase of public libraries the citizen secures the vastness of literature for next to nothing. Under equitable circumstances one should watch the mounting rate of taxation or the increase of income of socially owned enterprises with real satisfaction, not to say enthusiasm, and realize that the day of common wealth dawns.

To be consistent in the dread of taxes the citizen should flinch as little from direct as from indirect payments; but the atavistic nature of this fear is evident when one considers that a dollar paid out indirectly under the tariff is as really spent as if paid to the tax collector. The future psychologizing historian may well class among the monstrous incunabula of humbug the indirect tax and exclaim at its actual popularity in various forms. What changes would follow the translation of every indirect tax into direct taxation! Then the seemingly sourceless money so prodigally spent on battleships would seem to be dug out of the private purse, and peace would be popular.

The fallacy of indirect payment appears likewise in the reserve attending the compensation of public servants as contrasted with the prodigality of incomes paid indirectly. The community which would cavil at paying a public servant three thousand dollars a year pays uncomplainingly perhaps ten thousand dollars to the president of the local bank and beholds with equanimity the gathering in of the unearned increment on a township of land by a prominent citizen amounting to scores of thousands of dollars annually. In either case the public pays, but whether directly or indirectly, whether by formal act or merely in reality, makes a difference.

The farmers of a state pay with acquiescence their contributions to individual commercial incomes ranging upward to hundreds of thousands of dollars a year, but demur at the payment of more than meager living expenses to men employed in state universities, who, if properly buttressed financially, might declare an intellectual independence taking the shape of a more active espousal of the interests of citizens of small means.

That the origin of wealth, under organized political and industrial society, is social is beyond question, and the payment of incomes to individuals is as truly by society when in the form of dividends or profits as when voted by public boards and paid on warrants drawn by public officials. But the popular reaction to incomes paid directly differs widely from the reaction to indirect payment. Thus it comes about that while the man who markets a scientific product may receive an income of a hundred thousand dollars a year, the nation pays the director of a federal experiment station less than five, and that while a member of the cabinet whose work relates to manufacturing is paid twelve thousand dollars a year, a beneficiary of the steel trust is awarded by the same public an income which permits the easy gift of library edifices sufficient in number to serve as mileposts from Salt Lake City, Utah, to Providence, Rhode Island.

6. Competition and Character

Emphasis upon private possession and failure to conceive the larger freedom of cooperation result in an unnecessarily severe subsistence competition, in which the aim is to get the most for one's self regardless of how others are affected. Tricks and cruelties of trade are inevitable under the conditions.

It would be fortunate if conditions were arranged to bring out the best in people. Human nature has its fundamental and abiding tendencies and also qualities which are simply reflections of environment. Whether a man becomes a prize fighter or a soldier of the Lord depends upon guiding influences. The channels of expression afforded by one's social setting lead to large consequences. A power of imagination which under right culture might issue in scientific hypotheses may under a wrong culture qualify the consummate liar. Mere exhortations to integrity have but slight effect if the whole pressure and argument of daily circumstance are to the contrary. The individual is responsive to conditions under which he must maintain himself, even to the disregard of ideals. The iniquity of circumstances is as real as the depravity of men. If one manufacturer puts shoddy in his cloth others are likely to do the same or go out of business; we are good or bad together. There is scarcely a lawyer who would not prefer to fight the battles of the poor— if he could support his family as well.

With physical maintenance assured, and in the absence of disproportionate private wealth, competition would assume forms now barely possible. Instead of being controlled by financial considerations, the individual would be relatively free to apply his energies to ideal tasks. There are millions today whose aptitudes for creating things in the spirit of art are stunted because of dog-eat-dog economic conditions. To compete in advancing the common good under a system permitting cooperation rather than resulting in collision and the neutralization of efforts would amount to being civilized. The desire to excel may be enlisted for social purposes. It is a matter of social organization whether two retailers or physicians hate and envy or pull together. People prefer to compete for good opinion but they have to live first.

That an unpleasant competition for subsistence must prevail is a fallacy of the popular mind. Harmonious relationships and enterprise would be possible were there social provision for physical maintenance. For a higher civilization a minimum subsistence must be assured, that energies may be set free for better forms of effort.

There is about as much moral excellence in the world as there can be considering the stake in making money. Without a better economic order one can imagine the people of ten thousand years hence cheating, grafting, adulterating, skinning jobs, hiring lawyers to find loopholes in statutes, swearing off taxes, and gouging the helpless. A low form of subsistence competition emphasizes these activities and gives the trader a foxy air.

It is not to be argued, however, that what Stevenson calls a "strong sense of personal identity" is not a valuable social asset. Unselfishness is pleasing, so let a word be spoken for selfishness. The preferring of others to one's self has bounds beyond which the results are harmful. Whenever individuals in a class are content with little they place a ball and chain upon others who have spirit and ambition. The school teacher who is willing to work for forty dollars a month, because of undeveloped wants, supplies an element which causes professional solidarity to crumble, and through a consequent weakening of education tends to defeat the very aims of civilization. The workingman who does not mind eating from the confines of a hot tin pail delays the arrival of an industrial commissariat and the uplift of labor. The assertion of self is self-respect, and one cannot properly respect others until his own wants are positive. A willingness to be nothing is a crime against mankind. The amount of actual damage which the humble and contrite of spirit can inflict upon the class to which they belong, upon the coming generation, and upon relatives is equaled perhaps by nothing short of war and pestilence. To fail of self-assertion is to carry backward the hopes of others.

But with selfishness discredited there must be offense, and for selfishness without imagination little that is good may be said. There is self-seeking in whose defense no one can speak. It is the altruistic variety of self-assertion which may be commended. Let us work for pure milk, for if others' children are safe mine will be. Here is the circle of considerations which enlightened selfishness, more reputably known as altruism or social service, pursues. To be selfish in a large way is to help others. In seeking personal ends with imagination advantages gained overflow to the general good.

CHAPTER XI
A SENSE OF HUMANITY

A CALAMITY in any part of the world affects every other part. War and waste, flood and famine set up influences that reach far. The retardation of any nation, its ignorance and illiteracy, similarly menace other nations through diseases brought in at ports or through an immigration carrying with it low standards. A country cannot long maintain a civilization far above the average; no country can safely be insensible to conditions prevailing elsewhere. A highly cultivated family living among the ignorance and dirt of neighbors is constantly menaced. So with a nation. It is important that there be no backward nations, for they are a drawback to civilization the world over. The evolution of the working class is hampered by the existence of serf states of mind in the farthest country on the map. To better one's own condition one must think in terms of fraternity. Brotherhood is dictated by economic considerations. It is necessary that parochialism and provincialism be done away with, and that a ruinous patriotism, out of which conflicts and hatreds rise, be dispossessed by world consciousness.

This consciousness is appearing, to a large extent arising from causes not deliberately set in motion. International commerce has developed a non-provincial point of view. To become friendly when there is mutual understanding is as inevitable as once to regard the stranger as a natural enemy to be defrauded, killed, or eaten. Acquaintance and communication make for a world sense. Hence the advantage of the convening of international congresses to consider scientific and other subjects not confined to national boundaries. The interchange of instructors among the schools of various countries is of promise, and the development of fraternalism represented by the international socialist movement, which binds together the working classes of the more developed peoples, is a contribution to world betterment whose importance can hardly be exaggerated.

It is especially desirable that there be appeals to the emotions in behalf of internationalism. The man who thinks knows already that there is everything to gain by world concord, so it is the man governed by other people's ideas who needs to be reached, and he requires a training of the emotions. An international flag would have possibilities an international emblem, always to float above the flags of nations, which now stand in part for the concentrated prejudices and hatreds of centuries, fortifying evil moods by perpetual reminder.

The emphasizing of the social rather than the national aspects of history weakens virulent patriotism and establishes a better outlook. National egotism is inflamed by attention to old-time military episodes and by the selection of historical materials which, as in Germany, may be designed rather to form willing recruits to the colors than to make intelligence impartial. While rational people usually claim recovery from early impressions received from textbooks in history, a recrudescence of juvenile prejudice perhaps awaits but the blare of the band, and Fourth of July oratory and reminiscence are not without saddening implications.

Membership in clannish groups makes for anti-social states of mind. It is natural to form clans and groups, but it is important that the sense of kinship shall not be too limited. The member of a gang is unfitted for society because his world is too small. If his loyalty extended to the general public he would be a good citizen. The politician whose world is confined to his "friends" is, let us hope, to be superseded by the servant of the public whose devotions are not even confined to his "party." So the individual content to hurrah only for his city, college, baseball team, denomination, or country should be regarded as having stages of development ahead of him. The highest attitude is expressed in the words, "The world is my country and to do good is my religion."

1. Instinctive Basis of War

The chronic impediment to world fellowship is war, or the spirit which outcrops in war, a spirit whose basis is in instinct; for there is no reason, no logic, for war. It is an instinctive reaction to a situation. War does not improve a race; it does not improve morals; it does not in general help business; it does not add to happiness; it has not a single rational justification.

On the other hand it combines evils so almost scientifically that it might be regarded as the masterpiece of diabolical intelligence. True, it intensifies national spirit— and thus prepares for more wars. There is no well-reasoned and uninspired support of war, and it is the problem of dealing with its peculiar psychology that is today uppermost.

It is instinctive to react to an affront by the most direct method, to strike back. This native response, hardly exhibited at all in the shooting of strangers in long-drawn-out campaigns, appeals especially to intelligence little prescient of results and impatient of reason. The physical rather than the mental resolution of a difficulty implies an absence of rationality. Worsted in debate, the undeveloped man may ejaculate, "Well, I can *lick* him anyhow"; failing to repair a machine, he feels like smashing it; unable to command the intelligence required to deal with child or horse, he "gives it a good thrashing"; whenever intelligence fails to solve a problem, force is resorted to. To be sure, either party to a fight may alone be the undeveloped individual. But in every case a fight is a resort to instinctive rather than rational alternatives, and every conflict implies either primitive mind or a bullying for unfair advantage.

The psychology of war is primitive, and primitive mind is found in adolescents. The armies of the North in the Civil War were made up largely of boys— virtually constituting a children's crusade. Boys like nothing better than war tales, this selection representing their sharing in the emotional life of primitive man; however, except in cases of a virtual arrest of development, sometimes even appearing in men of otherwise consistent maturity, youth is likely to outgrow the militaristic stage and acquire peace traits.

2. Desire to Travel

So far as wars represent the willing participation of the private soldier, the motives are not far to seek. The travel impulse is a dominant one among adolescents, the desire to see new places being among the strongest of interests.[1] Enlistment has been a means of securing travel, which historically has been beyond the purse of the average youth. The appeal is made to young men to join the navy in order to "see the world." One can imagine the downright delight of the adolescent in former periods, before the days of the

---

[1] Professor E. L. Thorndike in his *Principles of Teaching*, A. G. Seller, New York, p. 101, gives a list of ten interests; viz., being at a party; eating a good dinner; playing indoor games, such as games of cards; playing outdoor games, such as baseball, basket-ball, tennis; working with tools, as carpentering or gardening; hearing music, as at a concert; being present at a theater; reading a story; resting, such as lying in a hammock or on a couch; traveling or seeing new places. It is the experience of the present writer that when adolescents are asked to indicate their preferences in order among these interests the first choice falls to traveling or seeing new places, with hearing music in second place.

locomotive, when a call to arms meant an excursion from England into France or from France to Ireland. During the period of chronic wars only the rich could travel, and the migratory instinct, of which the railroad today is the principal outlet, was corked up. Even the known dangers of arms presumably barely dampened the ardor for such seeing of new places. The time is now scarcely past when one who had been abroad was venerated and envied. The talk of the young men who volunteered for the Spanish-American War was of seeing Cuba or the Philippines, while the dangers of war were appropriately minimized. In the time of the Civil War, few northerners knew much of the South, and the romance of a strange land, uniting with the music interest, swelled enlistments. Lacking such incentives, the call to arms, North or South, would have perhaps met with an indifference which would have dictated a reasoned settlement of differences.

Cheap travel accordingly tends to let the gas out of the bag of militarism. In view of the fact that the desire to see new places is so strong that life will be risked, the cheapening of transportation is important as a peace measure. The desire to liberate the Cuban *reconcentrado* might, as a result of intelligent travel to our great cities, have given way to an interest to deliver millions of Americans out of rotten slums.

The peculiar susceptibility of adolescence, with its impulsions and ignorance, to militaristic expeditions suggests the wisdom of quarantining society as much as possible against such influence. The very fact of adolescence will permanently afford some basis of appeal which may be made use of by such interests as would keep the world armed, though we can hardly know how successful would be efforts to teach children from the first the advantages of peace. But if war were declared, not by monarchs, nor by Congress, which, while thought sometimes not to be sufficiently responsive to public opinion, is often unduly subservient to

mere opinion, but by popular election, to be participated in
only by voters above the age of twenty five years, with
cumulative voting by parents, the likelihood of war would be
vastly diminished. Such voting would represent deliberation,
which is always fatal to a fight.

The spirit of youth is in league with militarism because of its
adventure, its novelty, and its opportunities for heroic action
and display. There is a subtle thread of sex interest. A youth
will perform strange feats to win favor, and not only heroic
actions but heroic appearance counts. Feminine admiration
of the uniform has had its effect, but if every maid realized
that every fruitful bullet appointed an unfruitful woman,
feminine influence would be cast for civilization. Every man
killed means an "old maid" or a widow. A woman's life is lost
with every man's.

3. Better Use of Fighting Tendency

But is there not a still deeper reason why men fight?
Is it not a struggle for life? Nothing that is now meant by life
can be as well secured by fighting as by united effort. Mutual
help brings life. Life is to be had by cooperation, even as the
cells of the body cooperate in health. Fighting is a luxury.
The world cannot afford to fight.

But the fighting tendency, directed to suitable ends, is
valuable, indispensable, for it supplies motive power. A
substitute for fighting against people may be found in
fighting against evils, with mankind enlisted under one
banner. It is the condemnation of war that its targets are
people. There is surely enough to fight— poverty, disease,
ignorance, ugliness, erosion, weeds, bad roads. We can fight
for an economic system which would enable producers to
consume as much as they produce, thus doing away with the

prime cause of modern wars— foreign markets. Let wars be made against evils, not against people. The fighting against people, when there are so many evils to fight, is dire waste.

It is inconceivable that the intelligence of the world should not ultimately prove sufficient for the abolition of war, even though there is still war and preparation for war. But much of the keenest intelligence is aligned with private interests which profit in some way from militarism. A great mass of people, the successors of vast slave, serf, and peasant populations, possess an outlook which exposes them to manipulation for military purposes. War lives because there are millions who do not think on some subjects. Wars may be "pulled off" by the action of a few who are in a position to manipulate certain elements of population. But ignorance is lack of nurture, it is not necessarily incapacity; there are relatively few feeble-minded. The teaching of peace is all that is lacking to make war impossible. The suggestion may be caused to prevail that it is better to sign the inevitable treaty of peace before rather than at the close of hostilities, and that the interests of the workers of the world are one.

Social Antagonisms

ORIGINALLY EDITED BY
Dr. Frank L. McVey, LL.D.
President of the University of North Dakota

FIRST PUBLISHED IN 1918
BY A.C. McCLURG & CO. OF CHICAGO
AS PART OF "THE NATIONAL SOCIAL
SCIENCE SERIES"

CHAPTER I
THE WAR OF WANTS

THE wants of modern man— and woman— are more numerous than those of their ancestors, for we know more, and knowledge breeds wants. The early savage who fell sick presumably wanted to get well, though it perhaps did not make much difference to him. The medicine man was sent for, and the evil spirits of the colic or gallstones were sought to be driven out; but if the complaint was serious enough the savage died.

1. Knowledge Breeds Wants

It was all a comparatively simple matter. The afflicted desired the wizard of the tribe to rattle dried beans in a bag over his suffering frame; nothing more. He did not ask for a trained nurse, because she was unknown. As there was no large city to which he could wire for a high-priced doctor, he died inexpensively. Not having any property to leave behind, he called no attorney to commit to paper his last Will and testament.

From our knowing more, death is fought with all the weapons that ingenuity can devise and money buy. It is fought off in the forties by golf sticks among the wealthy and by dollar-a-bottle dopes among the lowly. Knowing that there are ways of fighting for one's life, and that some of these have proved of service, and all hold out hope, the man of the twentieth century creates a drain upon financial resources through his many wants when taken sick.

Many of our wants, and civilization consists in their increase, are due to the realization of actual needs, needs which have long existed but have not always been thought about. The ignorant man needs books, but does not necessarily want them. He should want them, but he is not always conscious of the need; when he becomes so he takes a long step upward. The small boy may need to visit a dentist, but he has no want to correspond; rather he would glory in a mouth having a few gloomy spaces where teeth should be. If we had known as much about dust as we now know there would have been vacuum cleaners aforetime. A want is often a real need that gets into consciousness. Ages ago there were millions of needs, let us judge, though fewer wants. There are more today.

It is an axiom in economics that the consuming power of the public is indefinitely great; ever beyond the purse. The same truth has been expressed inelegantly under the figure of a champagne appetite and a beer pocketbook. There are wants upon wants; wants pyramided to the skies, with the apex earthward. Moments there may be when one thinks that all his wants are satisfied, but such moments are deceptive; within fifteen minutes one may think of something that would cost the savings of a lifetime.

The stoics? Yes, they renounced wants; they made themselves rich by wanting nothing. Thoreau on Walden Pond was a stoic, having nothing and wanting nothing. But Thoreau was not married. He also went back to town. Keep your eye on the man who has considerable money and no wants; pretty soon he may splurge.

The approach of wants is seductive and free from alarm. The victim does not see the full number before him; he sees merely one or two in a clear light. It is felt that happiness will be nearly or quite complete when some particular want— involving just a little more than one can afford— is satisfied. Little does one realize that when one want is satisfied others will replace it automatically, a tandem procession in thin line or boisterous groups.

2. The Order of Wants

The procession of wants comes partly from their inter-relationships; if a man buys an automobile he must have a place to house it; and if he runs it away from home he must pay more for his meals. It is proverbial how the purchase of a new piece of furniture may lead to the replacement of all the other furniture in the house. The decoration of one room suggests the retouching of others, and perhaps the ultimate result is a new fence at the back of the lot. Whenever one changes his environment, which he does when he buys, he finds that he has disturbed his habit world, and he is likely to have to propitiate the gods of fitness by drawing still further upon the bank account. One wretched way to avoid wanting more things is not to secure the first one.

Let us suppose that the citizen fares forth; he goes somewhere, perhaps to congress, or to Los Angeles. Having thus changed his *situs*, he must be prepared to suffer the consequences. He will want many things that he never thought of before. These things are required or made desirable by new environment. If the statesman had stayed at home he might still be getting his lunches for twenty-five cents at the Grand Cafeteria, but in Washington he must eat as a lawmaker. One may wear old clothes on a farm, at almost no expense for garb, and with some pleasure, for old clothes invite to the fields, to the blackberry patch, and in March to the sill in the sun on the south side of the bam. There is joy in old clothes— in the country. Upon setting foot in the city, however, one loses his delight in seedy suits. What we spend depends much upon where we are; city or country, this street or that avenue, with cigars or pipes.

One cannot travel as cheaply as he can stay at home, if he has an economical wife. One cannot choose or leave alone so well when away. Others then gauge one's needs, indicate what one should want, and set the price. In leaving one's native heath there is left behind the little authority to govern oneself which still remains.

To be sure, if among strangers one is free from one of the greatest incentives to bankruptcy, social competition, and the eyes of acquaintances. People who do not stay long in one place may escape this burden, having the fewer wants therefor. It is not pleasant to drop below the standards maintained generally among business, professional, or social acquaintances. One is uncomfortable under the look of surprise; we like the surprise which compliments, but not the other kind. Often it is expensive to get acquainted.

3. Social Contact and Standard of Living

But there is less and less possibility of scorning conventionality, for the world is becoming smaller. Local standards and peasant dress disappear. The press brings to everyone new ideas of consumption, and even the most removed villager is no longer immune to the example of how others live. The social pull, than which nothing multiplies wants faster, produces a response to fashions and standards of living set up far away and upon higher financial levels. Suggestion and the spell of the leader, operating through all the channels of publicity, throw down upon the masses showers of new wants.

Hence, there is found the world over a rising standard of living. The light of the world has dawned upon the heathen Chinee, and he procures a kerosene lamp of small bowl and puny wick. A tribe might be economical forever if

it lived in ignorance of the rest of the world, but when
people, even the most lowly, learn there is something which
they do not have, there is desire, possibly action. The diligent
statisticians of Germany show percentages of increase in the
popular consumption of many an article of food which the
upper classes have known for a long time was pretty good to
eat; chocolate, for example. There are no localities or
countries heard from where people want less and less, always
more and more.

A miraculously elastic consuming power, upon which
purely psychological foundation modem industry and
commerce rest secure, has many roots, one of which is taste,
a faculty or frailty which makes one distressed with a chromo
after having seen an oil painting. When Good Queen Bess
jolted over the frightful roads of her kingdom in a springless
wheeled vehicle far inferior to a good farm wagon, her
conveyance was in a class with the chariot of Apollo; it was
the best there was, and it was all right until a better carriage
was built. Christian princes would no doubt have been
willing to sick their subjects on to war for the possession of a
two-cylinder auto, model 1900. But when the annual
improvements appear, there is dissatisfaction with last year's
machine. Think of it— the great fundamental importance of
a utility lost sight of through the revolutionary antics of that
wild bucking broncho taste! It seems like baseness to
disparage anything that will run on wheels and keep between
fences. Why do not we appreciate the primary, the basic
values, and cease from being troubled about niceties of detail?
A roof over one's head is a roof; why not take comfort from
that fact, and swear indifference to beamed ceilings and
indirect lighting? If one were pulled out of the sea by a rope
would it be sensible in him to criticize the strands?

Having taste, however, which is all things with all
people, we cannot rest when once we have gained the
substance of a thing; we must after its shadow too. My watch

was once my pride; I did not know any better than to be
perfectly satisfied with it, even feeling gloriously superior.
But that was before the day of the thin model. Now my
watch is ugly; taste has bucked again. It is the tragedy of last
year's hat, once so sought after and so ecstatically embraced;
now none so poor as to do it reverence. The poison of
luckless suggestion or an inner ripeness for change causes me
to dispraise that which I before adored.

From this variable factor of life esthetic vagaries
multiply. There is little constancy. We are hopelessly fickle
when once we get out of the familiar field of beefsteak and
boiled cabbage, where the verities endure. Few will agree
upon the artistic qualities of anything, and one will rarely
agree with himself two days in succession. If I gaze upon a
painting, a very devil of perverseness and impertinence may
lead me to dwell upon some disturbing detail that upon
another time would not be noticed. In fact in every re-seeing
my thoughts go coursing about by novel routes, delighted
with newly discovered aspects or stumbling over annoyances
unperceived before.

The consistency of regard with which we perceive the
humbler objects, like overshoes or the dictionary, is probably
due to our looking upon them chiefly in the light of their
serviceableness. One never stops to think if the dictionary is
not a trifle stout and ill-appearing; the genuine, whole-souled
service of this utility, rendered through its copious
vocabulary, reconciles one to inartistic overweight; rather it
causes one never to give a thought to the book as a work of
art.
Yet if the choice lay between two dictionaries, one artistic
and the other unattractive, the former would surely be
chosen, the contents being the same in each. And do we not
have here one of the reasons for the rising tide of wants?
Objects of substantial utility have impressed upon them by
the makers esthetic characters. A gas range is not only a

utility but also a work of art. Perhaps the old range in the kitchen really works about as well as the new styles; but having seen one of the more attractive types, the housewife soon proposes an exchange or telephones the "second-hand man."

4. Case of the Ulster

An ulster is an ulster to the man who has never had his attention called to the different ways the collar may be cut, or to button arrangements, or to single- or double-breastedness, or to the nap of material, or to linings, or to colors of this season or that, or to the placing of pockets and their character. He who goes to a tailor to have an ulster made, thinking that it is a simple process, comes to see its complexity; he who sought a means of keeping off winter winds and shutting out polar temperatures finds that he has entered the field of art, where nice choices are involved, and he may totter with fatigue after the ordeal of trying to make up his mind about a coat. If the tailor had kept still about the fine points it might have been all right; but even a slight draught, a mere swig, of the Pierian spring produces intoxicating effects.

Women know better than we. They take shopping in dead earnest. They know it is a matter of life and death— by exhaustion. Anyone can buy any useful article if he has the money, and buy it easily if he does not know too much. Those were happy days when there were only rag rugs and Brussels carpets. But art has come into the world with all our woe.

Only by keeping the tightest possible check upon the frisky tendencies of appreciation may any of us live without friction between self and income. Even Croesuses sometimes take exception to the looks of nature and set gangs to work remodeling landscapes, creating lakes, uprooting forests, and moving mountains. To such deisticalness is the money lord driven through unquiet tastes. The expense for the things that are of subsistence value can far more easily be met than that for the things which appeal to taste. In our unmeasured esthetic appetites lies a market big enough to engulf production for a million years. Every clothesline in every back yard in the world Would stretch beneath the weight of oriental rugs on cleaning days, provided the rugs could be had, and the people knew rugs, and there was the money to buy— after getting the things Father wanted.

5. Shapes and Colors

All sorts of stimulations work upon our esthetic natures. The exchange of ideas results in new standards, as does the contact of civilizations. The seeing of two things instead of one makes for comparison. If there were only one shade of red we should be satisfied with that shade— happy to paint a bam or dye a cravat in the one and only hue. The more shades of red are called into commercial existence, the more our color wants are refined and multiplied. And as color is capable of entering into relations with form, structure, and composition, the resulting number of choices would baffle anyone whose mathematics falls short of the uncanny permutations and combinations of numbers juggled in the pride of algebra. If all pencils were round, and there were only one color, green, the only pencil that a man could buy would be a round green pencil— and he would be satisfied. But with two colors, green and yellow, and two shapes, round and square, there may be a round green pencil, a round yellow pencil, a square green pencil, and a square yellow pencil; four instead of one.

Introduce other colors and shapes, and the number of choices goes upward like a skyrocket, and introduce in addition such factors as grades of lead, and erasers, and still other factors, and the skyrocket, flaming but unconsumed, spurts off toward infinity. There is a deadly geometrical progression in this. And every change in the article corresponds to a latent preference that somebody has in his nature, and brings it out as a want.

Applied to the innumerable articles of trade and commerce, this principle of psychological crescendo gives us at least a starting point in the wild economics of consumption.

Little do we know how much we are capable of wanting until we come into the presence of things, whereupon one knows the tempter. The child wants everything it sees, and in this transparent response perhaps is a clue to a better understanding of ourselves. The child reaches out for experience; he is impelled by curiosity and a hunger for contacts. To lay hold of objects, to possess, to absorb, to chew, is life; it is experience, development, excitement, action, exploration, adventure, and conquest. Even so does the spirit of his elders reach out for the untried, striving to enrich and enlarge careers. The higher life consists in kicking over the traces of the habitual, a feat involving the satisfying of new wants. It is idle to expect people to be satisfied under fixed conditions, however delightful at first. The most insistent of wants is that for a continuing development.

The identification of wants with life itself is made surer upon perceiving how the competitive principle, the law of self-exaltation, enters into consumption. The extent to which one commands the means to supply wants is a measure of his fighting ability, a test of his hunting prowess. The urbanized savage of the wheat pit or the jobbing district is reputed according to his skill in bringing in game and in vanquishing adversaries; he is successful according to income.

6. Display

Once in possession of the means of purchasing, the next step is outlay in forms which, in open or subtle ways, impress the world with the victory. The fisherman does not hide a superb string of fish, nor would the moneymaker give the impression of being financially unskillful. Even if he is modest his talents are likely to be advertised by members of his family.

The most obvious reaction in the neighborhood is for other men to show that they are equally good men and brave; that they can hunt too. Some may be good hunters and some poor; some may be poor hunters yet bring in game luckily trapped, and some good hunters may return empty-handed; and some may find the game has a fence around it. But there is strife to be among the first. And as the one sure way of securing the recognition accorded the strong, let evidences of strength and power be shown in expenditures.

As no one would appear weak— and there may be more chagrin in poverty than in crime— the temptation is to seem as well able to buy things as anybody else. There appears, accordingly, a tendency for wants to multiply purely from competitive causes, irrespective of the actual agreeableness of objects. Among large numbers of people competition has long since passed beyond the stage of struggle for enough to live on, as among the hungry hordes of antiquity or among the too numerous underfed and poorly clad of today; it has passed over into a competition in largeness of life, a competition in luxuries, in eminence, in display, and in what embraces all these— power.

A very considerable percentage of wants today are those which the individual feels because of the publicly registered success of competitors. Many of the things we should like to buy are regarded with an eye to effect; true even among the honest— and therefore poor?— although the spectacle of high-geared competitive consumption is reserved for circles of plutocratic surplus.

If we did not have to buy for the neighbors, and keep up with heartless pace-makers, many of us could be just as happy on less money.

7. Psychic Poverty

Let no one hope to find surcease of wants through opulence. It comes on good authority that the more one has the more he wants, and, singularly, the things one wants as his purchasing power increases always cost more than the things which satisfy upon a lower financial level. The tendency to put on all the traffic will bear is irresistible among dealers, which is interesting. But also the things which one is disposed to have are measured in larger numerals as one mounts the scale of material satisfactions and of spiritual ones resting on a cash basis.

There evidently is no escape from the want-fiend through the mere getting of more money; poverty is a psychological state which may afflict the opulent as well as the wholly or partly submerged multitude. It is a state in which one is aware of things just beyond his reach and just within some other fellow's reach.

If there is escape in the few years that remain to one after reaching the age of discretion it lies in a different direction. There must be a regulation of wants, a disciplining of them; they may need to be spanked. If there is a poverty which is purely psychological, it should be curable by psychology. Is not the hair of a dog good for his bite?

Monks have renounced the world, the flesh, and the devil, but that is asking a good deal. Philosophers have told us to want less, which advice is contrary to nature. To curtail wants is a mild form of suicide. We live by reaching out in wider and wider circles; no, the human race is not ready to draw into its shell— if it has one. Let us live.

Salvation must be on other terms. We might, for example, learn to want those values which are open and free to all comers, never having been impounded by smart dealers and monopolists, like fresh air. It may seem cold comfort to turn away from manufactured articles to the contemplation of nature and the ways of folks, but what else do prices permit? If one could wish to see the spider's fantastic geometry as heartily as we insects of an hour want to see things far away, the economy would be considerable. And that is just the sort of appreciation which we must learn or be consumed with futile aspirations and bitter envies. Not that one should submissively choose nature and let a privileged class make off with everything else. But as an element in happiness the appreciation of things for which there is no charge for admission is to be commended. Given the disposition to pick up values at every turn of the road, and ownership makes less appeal; happiness becomes more a possibility.

It is through the governing of wants that one may ever win happiness, and also through the making more accessible of things which are universally desired but which few can afford. A model city provides for its population many forms of goods which in the past have been secured privately by a few individuals at much expense. If one were asked to name the things he would obtain if given unlimited funds he would be sure to name many utilities which are now open to the general public in the more advanced municipalities. Books, works of art, parks and forests, fountains and baths,

birds and beasts from foreign lands, and the rest, are
common social assets.

The citizen may not feel just the same about this kind
of ownership as about private ownership. There is a
difference. If the citizen owned the buffalo in the municipal
zoo, he might upon occasion sell him and buy something
else. Or he might put the money in the bank. While social
ownership satisfies wants, it does not have the flexibility of
private ownership; it is not such a means of personal security.

It remains, then, for the governments of tomorrow to
rid the individual of any gnawing anxiety as to what will
become of him upon being taken sick, being thrown out of
work, or upon growing old. With fears for maintenance done
away with, it would be found that the private ownership of
an object would in a great many cases be unimportant. A
larger number of legitimate wants could then be satisfied. A
book in a private library may satisfy but the owner, while in a
public collection it may be read by hundreds.

It is not comfortable to be in need of things, to lack
things of sane utility, and find them out of reach— perhaps
with someone else enjoying them. It is one of the marvels
how those who "have", have so successfully persuaded those
who have not to lean upon the hope of possession some time
in the future.

But rising standards of living show that hope deferred
is losing in popularity, that the masses want. They may get
more outright; they may level incomes. Or more enjoyments
may be realized through including in wants those manifold
values never under lock and key, and those satisfactions
which social purchasing increasingly provides. A social
engineering may some time in the future help to the
reconciling of man and his wants, as by assurance of
necessaries, the shifting of competition to service instead of
accumulation, and the bottoming of esthetic choices upon
something other than caste indicia and vagaries of leisure.

CHAPTER II
ARTFUL SELLING

THE person who "goes down town for five cents' worth of something and comes back ten dollars in debt" gets far less sympathy than a hypnotized person should receive; for buyers are often as if hypnotized. The essence of hypnotism is to hold a person's attention to a given idea until that idea is acted upon. The normal course is for ideas to result in action. Very often a given idea does not result in one's doing something, because some other idea interferes; leave an idea alone and it will issue in movements; there is no escape. It is dangerous to live with a single idea, for we are bound to act to correspond. Our safety lies in having other ideas get in on the main track and cause the first idea to take a siding.

1. The Hypnotic Salesman

The strong desire to sell goods, which the reader may have observed, has brought out hypnotic qualities in salesmen, who seize upon a "talking point," concentrate our minds through enthusiasm, bring up reserves of arguments when we glance toward the door, make us believe we cannot live without their wares, offer to take pay in instalments — and a dray delivers the purchases that afternoon. They are hypnotists, and, in regard to the instalment plan, gay deceivers, making it appear that it is a painless way of parting with cash. Painless! A medical student nearly went mad over the rhythm of payments for a many-volumed work.

Ordinarily we have a fairly wide field of consciousness and we meditate in generous circles, especially if we have a large subject— ourselves, for example— on which to meditate. Our thoughts trip gayly about in green fields and by running brooks. One idea chases another in an inconsequential and even blissful game of tag, in which no player ruthlessly dominates— in which, by gentle neutralizations, the performers keep one another in check; and we go on in even tenor, quite within the proprieties of the law and our pocketbooks.

But let one enter a store, and all is changed; even before entering, all is not the same. Intimations and influences begin even in the suburbs, and the streets and window displays converge to a focus of suggestion. Goods are placed on counters, which one must always pass in great numbers before reaching what he wants to find, and someone has designed a maze such that the distance traveled by the fly is immensely increased over the rectilinear arrangement which has seen the finish of flies innumerable in the past. And the crowning ingenuity is achieved with a tempting display of toilet articles, which possibly includes fishing tackle, placed under the glass table-top from which one drinks root beer.

The artful seller limits one's field of consciousness. One loses sight of his past and most of his future, his friends and dependents; he has merely an eye single, and this is applied to a knot hole. The broad earth, the majesty of the heavens, and the bottomless pit— the last particularly— one loses sight of. The merits of the article are all that he sees— all that the seller wants him to see.

Such is life; and suppose it were not. Imagine salesmen trying to get away from the importunities of cash customers. Picture the buyer, roll in hand, hunting out the dealer from behind bales of modestly concealed goods and cajoling him to take a price, any price. Timidity and protective coloration would be the highest qualifications of clerks, and fabulous salaries would be guaranteed the reticent and shrinking, and even the deaf and dumb.

2. Narrowing Consciousness

The art of one kind of salesmanship resolves itself into one principle: limit the field of consciousness. Whatever the means employed, whether persuasion, innuendo, frontal attack, or visions of heavenly delights, the controlling principle is the same. So compelling often is invitation to buy that one experiences a momentary ecstasy of faith that in possession of the proffered article there would remain not the slightest impediment between oneself and perfect bliss. Automobiles are purchased in the extravagant but glorious misapprehension that they will transform life— milk the cows, weed the onions, discipline the children, crowd one's brain with knowledge, cure grip and colds, keep accounts, and climb trees, which last unfortunately they may attempt. The salesman knows the weakness of facts in the face of imagination, and profits thereby. Any misgivings are dextrously quieted, and possible deficiencies of performance or evident shortcomings of construction are parried with perhaps specious reasons readily assented to by the swaying victim. Reduced to a single thought, and that man's age-long quest, delight, he who came to look remains to pay.

The reasons why salesmanship has acquired its unique importance in this age belong rather to economics than to psychology. There is that in the social order which results in a wide disparity, on the part of the many, between appetite and menu. Restricted incomes among the many impose upon sellers an unrelenting struggle to be the first and most frequent to reach the consumer. Goods accumulate rapidly as a result of the marvelous productivity of modem industry, much more rapidly than purchasing power has increased among the masses. Push, a word which may well stand for commercialism, is therefore absolutely necessary to accomplish the feat of getting goods off the shelves; and lack of push, whose aromatic quality is the gentle art of selling, leaves goods unsold. There are times, as every salesman knows, when it is easy to sell goods. The fish hunt up the bait, swallow it, and swim to the boat proudly, hook in mouth— no landing net necessary. This is in periods when the crops are good and labor is fully employed at "good" wages, or when the opening of some natural source of wealth generates golden dreams. When times are poor, extreme effort is required to effect sales except for a minimum of maintenance.

Suppose that in a night everyone's wealth were doubled, would books cease to be written on the psychology of salesmanship? Not at all. At first there would be ready purchasing. The consumer would proceed at once to supply certain needs of which he had long been conscious but had never before been able to satisfy. The next stage would be the arousal of wants which at the lower level of income had not been felt, whereupon a war of wants would ensue. In the war of wants the art of salesmanship rests upon sure foundations.

Take heart, ye salesmen. Not that you are faint-hearted— there is no little courage in making people buy things they cannot afford. In stimulating wants you are upbuilding civilization, provided you make us want what we ought to want. Ply your adroit art, for it will be a long time before desire shall cease.

CHAPTER III
REACTIONS TO ADVERTISING

THE consumer may not be the best judge of advertising, but it is for him that advertisements are prepared, and he is likely to have his impressions of the art. The final test of advertising is supposedly that of the cash box, by which so many other things are tested. A literary masterpiece which did not pull trade would soon be discarded for the paragraph which brings in buyers personally or by mail. No doubt the advertiser frequently consigns to the waste-paper basket many a. bit of copy good enough in itself but lacking cash magnetism. Perhaps he and the consumer would not always agree upon what would appeal; perhaps he would be right and the consumer wrong, but he will pardon the presumption if the consumer has his own impressions. After all, the way the consumer feels is the fact in which sellers are interested.

1. Mere Publicity

One frequently sees advertisements which merely gives publicity to a man's or a firm's name, or give little in addition to a name. Advertisements of banks are often of this kind. The assets and liabilities and the names of officers often appear too. Perhaps these are enough; but with a modesty which is the keynote of this commentary, a modesty which for the sake of avoiding its becoming a nuisance will not be referred to again, let it be said that such bald facts do not seem to constitute a proper advertisement. It may be beneath a bank's dignity, and banks have that, to speak to the public in a pleading tone or to employ winsome phrases; but it would appear that a little more good cheer might not be amiss, especially as it often tries one's nerves to venture into the marble fastnesses of the glorified strong boxes known as banks. Next to a church there is possibly no edifice which more thoroughly terrorizes the shrinking than a bank. One may enter the grocery with some assurance; but a bank! It seems almost like an indignity to offer peanuts to the caged financial elephants— to contribute such small mites to the swollen pile behind the bars. And as for venturing to ask for a loan, even with blood and real estate as collateral, this is not easy, unless it be for the hardened business man; we prefer to borrow from our friends— without security.

Could not banks unbend? Tell us what car to take; tell us to bring the children; promise to have an employee turn handsprings in the lobby; say that you have the best blotters in town on your writing shelf; reveal unto us what the cashier eats for breakfast; and say that the richest director always fires his own furnace and carries out the ashes. Then will we come. But make us feel at home; if you don't—

It may be all right for the professional man merely to give his name and state his business. The doctor would not profit much by a pen picture of an operation or a published count of his pills. Things are bad enough when one is sick; no need to anticipate; and if one were assured in advance that there was probably nothing serious the matter, one would stay away. The doctor and the dentist know their business; they say little to the public, just a hint, and the office address. Let others extol; let others speak of the phenomenal dexterity of Dentist So-and-So in extracting fearful fangs, but let the dentist himself be silent; nor let him repeat the mistake of one who had as his sign an immense gilded tooth small above the gum line of the lower jaw and big below. If a wooden tooth is to be used for a sign, it should be constructed with a large body and slight roots; then one would expect that in this particular office the dentist would relieve him of an aching molar by the simple operation of tapping one side of it with the handle of a small mouth-mirror— about whose sterilization one rarely fails to be skeptical. It may flatter the dentist to hang out a sign which implies that he has the strength of ten because his heart is pure; but if he wants me to come to him he should not emphasize his own muscle, but charm me into believing that teeth rest lightly on the gums, to be bowled over and out like small tenpins.

2. Watching a Space

Occasionally one sees an advertisement which exhorts the reader to watch a certain space, in some cases the name of a concern being given. Where there is no name given it would seem that money could not be spent more foolishly. Who is going to watch a certain space? Very few readers could tell twenty-four hours later the exact location of a given space. If the concern's name is given, the advertising money is not spent wholly in vain; but even so, the failure to connect wares with the dealer's name makes the proceeding an unwise one. A good many things happen in twenty-four hours. It is much better to make as complete a case as possible at the moment when the reader's eye falls upon a given space. The use and abuse of illustrations is a fascinating theme. The art of illustration has reached such a stage of perfection that many magazine readers look through the advertising pages before they look through the reading matter in the magazine proper, and the need of buying illustrated children's books grows less with the increasing delight of the child in lying on the floor and turning the advertising pages for the sake of the pictures. The illustrations invariably illustrate; they attract the eye; they please; they charm. In fact many times they appear too attractive; they absorb attention so fully that the products advertised may be overlooked. Where the illustration is closely associated with the goods it does its best work. Investigation shows that readers may retain a perfect picture of the illustration and not have made the slightest association between the illustration and the reading matter. The advertiser may succeed in attracting attention but fail to carry that attention over to printed statements. The illustration should be subordinate and explanatory; it should pertain.

3. Lack of Evidence

The irrelevant illustration is matched by unsubstantial reading matter. The consumer is interested in evidence, which is lacking in many advertisements. Large claims and preposterous self-admiration abound, but what of proof? There is much eulogy and little demonstration. If space is too restricted to show proof, then give us sources to which we may go to satisfy ourselves. The avoidance, generally, of anything that looks like proof makes a bad impression. We know that sellers are going to speak well of their goods; that is to be expected. All sellers do this; sellers have always done this— but tell us how the thing is made; tell us of someone who has used the article for a convincing period of time; give us more facts, that we may come to admire through conviction. Declarations of lowest prices mean nothing, nor do claims for highest quality. These expressions have been used much; they are pointless and conventional. Every dealer claims lowest prices, and no one has ever heard of a systematic comparison of prices. One is forced to believe that dealers are uniformly too much given to self-adulation; too little to producing impersonal evidence on which the consumer could base his own conclusions.

It was a convincing statement that appeared in an advertisement of rain-proof coats. The reader was assured that a member of the firm had driven for miles in the face of a heavy rain storm wearing the woolen fabric in question, which was so woven that water would not penetrate it. One was convinced by this recital of personal experience; this was evidence that would convert the most skeptical, and it was somewhat disappointing to find that this choice bit of evidence was not supported by the test of holding a sample of the textile under a water tap. But the advertisement was good, it was fine; the disappointment was simply in the textile.

4. The Principle of Change

Change is an important principle in advertising; we soon come to be oblivious to the familiar and the unchanging. If a new sign is put up we notice it at once, but after we have passed the same sign a few times we become blind to the object. New things are noted because of a possible bearing upon welfare. It is instinctive to take an interest in the unusual; but once we learn that the new object is what it is, that it is merely such a thing and that it will not bite, then we go along about our affairs giving little or no further heed to the intruder in the field of consciousness.

Hence it is that we cease to observe the usual. A child is often thought to be a better observer than his elders. He does see many things that his elders do not notice; he sees them because they are new. Nearly everything is new to the child and he goes about with prying eyes. Most of us pay very little attention to our surroundings after we once become acquainted with them. People are often unable to give a description of objects in daily use. It is possible, in fact probable, that a person buying a jackknife would be much better able to identify it on the day of its purchase than after using it for some time. There is real difficulty in identifying one's umbrella. The checkered careers •of umbrellas are not wholly due to moral depravity.

The principle of change applies to advertising. It is not the statement that appears over and over which impresses most. It is true that we learn by repetition, but it should be repetition with change. Change may take place through a change in the copy or illustrations, or through a substitution of readers and observers. A sign painted on a wall is a new sign to every person who passes it for the first time. There is not much need to change copy for changing observers.

Akin to novelty is movement; the moving thing always attracts attention. Nature has disciplined all living things into a quick response to whatever is in motion, for danger comes with movement. The experience of our prehistoric ancestors and their remote ancestors, and of all ancestors, that creeping, flying, jumping, and pouncing creatures may be dangerous, has made such a deep impression on the nervous system that we are quick to see motion. Mechanical contrivances, guinea pigs, and acrobatic mice displayed in a shop window instantly arrest attention. The sandwich man in motion is more interesting for the moment than the greatest philosopher in a statuesque position.

It is not only necessary to attract attention, but to create a desire to purchase. No one would think of framing an advertisement which would merely attract attention. Illustration or text is intended to attract attention and to give an agreeable impression. A manufacturer of ladders would not represent one of his ladders as broken nor show a picture of a workman falling off; he would strive so to advertise ladders that the reader would feel like securing one because of its advantages: its safety, its ease of operation, or the good qualities of the materials used in its construction. If a food is advertised it should suggest pleasant results, as plumpness and health. Some years ago a breakfast food was advertised through the picture of a skinny and apparently somewhat idiotic man wearing an extravagant grin; that was bad advertising. One would prefer to use a food whose implied results were not so palpably undesirable. The advertisement of a photograph gallery was injudicious for similar reasons, a bulbous-nosed caricature serving for illustration. The association of a distorted countenance with photography is not attractive; we want our photographs to look as well or better, especially better, than ourselves. If there is the slightest intimation in a photographer's advertisement that our pictures are not going to flatter us we may lose interest in having our pictures taken.

A curious example of appealing to delightful associations appeared in the pages of a stock journal. The proprietor of a stock farm, in advertising horses, used terms applying to the most delightful foods. Certain of his horses were described as "peaches and cream," and the most provocative dietetic vocabulary was used, freely followed by exclamation marks. Peaches and cream had not the slightest relevancy to Percheron horses; but this dealer's advertisement provoked interest and wheedled the reader into a favorable state of mind; the impression made was that the horses advertised were most attractive creatures, and the novelty and cheerful absurdity of the appeal produced favorable results. We are won by spirit and enthusiasm, and recollections of table delicacies are oftentimes glorious.

5. Gratuitous Help to Competitors

There are advertisements that persuade, but do not persuade especially to the profit of the one advertising. Preachments of saving money by one bank advertise all banks, not merely the one paying for the advertisement. If the public is urged to secure umbrellas for a rainy season this advice inures to the benefit of all dealers in umbrellas. One man's advertisement may promote the interests of all other dealers, he shaking the tree while others as well as himself gather the fruit. Presumably all that a retailer wants to accomplish through advertising is to increase his own sales, and under competitive conditions he would even prefer that the sales of others should not only not be increased but be reduced, so that his own sales might be heavier. If the dealer is the only one carrying a certain commodity he can then safely urge its use in general terms. It is only when there is a monopoly that a certain kind of exhortation to the public is most profitable. The competitive dealer really does not care whether the public uses a product or not unless it is purchased from him and him only.

The dealer does not pose as a philanthropist. He is interested in his own income, and, unlike the promulgator of reform ideas, who seeks the world as an audience, he is mainly interested in reaching the possible buyer. To do this he must shout when others whisper, and whisper when others shout; he must set himself in contrast to others; if other advertisers use heavy type, let him use small type; if others use a variation of type, let him print his advertisement in uniform type; let him do something that contrasts with what others do. If most men were giants the man of average height would attract attention; among men of average stature the dwarf and giant are beheld by all beholders. The field for ingenuity in applying the principle of contrast is as boundless as the sea.

And yet in one matter the advertiser should not be very different. The atmosphere of sincerity is a universal attraction. To appear to be sincere is not easy; it is not always easy even for persons who are sincere to make others think that they are sincere, and it is to be supposed that if one does not have a good case sincerity could be simulated only with great difficulty. When one reads an advertisement that seems to come straight from the heart he is haunted by its message. Many advertisements are too smooth; too well edited; the hand of the advertising expert is too apparent. If an illiterate dealer were to blurt out in print what he has to say, the very crudeness of his expression would win favor. Directness, brevity, and genuineness have power.

There is a suggestion of insincerity in advertisements that cost a great deal. One fears, too, that the seller is incurring a fearful advertising expense to be recouped out of the purchaser's pocket. One does not like to feel that the firm with which he deals is throwing out thousands of dollars upon expensive announcements. There is somewhat the same feeling as there is with reference to big stores. One hopes to secure the better bargain in some unpretentious establishment on a side street than under a vast roof. One associates a big concern with big expenses, and inclines toward the smaller establishment. The display of wealth by the seller, either in establishment or advertising, reacts unfavorably, just as the extravagant dressing of the wife of a physician or a lawyer causes the average person to wonder if fees are not likely to be too high. The simple and economical administration of the household of a professional man is an attraction to patrons of moderate means.

There is a certain suspicion in regard to all advertising. We have heard how businesses have been built up through daring advertising, and one fears that there is a good deal of bluff in the matter. We suspect big dealers of securing returns through the mere force of publicity and somewhat regardless of the actual merits of things advertised. We expect them to overstate their claims, and we often seek to find out for ourselves about the commodities offered. There is a wide distrust of printed statements; we read about a political meeting, and then hunt up someone who was there to tell us exactly how matters stood. Full credence is by no means given; yet even extravagant advertising seems to produce results. Notwithstanding unfavorable reactions, the din of the advertiser succeeds in impressing upon an impressionable public, names, trademarks, and products. We buy things because we have heard of them, and we do not buy the unheard-of thing unless it be before our very eyes. With all the finespun ingenuity of modem advertising, and with all its lavish expenditures; with all its utilization of commercial psychology, and its appeal to contrast, repetition, movement, color, change, pride, and delight, the most compelling argument for purchasing rarely appears: they do not tell us how to get the money with which to buy.

CHAPTER IV
THE FITNESS OF VOCATIONS

I CONFESS to a yearning for the job of being a janitor. There is lure about being in basements a good deal, and sitting on a packing box and smoking a pipe. From a basement window one may peer out at about street level and see who is coming — much as the cave man might have done, and with less apprehension. Possibly it is the cave man soul that prefers underground retreats. Then the janitor has more or less to do with fires— smoky lamps and lanterns and heating systems and sissing steam radiators. Being a janitor or fireman, one could always be sure of a good excuse for not attending lectures. Even on Sunday a man thus employed might have to leave the house to look things over during that part of the afternoon when most domestic situations of a strained nature arise; for there is nothing like idleness and reminiscence to start an argument.

But aside from the attractiveness of subterranean life, when much of the work is done by machinery and in dim lights, amid happy confusion and with accidental sociabilities with great men, for these may come along, there is also the incentive afforded by not being perfectly contented with one's own job.

And was there ever a man whose employment fitted him as does a tailor-made garment? There are such as say they are perfectly satisfied with their work. Assuming that all men are truthful— but it is hard to assume it. Assume it anyhow. Then there are the ninety and nine who do not think that their work is perfectly fitted to their natures. There are far more people who fear that a mistake has been made in choosing a calling, or in the thrusting of one upon them, than would declare they were satisfied. Most people

are not so sure that they would take the same course if
returned to the starting point. They have doubts. They want
to think it over. Some even zealously assert that theirs is
positively the worst occupation known among men. And the
strongest complainers are often notably successful as the
world goes.

No, the correspondence between one and his job is
not always nor customarily, nor ever except in the rarest
cases, of the uniform and silky pressure of a perfect fit.
Vocations do not often counterfeit the liquid environment of
a happy cork, moist, bobbing, and serene. The discrepancy
may lie either in the supporting medium or in not being a
good cork.

1. Types of People

Which leads to the truth that while there are many
kinds of corks there are not so many after all. It is said to take
all kinds of people to make the world. On the contrary the
world is made up of a very limited number of kinds of people,
a far smaller number than that of the employments which the
modem world requires. Vertically, there are grades of ability
and intelligence, ranging from the feeble-minded, without
whom modem psychology could not get along, up to
individuals of the largest brain boxes and superlative talents.
And, horizontally, people differ in temperaments and special
aptitudes. That is to say, people of the same level of native
intelligence will be found to possess minor or important
differences. No two people are quite alike, it is true, but one
individual's mental map does not differ from another's as
widely as occupations differ from one another. The original
differences of human nature are less numerous and less
radical than the differences in employment brought into

being and endlessly multiplied under the division of labor.

2. Occupations Make People Different

It is the original nature of man, his inborn traits, that are meant. People of fifty or sixty, or even thirty, years of age are found to differ about as widely as occupations. But these differences have been grafted upon a rather common human nature. At the finish there are more nearly as many kinds of people as occupations, but not at first. Training, environment, money-getting experience, and wind and weather combine their force upon the individual as soon as he becomes a banker, rancher, physician, or janitor, and differences result as you see them.

Even in one's earliest years the effects of occupations are registered, through the conversations of people known to the family and especially through the very tools and appurtenances of the employment of the male head of the family. The viewpoints established in childhood through these influences can scarcely be overthrown later. Thus from the very beginning of one's life, occupations add to the differences among people.

But the early or late weathering effects of occupations are rarely quite sufficient to efface the paint of heredity. The plumber who would have become a lawyer if he had known in early life that there were lawyers— if his father had talked about courts at the supper table— never fully loses the legal bent; and the boy with the gift of phrasing who is short-circuited to the farm grasps the plow with fingers that itch for the pen.

There are enough odds and ends of native and unsatisfied preferences left in nearly everyone to cause friction under the requirements of most of the tasks which society has at its disposal. I may have a preference for basements and no affinity for stargazing, yet inhabit an eyrie in a very tall office building. Green fields, brooks, birds, and soil are not for the engineer in the hold of a lake freighter. The satisfactions for certain deep-seated ancestral likings for the things of the old earth are not at hand for the millions whose work imprisons them in cities.

One's nature is so varied that only a highly varied employment would fit perfectly. But such employments are far from usual. The tendency is distinctly to the contrary. Those who are thoroughly satisfied with their occupations have work of a changeable and refreshing type or take kindly to bit and harness.

Not only is the love of nature sorely upset by urban environments, but the free-roving spirit of man chafes under enforced monotonies. Dr. Eliot, president emeritus of Harvard, makes the astounding statement in one of his books that after a while the work of a university president becomes as monotonous as that of a blacksmith. If men were to have full range for adventure, curiosity, conflict, surprise, and the desire to travel and hunt, it would be necessary to piece together a good many occupations, with but a fitful tenure in each. The jack-at-all-trades appears to have the most comfortable career, except for money getting.

3. The Pay Motive

And it is money getting that controls. We all are doing things which we should not be doing if the fleshpots did not send up their delectable odors. Money is not only a root of evil— a large thrifty taproot— but it is the root of good works done in the name of industriousness. Taking up an employment is not without regard to compensation.

Hence one may be found working at something which does not appeal to taste or satisfy the cravings of his nature; from which fact arises discord. Unattractive work which is profitable must be chosen as against that which would afford more delight but less cash.

The early world probably suited the savage very well; it was the world of his ancestors. But the modern world— the world of posterity— takes the skin off. We stuff ourselves into narrow employments, and the superintendent comes around and trims off any portions that stick over. Such is specialization.

The laws of nature keep on working, however, and as one ages, his irritations burn low and tasks come to rest lightly upon the nerves. Habit chloroforms. Then, too, the savings bank account and the balance sheet unfold increasing charms, to the end that early distinctions are largely lost. One tends to become reconciled to his lot— if it pays.

There is also the chance of asserting one's nature even under forbidding conditions. Many employments, and may their tribe increase, allow somewhat for personal growth; the incumbent may make his own job. One may translate his occupation into personal terms; he may elect as his own this or that phase of a standard employment, and come to be valuable by commercial tests. Opportunities exist for building the nest to suit the bird.

Interests also change, for interest follows whenever one applies his mind closely to a subject. A certain line of work may at first be most unattractive, yet upon being given genuine attention, come to be pleasant. It is not the easy task that has the largest possibilities of satisfaction, but rather the labors which tax one's resources and kindle latent joys. The closer the application, the greater the prospect of quiet but absorbing delight. The superficial pleasures on this planet are soon exhausted; if one would be happy let him get hold of something that pulls back.

The job pessimist not infrequently confounds the limitations of employment with the general limitations upon human life, just as certain feminists think that man, especially through the denial of the ballot to women, is the prime cause of feminine unhappiness. Yet with the ballot—who should not blush for its denial? —and a servant in the house, and the budget system in the family, there still remain old age, death, and fat. One should make sure, in kicking against the pricks of occupation, that he is not kicking—though he might have reason to do so, very likely— against the order of the universe, which, however ill-contrived or unacceptable, is beyond speedy repair or substantial alteration. Freed from every oppression we should still be uncontent, for freedom is disappointing.

Yet with all that may be said in praise of the gradual adaptation of the worker to his work, the disharmonies are sufficiently serious. That a man has to work at all is not a universally popular imperative. Then the mistakes made in getting into employment are not a few. What more serious choice does a man make than that of occupation? There are too many square pegs in round holes and round pegs in square holes, and altogether too many holeless pegs and pegless holes, in the world to warrant any depreciation of the art of choosing an occupation, if occupations are really chosen.

Of which there is doubt. Economic conditions in a vast number of homes compel children, as they reach the age of earning, to accept any work that offers. Usually there are more applicants for employment than positions available, and the work that can be had first is that which is entered upon, often to be followed for life. There is little real choice when hunger forces the balance.

4. Ways of Choosing Vocation

For a real choice certain conditions are necessary. One must know about the different occupations, know that there are many, some of which, like law and politics, are double cousins, and others of which, like accountancy and literature, are not on speaking terms. It is highly important to know early in life that there are various occupations, and to know of the inwardness of these occupations— to have information serving to bring out a reaction in the young person; anecdotes from the professions, descriptions of engineering works, sidelights upon commercial and financial careers, and endless modem instances, as touchstones to preference. Wide opportunities for the discovery of affinities are required in simple fairness to the rising generation. Children should be taken to visit all sorts of business, industries, and farms. Those in the country should have excursions to great centers, to seaports and mines, and those in the city should be shown the country and its pursuits. Representatives of the various employments, workers as well as employers, should lecture before bodies of young people. Thus informed the young person would have a spur to ambition and be definitely guided.

Not only is such information important, but the time when it is seriously listened to is equally important. While there are those whose bents are apparent from the first, there are a multitude whose predilections shift and flicker until late. Usually the occupational affinity of the boy bears small resemblance to the love of his maturity. If the choices of boys and girls were true to their later selves the world would be overcrowded with policemen, locomotive engineers, draymen, acrobats, bass drummers, clergymen, and lady missionaries. Individuals often run a gamut of preferences from childhood up to the age of eighteen or twenty. The

German caste system in education, which fixes occupation at fourteen or before, and the imitation of that system proposed in this country by those whose philosophy is derived straight from the manufacturing industries, are wholly inhuman and unsound. Premature commitment to occupation marks the downfall of equal opportunities in this world and is a crime against the young.

Even with the best of early conditions the possibility of error still exists, for one may misinterpret the inward signs. Some contortion of vanity may convince one that he would succeed where his failure is inevitable. Perhaps he should plow who would preach. Like the believer who is baffled in interpreting the signs of pardon and guidance, the youth often finds it hard to distinguish between true and false lights, and may even lay out his future by a will-o'-the-wisp. Numbers enter professional schools who have not the required abilities and traits, soon to drop out, and many in middle life change from one pursuit to another— are late in finding their niche.

This sort of wastage can be partly overcome by good advice and scientific tests of abilities. Certain types of imagery are required for success as a typist or stenographer, for example. Tests of the ear would decide early in childhood whether it would be worth while to seek a thorough musical education. Tests of imagination can be made to determine fitness for occupations involving creative ability. The person who makes snap judgments can be directed to an employment where execution is required, while the slow-moving logical mind can be pointed to a calling where persistence and study are more essential. It is a matter of common observation that some who fail in one kind of work are phenomenally successful in other kinds. One's own first choices are by no means final; hence the need of correcting or anticipating false starts through the tests of the psychologist. The fact that one wants to be something in particular indeed creates a strong presumption of fitness even when observation tends to the contrary. But there is a field within which scientific tests are important.

5. Advantage of Disadvantages

Yet the individual is so complex that there must be extreme caution. There is such a thing, for example, as making a deficiency pay dividends. The would-be orator unpromising in his speech— *vide* Demosthenes and Henry Ward Beecher— may by sheer effort acquire fluency superior to those who would pass a better vocal examination. One would think that a traveling salesman should have good hearing, but one man made deafness contribute to receipts through a chronic facetious misunderstanding and exaggeration of the customer's orders. Modern Germany became a "model and a menace," not through natural resources, but because of their lack. A poor soil and inadequate water connections are largely responsible for a tremendous agricultural and manufacturing development and the creation of internal waterways, one of the results of which is to make Berlin, 400 miles from salt water, a great port. Deficiency or no deficiency, look out for the man who wants to be something, and wants it badly. If genius is another name for hard work, it is as important to observe purpose as talent. Card tests may stop a few unfortunates from attempting the impossible, but so many other factors besides apparent ability enter into actual fitness that testers should be modest.

Any effort, however, designed to bring about better relations between taste and talent and employment is hopeful, for it may lead to examining occupations themselves to see how much they offer a rational being. It were better oftentimes that jobs be made to fit than that people be made to fit.

Positions should satisfy normal men and women. With work organized, diversified, and alternated to provide fuller human expression the choice of vocation would be less hazardous or ill-fated.

But this, of course, while devoutly to be wished, is for a later generation. Today it is step lively to have a job at all, and those who can afford it find a life in avocations often unhappily denied in the vocations by which they earn their bread.

CHAPTER V
PERSONAL ATTRIBUTES

A MAN once studied contracts for a year under one of the ablest teachers of law in the country, and then said that it did not seem to him that he had learned anything. He was mistaken; he had learned much, but on the spur of the moment he could not summon up remembrance of the past. If this man had been well questioned, and his mind explored systematically by a psychological X-ray, an abundance of learning would have been discovered.

1. Underrating Our Knowledge

Learned men, experienced men, wise men, may feel empty. The salutation. How do you do? is vastly more humane than, What do you know? The former does direct attention, but the latter leaves one wriggling in a sense of mental impotence, without a single starting point for recollection.

We are always doing ourselves an injustice by underrating our mental stock. Someone will counter with the case of the sophomore, but the interruption is groundless. One simply cannot climb any height from which he may get a full view of what is stored in his brain.

We never know how much we know until we are placed in situations which call forth our resources. The feeling of inefficiency is often highly inappropriate, and is no sure test of ability. Suppose a person were given tasks like this: tell all you can about people, or, write about business organization. It would be with extreme difficulty that one could set himself going to say anything. But let the interrogator produce specific queries searching the pigeon-holes of the brain for the information filed there, and one would make a better showing.

2. Questions Stimulate

But if the question never comes? Then we never recall our knowledge. There are thousands and thousands and millions of things in our experience which for want of suitable challenge are lost. They are in the mind, but we do not know they are there and never may know. Once in a while, by chance, a memory button is pushed in the meeting of an old friend or in stumbling upon old correspondence, whereupon cobwebby doors fly back and we are amazed at unexpected revelations of recall. There is a touch of sadness in the knowing that we shall never fully recall what we knew so well. Buried and forgotten lie a hundred selves in a cemetery where even the ghosts forget to walk.

The needs of daily living determine what shall survive from all the mass of personal experience. If the physician forgets something he learned in the medical school, it is because such knowledge is not in ordinary use; he remembers that which is involved in his daily practice. The mind eliminates; it cleans house. That which is not required for present occupation is brushed aside in favor of the bright and shining facts upon which our bread depends.

But the essence of forgotten things is not lost. Many of the principles and sentiments by which one is guided are derived from materials whose gross form no longer can be recalled. Choices are made in the light of former experience whose separate elements are no longer distinguishable. At one time, perhaps, the cook could tell how many spoonfuls to put in, and the physician could tell how to know this disease from that; but, long since, a happy and economical intuition took the place of studied exactness, which stage of intelligence is last and best.

The sense of ignorance lends itself to saying we do not know when we really know, lends itself even to an affectation. No one can keep his eyes open without learning enough to warrant holding his head up, even in an age when the ponderosities of specialization loom on every hand. Let us not be cast down; we know more than we think we do, and perhaps more than we are given credit for.

3. Writers Show Us What We Already Know

The writer of books takes advantage of a simple device and gets himself an unwarranted reputation for learning. By casting a net of organization over information largely common he brings under heads and subheads that in which we all move and have our being. We already know much of what we read, but it never occurred to us to frame it. The appeal of the successful author is in the saying of things whose reality we recognize. He puts together that which is chaotic and unorganized, but his materials lie all about us— if he sells 10,000 copies. Everybody has one or more books in his makeup; but only a few persons ever catch the trick of heads and subheads. Those rare phenomena who are styled walking encyclopedias are not really unique; all the people we see, even the illiterate, are walking volumes, some being sets, others single books, and some pamphlets— literature world without end. According to one's experience is he a work, and according to his skill with the lariat of paragraphs is he an author. Do not worship a book— you would not if you could see the author, says one; good advice, for authors are like everybody else, except for rhetoric and the exasperating knack of dragging forth from semi-oblivion the escaping culprits of ideas.

We shall go to our graves skeptical of our own attainments— with a few bright trinkets of thought on the counter before us, and with bulky shapeless masses of mental possessions in the unlighted recesses of the warehouse. But knowing this illusion of ignorance, we may counteract its evil influence; and whenever a task presents itself we may attack it boldly in the faith that in the doing of it hidden resources will become available.

Not only is there such illusion of ignorance, but there is also, as a disconcerting factor, the sense of awkwardness inseparable from new experiences and promising attempts.

4. Novice Is Awkward

Like a fish out of water, is a term of comparison which has done duty these many years; and while old phrases have to fight for their lives in a university age, it is doubtful if ill-at-easeness could be more effectively represented. In the water the fish is in its element; out of that medium it flounders, is confused, embarrassed, and awkward. There is everything in being in one's element, as men as well as fishes prove.

If one has ever seen a man accompanying his wife to a millinery store he will not ask for other illustrations, but they are plentiful. In his office the attorney is awe-inspiring; out of it he may appear unsure. The newspaper man who is inveigled into talking before a girls' school may enter the gates in a partial swoon and feel the need of stimulants. The chemist who for the first time takes the witness stand makes a showing which would brand one of his students as a freshman. The inexperienced speaker makes a mess of his opening sentence, perhaps, as in one case, "rising to speak to his feet." Let the fair maid whose lover makes a clean job of revelation beware; it is not human to get it right the first time. Getting married is a fearfully new procedure, oftentimes; one thoroughly competent and urbanized business man chewed out the fingers of his white gloves during the church ceremony. He could sell goods, but this was the first time he had been married. In training camps, business and professional men feel and act like schoolboys, petty official individuals lording it over them in all the brutal superiority of braid and *savoir faire*. One never feels himself to be the man he is until his feet are in his boots and his boots are on his own sod. Then let them come on; we are ready for all comers: the doctor in his office; the pilot at the wheel; the farmer in his fields; the professor in his classroom ; the cashier at the grating; the policeman on his beat; the jockey on his horse— yea, the pitcher at the well.

5. General Pattern of Behavior

One, of course, may acquire a generalized behavior suitable for new situations. The man who cannot make a speech may at least rise, bow, and sit down— oh, that some who can speak would do likewise. A mild-mannered reticence and willingness to let the other fellow lead go a long way toward adjustment. But let no one hope, in these days of specialization, for perfect versatility. Anyhow, what is more charming than embarrassment— in others? Childlikeness is charming, and a blush from inexperience is one of the most delightful, if one of the rarest, of phenomena. It is really graceful to acknowledge frankly that one does not know or cannot do. The disclosure may be made happily, and then think how others who know and can do take comfort out of your deficiencies. It is not a bad way to get along. It was the policy of Disraeli to surpass or to make no pretensions.

The awkwardness which one sometimes exhibits and always feels in new situations goes back to childhood. The little boy who is called up to the teacher's desk after a green apple excursion stands first on one foot and then on the other, if unsophisticated; twists the buttons on his coat nearly out of their moorings, holds his head this way and that and feels called upon to make sundry jabs and jerks. He may— spit— a time-honored practice of voiding nervous energy; also not obsolete. And long before the culprit reached the green-apple stage in his life history, as far back as when he began to walk, the same tendency to overflow in excess movements, characteristic of embarrassment, was present; in fact, in babyhood nearly all movements are at random and done to no purpose. A fund of nerve force presses for expression; the channels of habit for the outward flow are not yet opened at the muscles, hence the child seems subject to a series of internal explosions resulting in getting nowhere.

As one grows older he extends his government over the domain of false motions and ill-coordinated reactions; he acquires the trick of getting results and leaving out the flourishes. After a while the child learns how to walk without efforts apparently designed at uprooting the rug, punching holes through to the basement, percussing the atmosphere, or with generous sweeps of the legs including the wall decorations in a grandiloquent abortion of gesture.

The sense of awkwardness is painful, and one gladly avoids it. After one grows up he prefers few if any observers when first acquiring manual or pedal arts, for excess movements frequently appear funny to onlookers. In childhood, however, little thought is taken of the many slips and variations which characterize all that is undertaken in physical or mental expression. The hundred misplays and failures of every day of early life passed without comment or chagrin. But as years go by an ideal of precision grows up, impelling to exactitude and establishing a conventional fear of a grotesqueness of freedom.

6. Reverting to Childhood

Possibly it is this ideal which lies at the root of a certain timidity one feels when revisiting the scenes of childhood. It is scarcely possible to go about in the environment of one's childhood without shrinking into a feeling of helplessness; the conventional self of one's later years giving way to a revived sense of infancy, in which psychological collapse one would hardly resent, as age should require, being set upon and spanked. And certainly the old neighbors and friends never envisage us except as So-and-So's boy or girl; never see us in all the impressiveness of our real adult self-importance. Which being the case, to stay over between trains seems often long enough.

7. Childhood and Growth

But not to be childlike in venturing is to invite a stoppage of development. To be ill at ease is to be assured that growth is still possible. Unfortunate is he who has lost a vivid consciousness of maladjustment, whose antennae of curiosity are not ever bruised and raw f rem fresh contacts; stagnation is his portion. It is more comfortable to have a ready-made phrase or a ready-made action with which to come back, but ease is an enemy. It is better to seek places that prick and stir and burn us with the conviction that we are still as the child, still to be taught, still to be led.

8. *Truthfulness*

Misled by illusions of ignorance, and a feeling of awkwardness when we should felicitate ourselves upon a wholesome awareness of need of adaptation, there remains the factor of a downright partiality for fiction.

There are possibly three reasons why a certain odium attaches to the best-seller: it is fiction; its readers may be frivolous; and its author incurs that disaffection which belongs to a writer who is "too successful."

As to the first consideration, detractors may at once be thrown bodily out of court. There is the most clinching precedent; for it was observed of old that all men are liars, the last and noblest creation of the architect of the universe being, in fact, a work of fiction himself.

Who say that people are primarily interested in reality? Interest in the truth is an anemic youngster compared with the roaring delight in what is not true. Livy begins his *History of Rome* with painstaking accounts of impossibilities— whether told as jokes or not is not fully clear to a student fighting Latin declensions and conjugations. Early literature and "history" is so filled with the improbable that it would not pass muster as good fiction before the modem magazine editor or dramatic critic. Certainly our ancestors did not have any qualms about fidelity to facts, and we are their children, notwithstanding that one may fall in with a person who denies that he had any relatives living at the time of Cicero.

I was recently riding— in the smoking compartment— with an "oil man," a delightful person with gray temples, ample ruddy countenance, an oversize diamond, whistling silk patches sewed inside his trousers knees— to prevent bagging— and a fluent but ungrammatical diction. As it became evident that his auditor was ill-supplied with facts about the development of oil properties, he began to let out, the virgin current of truthfulness gradually expanding and changing color upon reaching the ocean of the highly improbable, his face in the meantime taking on a more beatific expression and his cheery eyes fairly dancing at last in the childlike glee of fiction. I knew he lied, but it was pleasant, and I parted from him with regret.

9. Telling a Good Story

Let anyone test himself for truthfulness, and he will find that the straight and narrow path tends to become as crooked as a ram's horn. At every point the tendency to tell a good story, which is a perfectly respectable motive, taken alone, asserts itself, and one finds himself touching up this feature and shading that in the cause of literature. If one owns seven acres of land and drives out to look at a rail fence, he feels a stealthy impulse to report the incident as that of going out to his ranch to see about an important matter of business. To the dentist the pulling out of a fang tends to get itself into the category of surgical operations, while the professor invariably conducts recitations by lectures. When a chance acquaintance tells you he attended college, subsequent revelation may show it to have been a business college, and was there ever a short-course commercial school of lenient entrance requirements that was not a college, if not a university?

No matter how cultivated and scrupulous one is in matters of fact, introspection will reveal a series of pressures bulging out this item and compressing that, the naive design of which is a smoother composition than occurrences warrant. And it is not often that the narrator suffers any serious eclipse in the telling of personal adventure; even out of a wreckage of failure or faux pas the teller will pull up some gleaming fragment of triumph largely redressing the balance of egotism. Try to recount any incident in absolute realism— the merest happening will serve, such as an exchange of repartee or an evasion of a book agent; what do you find? One finds his mental gait reduced to that of a person going through a strange passage at night. The attempt to be strictly truthful in such case, by giving full circumstance and guarding against claims of subtle advantage, is laborious. In view of which considerations, with what steam shovels of salt should one treat great masses of supposedly biographical and historical material? It would not seem necessary for newspaper editors to doctor reporters' stories, except for climax, for they, like others, cannot tell the truth anyhow— not at least and write rapidly.

10. Egotism in Narration

Truth-telling is often judged too much apart from personal interest and happiness. It is not to be overlooked that everyone has his own interests to guard in a world of tooth and claw. Speech and report are among the finer weapons of competition, and to make a good showing, to render a good account of one's self in words as well as deeds, is the outcropping of a deep-planted instinct.

Naturalists admire the deception which renders a larva invisible through its twiglike appearance, and the humming bird is in good repute notwithstanding the falsification of its nest, which can barely be distinguished from a knotty growth on the limb of a tree. The pickerel is dark and spotted and hard to detect from above; its body underneath is light colored and hard to discern from below. Protective coloration is one of nature's trump cards, as every weasel, prairie dog, hawk, serpent, and jack rabbit demonstrates. The reward for deception in these cases is life— survival. Insects and mammals feign death, and when the invader withdraws they presumably get up, stretch themselves, and tell the others how smart they were. The ground bird hops away as if injured, inviting pursuit, only to trick away from the vicinity of her nest.

With such precedent in nature, with nature rewarding deception and penalizing disclosure, we may at least take a biological attitude regarding tendencies toward deception in man, which, while often to be deprecated, may profitably be considered apart from the dazzling light of the ideal and in the familiar twilight of common sense and living conditions. Deceptive coloration is not confined to bees and gophers; one is tempted to cite the case of milady's complexion, but it is rather with reference to tricks of trades and the keeping up of appearances that the principle has its more serious applications. There is a desperate effort to keep up in appearances; good suits and poor blankets; an unpaid grocer and a fat subscription; a showy house and insufficient food; tips to the porter and a wife with an empty purse.

A good front, whether substantiated by back and insides or not, has a value or so much emphasis would not attach, and deception plays a part in modem society comparable to its part in the lower kingdoms. In particular it is the assertion of species, the often pitiful declaration of equality. The art which enables a person with no reserves of capital to look as well as the affluent is a hope of democracy. It is a merciful provision of science if cotton can be made to look like silk and paste gems to pass the unpracticed eye: gems may be trinkets, but if anybody is to have them let us all— we do not want to drop out of the species. There are enough human varieties with the best that we can do. Thank heaven for the man who first got up ready-made suits that look as if tailored, otherwise perhaps, by a base perpetuation of clothes differentiations, once enforced by law in New England, the crowd at the street comer might appear as heterogeneous as the denizens of the animal tent through which one passes to the circus proper— or improper. Cotton, paste, shoddy, fraud, and pretense tend to keep us all looking much the same on the exterior, pending that great day when we can all wear the genuine article.

11. Deception in Competition

But paste and shoddy on the counter signify differently. Commercial deception, which made the ancient Greek trader *persona non grata* among gentlemen, easily overflows the banks of even biological propriety, enhancing as it does the seller at the expense of the buyer. Even here, however, it is in the interests of survival, and this particular dealer deceives because he thinks he must. The terms of competition may be such in trade as well as in war that an overdevelopment of the deceptive quality may take place. Let us leave it to future generations, for this one has shown scant genius to this end, to fix the terms of subsistence so that the shriveled green apricots will not uniformly be found at the bottom of the basket, with only fair, Eden-like ones lusciously displayed on top. But that is an economic question, and not to be entered upon lightly.

Untruth not only enters into the struggle for subsistence in a physical and social sense, but it has its higher— spiritual?— significance; it represents a world of fictions more stimulating and entrancing than the real world has been found to be. It is remarkable how quickly the world of the obviously real is exhausted, but the world of imagination and artistic perception is illimitable. A child soon gathers the world about him into his senses, and is as filled with shapes and colors and uses of objects as the non-scientific adult. The vaudeville wag who said he would not mind losing his eyes, because he had seen everything, proved the wisdom of folly. If one were to become ten thousand years old he would never live more fully the scent of rain on autumn leaves or the colors of a prairie sunset; indeed, rather less with years, for there is an indescribable glamor in the sensation of childhood, a fairy web of charm which fades with the repetitious labors of the eyes and ears. No scenes are more luminous than those remembered in the light of other days.

Having eaten the heart out of environment through the senses, and with minds not yet filled and satisfied, there remains the world of the unreal, a world of equal if not superior delights for childhood and a realm wherein age may take refuge. The dusty way is transfigured into the golden streets of the New Jerusalem, and the stunted shrub, fertilized by an exuberance of fancy, becomes a tree bearing all manner of fruits, the shortcomings of experience being supplemented by imaginative and poetic elements. The abiding interests of mankind are rather with the imaginative and unreal than with the real, even the hypothesis of the scientist, related as it is to the pursuit of truth, being not infrequently but a fascinating misapprehension.

Beliefs are as often from interest as from conviction. We have all met the person who, without evidence, is rooted in certain views and equally averse to seeing the grounds of others; the person, both credulous and incredulous, who believes without reason and is skeptical without reason, and to whom it is not possible to attribute a preference for the stark truth, being, as are we all, to a degree, in this respect, like children, who first consult convenience and joy.

CHAPTER VI
THE CONFUSING OF MINDS

I F TELLING children myths and false accounts of
nature's operations were not so universal, so
conventional, and so written all over with current approval, it
would appear inexcusable. For consider what this practice
really means. The child arrives in a world which is new to
him; he has no standards, no principles, no experience; the
world is a mass of appearances before which he is mentally
helpless; his logical powers are in the germ stage, and it is
only slowly that he can perceive causal relations.

1. Children Need Help to Think Straight

Now if, instead of the nicest recognition of the
immaturity of his powers and the greatest possible assistance
to him in making out the sequences of nature, we furnish
him thought materials incorporating fallacies of all kinds and
degrees, we make it many fold as difficult for him to develop
proper knowledge and perspective.

Often the literature offered to children gives them the
imperfect views of primitive man regarding the world. Books
and readings for children contain collectively an immense
amount of folklore, fairy stories, myths, accounts of
supernatural happenings, and inaccurate reports of the
operations of nature and the behavior of animals. Giants,
ogres, nymphs, angelic and sinister spirits, personified
objects, witches, dragons, and ghosts represent some of the
concepts supplied. Whole series of volumes compiled of this
type of reading matter are published and employed in schools

and homes.

The practice of supplying children with such materials is due to several causes. In the first place, children are tremendously interested. Also a common argument is that these materials afford necessary exercise of the child's imagination. Then Herbart, G. Stanley Hall, and other educational writers have propounded the theory that inasmuch as children represent a stage of development corresponding to that of the primitive adult, the child's culture materials should be those of the primitive adult. The theory of culture epochs, which has had great vogue in educational circles, is that the child's reading matter and the materials of instruction should correspond with the stage of early development which is parallel to the mental stage of the child. This theory has governed the presenting of material to children which has no practical or scientific justification.

The weakness in the arguments above becomes evident upon close examination. The fact that a given kind of materials is highly-interesting to children is not a conclusive argument for it. Children become equally interested in materials of a more valuable kind. We are accustomed in the case of diet to pay little attention to the child's superficial choices. Governed by the child's preferences, we would serve candy three times a day at the beginning of each meal. If no other kind of literature could vie in interest with the myth the case would be somewhat different; but it is not proved, nor can it be, that wholesome and constructive materials may not be presented to the child so that they will charm him fully as much.

2. Myth and Imagination

As to the argument for the imagination, one upon which much reliance has been placed, there is like reason for skepticism. Not that the myth does not exercise the imagination, for it surely does. But other materials, less objectionable, also exercise the imagination. Let us take a particular incident in the mythological story of Orpheus. Orpheus was a great musician. The child is told that when Orpheus, who was the son of a god, Apollo, played his lyre the spiders stopped their spinning, the ants left off running to and fro, and the bees forgot to gather honey; the birds gathered around trying to catch the tune; lions, bears, wolves, foxes, eagles, hawks, owls, squirrels, field mice, and many other kinds of creatures gathered about him; trees tore themselves up by the roots and joined the audience. The power of Orpheus is set forth by Pope in the words—

When Orpheus plays, trees moving to the sound
Start from their roots and form a shade around.

Here is exercise for the imagination, rather delightful, it must be said, to anyone. But so far as the training of the imagination is concerned, like results could be secured if the essential images were woven into a realistic sketch. The imagination is exercised through the Orpheus story by picturing the different animals; by visualizing the trees, the spiders, the ants, and the bees, and by forming a mental image of a man playing a harp in the open. The conceiving of a tree pulling itself up by the roots is really no greater exercise of the imagination than the mental picturing of a tree in its normal position. But if it were to be argued that the imagination received a special touch from that part of the

story dealing with the movement of the trees out of the earth, that feature could be duplicated in a story in which a tree was represented as being pulled up by the roots, either by machinery or by a tornado; in fact, the digging up of trees and their transportation and transplanting in cold weather by the use of trucks and devices would, so far as the imagination is concerned, fully take the place of the mythical account.
It is worth while to examine somewhat minutely the claim that mythical materials furnish an exceptional exercise of the imagination. It would appear that not a single element in that part of the Orpheus myth quoted could not be successfully imitated in a story in which there were no nature-faking, no improbable occurrences, and no confusion of causes.

3. Effects of Nature-Faking

Now consider what the child does get out of this myth wholly apart from effects upon the imagination. While older readers would already have had sufficient experience to know something of the actual effects of music upon animals, the little child is certain to be misled on this point. It may be years before he will become sure that bees will not stop gathering honey even if Kreisler or Paderewski were to perform ecstatically; in fact, the child might thereafter always be confused and falsely informed as to the effect of music upon animals. Instead of getting the right of the thing he is indelibly impressed with false views. Perhaps it is not of the utmost importance whether a person lives his life in error regarding the reaction to music of field mice and eagles, but as the account is typical of hundreds of others, the fact of misinformation is not to be lightly considered. Later on in this same myth, so dear to children's books, Orpheus is represented in an unsuccessful effort to rescue his wife,

Eurydice, from the dark underworld where Pluto was king. At this point in the myth the ingenuous mind of the child receives an ineffaceable impression of a highly problematical region which, with trimmings, as hell, has terrorized multitudes of sensitive men and women.

There is clearly nothing in the myth in question which could afford a greater exercise of the imagination than might be had in any well-written tale. The reading of any account which necessitated the imaging of objects, persons, animals, and scenes outside of immediate environment provides the same sort of mental exercise as that provided in mythical literature.

The idea that the child when reading mythology reproduces the state of mind of primitive man is not to be accepted too hastily. A great deal of mythology represents the serious efforts of primitive peoples to explain the world. They did not get up fantastic myths just for the sake of entertaining themselves. Before the days of chemistry, physics, biology, meteorology, and other sciences, individuals labored under great difficulties in interpreting nature's phenomena. When the ancient said that the earthquake was caused by the movement of a giant in unquiet sleep within the earth he was probably giving the best explanation of which he was capable. It is very uncomfortable to live with a question mark always before your face, and the early thinker secured repose of thought through beliefs which are highly grotesque to us. Many of these beliefs were a crude form of science and represent efforts of the inquiring mind. There is no record to show that early man committed the folly of which we are guilty, namely, that of filling up a child's mind with ideas known to be false. The mythology and pseudoscience inculcated in former times represented serious convictions on the part of adults. The particular sin of which we are guilty is that of knowingly subjecting immature minds to false impressions.

4. Pointing to the Error

It would be a great advance over present practice if whenever erroneous concepts were presented the error were distinctly pointed out. If a fairy story is told with the explanation that it is untrue the undesirable results are fewer. Where the myth is narrated with the air of truthfulness the damage is greatest. Certainly no child should ever be told what is not true, no matter how popular the myth, without his being told that it is not true.

But even where this precaution is taken bad effects are not fully prevented. The writer remembers the case of a somewhat hysterical woman whose fears were sought to be allayed by the reading of a book of exposures of ghost stories. A ghost story would be related, to be fully explained away later. No one could read this book and draw from it any support for a belief in ghosts, yet the imagery and uncanny fascination of the tales would so work upon one's mind that he would scarcely feel like putting his head out of doors after sundown; one's emotions were not kept in check by the *exposé*, but on the other hand were inflamed by terrifying elements. The unwisdom was in exposing a sensitive mind to this sort of stuff.

So it is with mythical literature in general; it is a mistake to permit the mind to contemplate certain materials out of which spring wrong attitudes, unwise expectations, and deformed views. A girl may know the unsubstantial nature of the story of Cinderella, and yet be affected by it to the extent of indulging to an unwarranted degree in expectations of high romance. She may thus be predisposed to imagine a marriage with a prince, or to hope, as is not at all uncommon, that with marriage all cares, worry, self-dependence, and hard work miraculously vanish. Out of fairy stories has come a feeling for personages of royal blood which has had not a little to do with the keeping of monarchy in the world, and with the perpetuation of the theory of the divine right of kings. Hercules was the son of a god, why not the king?

5. Myth Affects Adults

The question of the wisdom of employing mythical materials in the education of a people may be approached from more than one point of view. It is not the purpose here to consider the extent to which fears may be planted in the individual for life through horror tales and accounts of ruthless and conscienceless mythical characters, but the toll taken out of human happiness by this means is very large. The delight which children experience in fairy stories is more than counterbalanced by the terrors suffered. Discussion of the effects of this kind of literature upon the emotions may be left to the domain of nervous disorders and psychoanalysis. The particular point under consideration is the effect of early false impressions upon the logic, mental attitudes, the concepts and opinions of people about us in society. Does early acquaintance with folklore and pseudoscience put kinks into the mental processes of adults?

In considering this question we must realize that first impressions are not only lasting, but that in various cases are final all the information that a person may ever secure on a given matter may be that gained in childhood. It is not to be supposed that early misinformation is in every case supplanted later by correct information. In the case of the Orpheus tale, to be specific, the child may never reach the stage of accurate information as to the effect of music upon animals. It is altogether an unwarranted assumption that all the false ideas planted in the child's mind in the shape of legend and superstition will in due time be ousted and replaced by real knowledge. A great many people never grow up. There is the case, now known to be frequent, of the adult whose mental age does not correspond to his physiological age; he may be thirty years old by the calendar and mentally a twelve-year-old. In such cases we could hardly expect that the individual would ever outgrow the effects of misinformation.

Now let us take the case of the person whose mind is normal; here there is no arrest of development in mental capacity, but there may be an arrest in the accumulation of knowledge; in fact, this happens universally. Along some lines the knowledge of each one of us has been advancing through all the years of life; but along other lines the growth of knowledge tapered off and ceased years ago. For example, here is a man whose knowledge of square root absolutely terminated when he dropped out of school, perhaps leaving his tattered arithmetic in his desk. Here is another whose knowledge of the French Revolution has never been expanded beyond that gained early in life from a paragraph on the subject in a general history. In hundreds of instances the mental life of the individual exhibits like conditions. To a large extent we are governed in mature years by information or misinformation thus definitely set off in early life. Early arrest at the stage of misinformation produces widespread evil results in the modem world. There is no nation whose development upward is not today seriously clogged and threatened by unsound mental products. Folklore, false conceptions, perverted history, fantastic legends, and the products of credulity form an almost impassable barrier to rational civilization. Grotesque and degrading folk-views lay a heavy burden upon progress in India, China, Europe, and the world. Forward steps in agriculture, sanitation, and medicine, penology, and in commercial, economic, and social conditions are taken with great difficulty.

6. Opposition to Science

The opposition to science illustrated, for example, in the case of Darwinism and the germ theory of disease arises largely from the fact that minds are filled up with faulty preconceptions. New discoveries are resented by those whose minds are already stocked with antagonistic ideas. It would be much better for a population not to have been informed at all rather than to have been falsely informed. The people who roared with laughter when Franklin read his paper to prove the sameness of lightning with electricity were thus moved to ridicule because Franklin's ideas were so different from those which they possessed. To a mind free of incorrect views of lightning the ideas offered by Franklin would have been as acceptable as any. The pernicious function of a vast amount of unsound traditional culture material is to stand in the way of actual knowledge. A Chinese boy might readily be taught the most advanced medicine and surgery known to the Western World, but it would be impossible to clear the superstitions from the mind of a typical Chinese doctor and get him to embrace what the boy would readily learn.

7. Baby Talk

An interesting analogy to this blocking of the mind by misinformation is the retarding of mental development through the use of slang and baby talk. These forms of language have much the same relation to speech development as has mythology to science. Where parents talk to their children in an affectionate jargon which violates all the principles of correct expression the child is placed at serious disadvantage. Instead of learning a given word correctly and at once, he wastes his energy upon an incorrect form which must be painfully changed later. There are cases where children have reached a considerable age while still using forms of baby talk, and the speech retardation in these cases is serious. On the other hand, if the child hears only pure English from the first he has an immense advantage. By the time he is eight or ten years of age he will have as wide and correct command of words as the average man or woman. A child can pronounce a word of four or five syllables just as easily as he can pronounce a series of four or five words of one syllable each. One can hardly overstate the advantage to the child of being exposed only to perfect pronunciation and well-formed sentence structure from the first.

8. Value of Right Culture

Consider the principle as applied to all the culture materials of the child. Surrounded by exact statements of general information and science, he would develop with astonishing rapidity from receiving only correct impressions. The time required to get correct impressions is not greater than that required to get wrong impressions. Then the energy required for revising a false impression is wholly saved. It requires no longer to understand that it is air pressure which raises water in a pump pipe than to gain a faulty idea of "suction." A child can learn as readily that the yeast plant releases bubbles of a gas which causes bread to rise as to learn, only to unlearn, that a fairy is operating in the bread dough.

The phenomenal development of various young persons

under superior culture conditions lends weight to the argument of Professor Boris Sidis of Harvard University, whose son was thus distinguished, that what seems to be precocious attainment is easily within reach of the average child if suitable materials for his mind to feed upon are provided. It is probably safe to say that we have but a slight vision of the immense possibilities of improving human conditions through the supplying in early years of only the best and most vital items of knowledge. The waste and misdirection of mind in childhood and youth through the careless choice and presentation of mental diet are beyond imagination.

9. Gold-Brick Mind

One does not need to look very far to discover in the general public evidences that the fairy story outlook does not fully pass with childhood. Every community contains at least a few individuals who have taken too literally the myth of King Midas. King Midas reached out for the bedpost and found that it turned to solid gold within his grasp, and likewise found, so the child is told, that everything he touched turned to gold. One would think that no one would be seriously affected by such a myth if one did not realize the number of investments made which rest upon some such belief. There are always people to be found willing to stake their money upon golden dreams, and the number of gold bricks purchased annually is by no means negligible. Now it is not likely that any investor, if pinned right down, would concede the possibility of a bedpost turning into gold. But such a tale contributes a certain influence toward producing a state of mind favorable to absurdly unwise hopes of profit. Six per cent looks like an insignificant return to the myth-

minded candidate for the sucker list. The net result of
miraculous tales of good fortune and great wealth is to
produce a credulous state of mind out of which the dishonest
promoter and the salesman of fake stocks reap a tremendous
annual harvest.

An excessive amount of myth and folklore, tradition
and legend in the culture materials of the various nations has
much to do with building up uncritical and inefficient mind.
The expectation of the miraculous is fostered and all sorts of
preposterous ideas propagate themselves. The medieval belief
in a panacea survives in the confidence reposed in various
quack nostrums, which, to judge by the advertising matter,
cure practically all diseases. The elixir of life and the fountain
of youth are still sought, and the magical properties of
trinkets are in high favor. Iron rings are worn as preventives
of rheumatism, and horse chestnuts are carried in the pocket
as another treatment for the same disease. The "thirteen"
superstition is sufficiently strong to cause hotel-keepers to
avoid this number upon rooms. The belief in talismans and
in lucky pennies and coins is firmly fixed. We are told that
more than a million charms were purchased by soldiers early
in the present European war. Hoodoos are taken with equal
seriousness, and the plumber who does a faulty piece of work
may remark that a black cat crossed his path that morning.
It may seem that such fanciful notions do not interfere in any
important way with the world's business, and that they
merely hover in the background and have little practical
force. Probably the plumber does not really believe that a leak
in the pipes was due to the black cat. But the results of such
forms of consciousness are nevertheless not a few. A clean-
cut rational type of mind can hardly be set upon a foundation
of erroneous early impressions. The slowness with which
modern science and modern thought make their way is due
in large measure to such unfortunate mental inheritances.

10. Social Effects

The mind factors underlying racial and religious antagonisms date back to peculiar instruction in childhood. Thus originate the fanaticism of religion and the race and national egotism which result in war.

A good deal of misinformation comes in the form of a too-literal interpretation of early literature. This has been especially true in the case of Hebrew literature. Eminent scholars, higher critics, assure us of the rhetorical or symbolic character of many of the accounts, yet the stories of the deluge, of Jonah, and of the passage of the Red Sea are accepted in a literal sense. The essential lessons of any literature are misunderstood through such intensely literal interpretation. Such a reading commits one to conduct and ideals which the modem world could do very well without, and hampers ethical and intellectual development. Faulty rules of literary and historical interpretation brought to bear upon childhood result in deforming the whole superstructure of adult life.

It is highly important that in the education of the young there be the most careful selection of subject matter. Germ ideas of error should not be planted in the minds of children. The character of civilization might be fundamentally changed if every effort were made to start children consistently along the road to enlightenment, science, and truth. To keep the race in darkness it is only necessary to keep on misdirecting and befuddling the child's intelligence, thus giving a false direction to the mental life in later years. All sorts of prejudices, animosities, and stubborn obsessions opposed to progress are traceable to absorption of primitive thought materials.

It is as easy to produce enlightenment as to

manufacture error. There is a plenty of material for youthful readers in which there is nothing to which objection could be taken. Consider the delightful and informing stories afforded by geology and paleontology. Books dealing with early and extinct types of animals and with the life of the cave man are of extreme interest. The life of the bee as described by Maeterlinck or Fabre perhaps transcends in fascination any ancient myth. The possibilities in scientific, geographical, historical, and biographical narratives are as broad as one could wish. Modem manufacturing, transportation, agriculture, and commerce abound in information which can be woven into highly interesting sketches. Indeed various writers have done a great deal to create a new kind of literature for children. But it can hardly be doubted that many of the shortcomings of the public mind are referable to a misguided instruction still universally practiced.

CHAPTER VII
IDEAS AND ADJUSTMENTS

A MAN may ride for days across the open prairie and rarely see game of any sort or think of game. Whether game in the open is scarce or merely invisible, unless one is thinking about game or looking for it he is not likely to see it. Now suppose one takes along a gun with the expectation of shooting something; then his whole attitude changes. Without a gun he may go by animals without seeing them, not being on the lookout; with a gun he not only probably sees animals but oftentimes he makes the mistake of "seeing" animals where none exist. In the deer season men and objects are mistaken by sportsmen and shot at for deer. If one is looking for rabbits he tends to see them behind every clump of weeds and in every bunch of grass; to take a gun and look for rabbits is to see them even where there are none. One sometimes sees a man with a gun starting out through town to reach hunting ground. Such a one may be seen glancing about even in the streets of the city as if expecting to see coyotes, prairie chickens, and wild geese; he may cast the hunter's glance at the eaves of a city residence as if there might be a good shot in that direction.

1. Force of Expectation

The tendency shown by the sportsman to see what he is looking for appears in all of us in everyday affairs and gives us evidence of the force of an idea. If we are looking for a face in a crowd, we notice that face sooner than would anyone not looking for it, although looking in the same direction. If we are looking for a person to come up the street, we may think we see that person several times before he actually appears. One may cross meadows a hundred times without seeing a four-leafed clover, but if he has the idea of observing four-leafed clovers he will find them without much effort; all one needs is to have his mind set for four-leafed clovers, in which event they will jump out of the earth at him. We see what we are looking for, and we sometimes think we see what we are looking for even if it does not appear. Surely if we want to see anything we should be ready to perceive it.

It is said that we get out of anything as much as we bring to it. If one knows nothing about baseball he does not get as much out of witnessing a game as one who takes to the game certain expectations. A piece of literature is relatively barren to a reader who approaches it without standards and with no background of experience with other literature. To appreciate anything one's mind must be furnished with materials and attention must be properly directed.

2. Vocational Application

In ordinary life one may look for nothing and see nothing, or he may look and see. Suppose a young man entertains the idea of becoming a great lawyer. Among the first results will be an almost automatic accumulation of knowledge about courts, cases, and lawyers. In casual reading the fact bearing upon the law will be particularly noticed; it will jump out of the page like a four-leafed clover in a field to one looking for it. With the addition of every new fact and incident bearing upon the law the basis for further observation is enlarged. This early accumulation of knowledge serves increasingly as a magnet to attract other legal ideas.

Thus one's preparation for a chosen occupation is made somewhat unconsciously, as attitude of mind contributes to the securing of necessary information. Items of knowledge and experience seem to drift to one who is interested in a given field; this is illustrated in the case of preparing to write an article or make a speech. When the theme is chosen one begins to accumulate particulars related to it, and the composition will partly form itself once the mind is directed to a topic. It is a good plan to begin weeks or months or even years in advance in the writing of a work. By making an early start materials which would otherwise escape notice come drifting by, and at last, when the moment of execution arrives, there are ready an organization of ideas and a supply of pertinent items. This slow preparation is the easiest and the most productive.

Strenuous methods are by no means the best. One does not do best that which he does with the greatest difficulty; the successful feat is oftentimes that performed with the greatest ease. We should make use of the principle of growth rather than rely upon severe impromptu efforts. The strenuous life is unwisely extolled; it is far better to live under the steady influence of governing ideas and purposes, and finally measure up to success through development instead of struggle.

The advantage of purposes which can be realized only after a long period of time is to be noted. If one lives merely from day to day he will never accomplish as much as if he directed his aim toward some object not to be achieved until after months or years. The pull of a distant goal is a wholesome influence. It is not well only to have purposes and plans that may be realized in the immediate future. By centering attention upon a distant end one's efforts become better organized and he grows toward the fulfillment of large results in a way that suggests cosmic processes; one gets the benefit of a kind of compound interest.

3. Action Results

The force of an idea is thus evident in its control of the field of observation and in its power to draw one toward a remote achievement. These things it does by its tendency to result in movement. The idea of doing a thing goes a long way toward getting it done. The idea is the beginning of movement, and the best way to make sure of accomplishing a thing is to dwell upon the idea. When a cat pounces upon a mouse the only idea in the cat's mind is the mouse; there is no concern as to the placing of the feet or of the contraction of the muscles— the idea is the thing. Similarly, if an athlete is about to make a broad jump he will do best by thinking of his landing place and giving but slight attention to anything else. Obsessed with the idea of jumping to a given point, all the athlete's powers are regulated to this end. If in such a case one were to fix his attention upon an intervening point he would surely fail to execute his best efforts. By holding the thought, as the Christian Scientists say, conduct is unavoidably influenced and directed.

What happens when one holds a wrong idea is seen in the tendency to jump down from a high place. When one is high up he may unfortunately center his attention upon the height and the danger of his position. If he does this he will experience a tendency to get down to safety, and as the quickest way would be to jump he finds difficulty in refraining from plunging headlong. The idea of getting down tends to discharge the muscles for this act. If one could shift his attention to the view from a pinnacle or engage in conversation or in some way possess his mind with ideas not related to getting down quickly, he would be perfectly safe.

It is the idea of falling which makes it impossible for the average man to walk a narrow plank over a deep chasm. One can walk a six-inch board for a long distance if it is an integral part of a floor but let it be taken out of the floor and placed over Niagara Falls, and not one person in a million could resist the suggestion of falling.

4. Idea of Success

It is evident that if we want to go anywhere over a difficult passage it is better to hold in mind the success of the project rather than let one's attention center upon possible failure. To believe that one can do a thing helps mightily to the doing of it, and to fear that one will fail sets the entire organism into an attitude favorable to failure. An idea is not a tame, harmless affair, but is loaded, and it makes all the difference in the world with what ideas one lives. One should select his ideas with the utmost care, choosing those which are consistent with welfare. It will not do to depreciate one's abilities or to sink to apologetic positions. If one does not believe in his own future, his future automatically contracts; but if he sets his aim high, he then receives the benefit of the dynamic forces which ideas represent.

Openness to conviction is important in view of the function of fresh information in effecting suitable relationships; but, unfortunately, new ideas often irritate and prove unwelcome. It can hardly be said that the people of the middle ages were hungering to know the movements of the earth or to learn about human anatomy, for the ashes of martyrs to science are hardly cool. Persecutions aimed at the suppression of new information do not speak highly of thirst for knowledge. Indeed the relatively small amount of science which existed one or two centuries ago seems to indicate that a common attitude was not one of burning zeal to know, but one of aversion, skittish if not malevolent.

5. *Attachment to Ignorance*

Ignorance is the natural state of man— that to which we are born— and the encroachment of knowledge is often successfully resisted. Men are curious, also incurious. In some there is abiding curiosity; but even so, there are required for it a training, an encouragement and coaxing, and a systematic direction.

The derogatory term, bookworm, indicates that love for learning has not taken full possession of society. There is a fear of learning and a dread of the wise. Candidates for public office lose votes if called professor or doctor. The desire for entertainment, amusement, sensations, and novelty is universal; but that curiosity which persistently attacks mysteries is rare. Even with the student, whose presence at a seat of learning implies a thirst for knowledge, it transpires that such thirst is often easily slaked and that the instructor must resort to polite coercion to keep him going.

When the first surprise of childhood toward the world vanishes there may be little further curiosity in regard to objects. Hence it is important, both for science and personal development, to keep alive the spirit of inquiry. A noted geologist traces his lifelong interest in nature to the observation trips upon which he as a child accompanied his father; interests thus shaped in early life bear fruit long afterward. Without direction and inspiration one may soon fall into a listless attitude, becoming indifferent and insensitive to the fields and their inhabitants and to cities and their activities. A visitor often meets some person who has lived many years near a natural wonder or a great manufacturing concern without ever having visited such.

Effort is required to keep alive that inquisitiveness which in childhood seems to have force enough to supply motives during the longest life. The thing desired is a continuing sense of wonder, otherwise expressed as a problem consciousness. One may look at workmen excavating a street for a water main and simply see human forms swinging pickaxes; or, having a problem consciousness, he may conceive interesting questions. Having the seeing eye, one perceives problems on every hand, and with accumulation of knowledge upon a certain topic, interest and curiosity increase.

One tends to excuse himself from being curious on the ground that men have already found out everything, no nook or cranny appearing to remain unexplored. What is left of the secrets of nature anyhow? Men in blue goggles have been pounding rocks to pieces and hunting specimens for these many years; and no insect has succeeded in developing a protective coloration perfect enough to make good its escape from the "bugologist."

The exercise of curiosity by reading of the findings of former observers is left, nor have all the secrets of nature been made out. We doubtless suffer from a gigantic illusion if we feel that nearly everything has been found out.

6. The Personal Element

Whether it is because we feel that nature has little more to offer the ordinary observer, or because we are naturally more interested in people than in things, it comes about that the keenest curiosity is with reference to people. There is nothing so interesting as other people's business. A man may care nothing about the interior of the earth, the composition of the stars, the life of the incorrigible microbe, or the feather arrangement of the hawk's wing, and yet be consumed with a desire to know what his neighbors are up to. As long as there is a flutter of mental activity there will be joy in the ways of people. Unlike the natural world, which to many appears uninteresting and barren of message, the eternal flux of history proves fascinating, and the history which is most attractive is that which is making near at hand. A much maligned interest is in gossip, the germ of an impressive science— sociology.

No one is without interest in what other people are doing, saying, and planning; we want to see not only how the other half lives, but how the rest of our own half lives. Even among families of like economic status there are possibilities of interesting disclosures. One's neighbor rebuilds his house, and there is the natural desire to know the point of view that governs him in making over his residence. There are enough conundrums in the lives of the people in one's own block to absorb surplus mental energy. Here is the field of the dramatist and the novelist, and to the extent to which these can look through roofs, walls, and doors, and divine the actualities of the inner lives of people, who seem so uniform but are so endlessly different, these writers secure our willing ear. The march of mind, which has been from astronomy to biology, is now to sociology. Curiosity was at first directed mainly to the heavens and to philosophy and theology; always the learned man was dealing with remote things. Later came the studying of natural forces and organisms, and still later comes the finding out about one's neighbors.

Hail social science. The world will become a much fitter place to live in by the redirection of curiosity, for instead of speculating on the appearance of the off-side of the moon we shall concern ourselves with the question of how many children in our town do not have milk on their oatmeal.

CHAPTER VIII
DIFFERENCES OF OPINION

W HEN Mr. Ford, the automobile manufacturer, sailed for Europe on his "peace ship" during the great war, he believed that the war was being kept up by bankers, munition makers, and the men higher up. On his return he was equally convinced that the men in the trenches were mainly responsible. While the latter conviction is interesting in that it concurs with the final convictions of a good many other people, the reversal of opinion on the part of Mr. Ford is interesting simply as a reversal of opinion.

One sees in Mr. Ford's change of opinion an admirable illustration of the fact that of the several joint causes of anything, one may be impressed today by a certain one and tomorrow by another.

1. Evidence and Opinion

The opinion based upon a stage of evidence falls before more evidence, and as there are all stages of evidence, endless differences of opinion arise. I believe one thing today and tomorrow another, having learned something to the point in the meantime. If one is governed by evidence, a fixed opinion is possible only by having complete evidence or by not increasing one's knowledge.

If opinions differed only with amount of evidence, full information would harmonize the world. But highly as evidence is prized by judge and scientist, it is not so heartily sought in the world at large. Many differences of opinion arise from other causes than varying quantities of evidence, yet differences numerous enough, surely, arise from seeing many-sided truth from a single viewpoint.

Questions of human life are intricate, and it is not easy to hold in mind all aspects of a problem. Does poverty cause intemperance, or intemperance cause poverty? If one knew everything about poverty and intemperance, looking down upon the world from a point of phenomenal advantage for observation, he would know all. But the man in the street knows a few instances only, and these he may cite according to preconceived notions. The result is that when two men discuss the relations between poverty and intemperance they may, unless modest, emphatically disagree, their bits of evidence not being representative of the whole subject.

One effect of the scientific method has been to make a trifle more popular the allowing for a possible shortage of facts. We learn to speak by what the evidence indicates, or to the best of our information, exhibiting a caution in the interest of truth of which the valiant devotees of fagots and thumbscrews would have been ashamed. But still, on the street and in the comer of the hall where spellbinders rail for party, one overhears the perfervid argument whose reason for being is inadequacy of information.

Let us not, however, hastily infer that opinions differ only according to degrees of evidence. This would be the greatest of errors. The mere mention of evidence may lead us astray. There is really less interest in evidence than one might suppose. Evidence is often wanted only to bolster up a cause, not to establish the truth. Everybody has use for evidence, but not everybody follows where it leads. Conflicts of ideas which originate merely in evidence or lack of it are trivial compared with those which rest on other grounds.

Long ago the wisdom of not disputing points of taste was recognized, and that one man's meat is another man's poison became one of the first discoveries. In many matters argument gets one nowhere and evidence is flouted by feeling. We prefer different melodies, colors, foods, and faces, and are unable to give reasons of weight to anyone else. The medieval knight who stationed himself at the crossroads and challenged to combat anyone who did not admit the superior charms of his lady love was taking chances. Differences in the appreciation of the human countenance are so numerous that even doubtful beauties may chance upon real admirers. Hope springs eternal, and with good reason— tastes differ.

Members of the same family differ in tastes, and the inherited tendencies in peoples, as would be expected, show far greater differences. Give a young Japanese, says Le Bon, exactly the education given a young Englishman; teach him every fact taught the Englishman— will they act the same under identical circumstances? Not at all. Never will the Englishman and the Japanese react exactly the same way. There is something in the composition of the brain which throws an influence into behavior which no amount of training can overcome.

All sane people agree upon the eternal verities of, say, the multiplication table and the pole star. Any biped who has come far enough toward the prevailing culture level to admit that there is such a thing as numbers will assent to the rules of arithmetic. There are axiomatic matters which to deny is to plead insanity or perverse incapacity. But once away from these universal agreements and embarked on the sea of instinct and feeling, uniformity ends. No one disagrees with me on the verities, but it is a lucky hour if I can find anyone, even in my own family, who will follow me in esthetic discernment.

We like very different things, and there is no use arguing about them. If the brain could be held up to view in its infinite minuteness we should find that one's neighbor's brain and his own differ as widely as countenances.

Disagreements in taste, which a tendency in nature

multiplies to the relieving of monotony, are, however, tame affairs compared with those which arise from conflicting interests. There would be few lawsuits if straight people did not see crookedly. Logic is a tool of self-interest. Political and economic literature is packed full of self-protecting arguments. There is hardly a book published on any economic subject that is not as lopsided and partisan as a lawyer's brief.

Competitive conditions govern thought, for the brain is simply an organ that has been evolved in the struggle for existence. The first duty is self-preservation, and reason swings into line when we are bent on getting something for ourselves. The monopolist does not think as his victims do. He has the same data that we have, but arrives at the honest but weird conclusion that God in His wisdom has elected him to rule anthracite. If the same man were a miner, his brain cells would develop a different sequence of ideas. As a man's income is so he thinks.

The animals have their own ways of saving their necks— the horns of stag, the claws of wildcats, and all sorts of epidermis and perfumery. We excuse these creatures in their unique defenses and prevarications. Horns, hoofs, claws, and all are represented in the supreme weapon of human defense and aggression— logic. An academic treatment of psychology has set reason upon a pedestal of impartiality. But talk with the first man you meet and see how impartial his reasoning is. It is as crooked as a ram's horn, and wrong at every point where his interests conflict with mine.

2. *Tyranny of the Stomach*

What Fabre, in his *Life of the Spider*, styles "the tyranny of the stomach" disturbs reasoning when not controlled by self-evident truths. Where there is the slightest flexibility in the evidence, conclusions will vary with self-interest. What is rightness, anyhow? We know that this changes with changes in social control. If the American Federation of Labor or the Socialist party or the Votes for Women organization or the Army and Navy League had the upper hand, "right" would mean something other than it does.

Is it "right" to provide old-age pensions? It becomes so when the call is backed up by sufficient power. Might makes right, the might whose symbol is numbers and ballots. Political truths are the products of a logic originating in the stomach, where for the most part reason has its seat

The stomach is not a modest organ. Its immediate capacity, it is true, is limited; but the possessor has a tendency to anticipate the needs of the stomach in the far future. He lays up stores. Opulent citizens, animated by the laudable ambition to see that their stomachs will have enough to go on, establish a claim upon the food supplies of remote futurity, and if these men were to live to be as old as the proverbial hills they would scarcely be able to gnaw through the outer crust of the food mountain implied in their bank accounts.

The desire for food is transmuted into a desire for power, whereupon there is no end of ambition. If one were satisfied when he had enough, if the fundamental needs were not succeeded by craving for domination, a stage would be reached at which men would think more in the spirit of science. But through ambition, or from force of habits of mind set up when hunger was a driver, men full of years are also full of selfish prejudice.

Even judges will think according to election returns, and ultimately come to believe in what is thus forced upon them. Outside the calm of pure science, logic is but a reflection of the will to live. The automobile salesman overlooks the deficiencies of his own machine, even sees them as virtues; mechanical principles in the science of physics are one thing— applied to machines upon whose sale a living depends, they are not quite the same.

CHAPTER IX
BUSINESS AS CONCILIATION

IT MIGHT seem that business, which aims at profit, would intensify the sense of opposition; but, on the other hand, it appears to have phases tending quite to the contrary.

Urbanity, being urban, can fairly be claimed to have a commercial origin, while unsocial rusticity represents a more independent career.

An eastern university offers a course upon the rural mind. One's first impression is that the instructor would be put to desperate efforts to distinguish successfully between the rural and the city mind, or any other mind; yet there is a basis for such a course. To a large extent mental traits are established by one's surroundings and practical interests. No one is born with a rural mind or an urban mind, but by being brought up in city or country one may acquire traits to correspond. In a sense there are as many types of mind as there are occupations.

It is difficult to set off confidently the traits of the business mind, inasmuch as everyone is engaged in business to some extent, employing funds or earning a living. There is an amount of business activity in every person's life; we are all in business more or less. Yet while business has a widely diffused influence, some who engage much in business possess minds which have not been early and principally shaped by business.

1. Relation of Dealer and Customer

But if we consider business in its intensive aspects we are brought face to face with certain tendencies; the occupation of the salesman or the dealer tends to shape outlook somewhat definitely. What these effects are upon the mind are of extreme importance, for the empire of business is of wide and growing extent. In what ways does trade stamp itself upon the brain cells of the young man who enters it at the most impressionable period?

A social consciousness is immediately developed, for a customer is implied in every act of the tradesman, who must visualize the consumption of his goods and think of what others need, for the needs of others are his opportunities for gain. He must put himself in the place of the buyer; he must imagine what the buyer wants and how the buyer will look at a given product. To some extent the dealer is like the actor, who assumes a character. He serves by understanding what other people require; he ministers, not like the clergyman, who does not keep books, yet he ministers.

An immediate difference between the business man and the clergyman is that the service of the former is not dictated primarily by considerations of benefit to someone else. The dealer is mainly interested in making a profit. To secure a profit he must first find someone to deal with, and tactics must accordingly, at least at first, be conciliatory, and the substance of the transaction is the supplying of other person's needs. The insistence upon a profit marks an ethical division between the work of the reformer or clergyman and the tradesman. The individual's need is the opportunity for unselfish service on the part of a social servant, but the individual's need in the case of the tradesman is an opportunity to serve plus one for making a profit. Business men are philanthropists in a sense, but not inconsiderate ones.

The business man who indulged a passion for rendering disinterested service would soon go into bankruptcy. As soon as the public found that he had a soft spot of benevolence there would be a swarming down upon him of impecunious customers and an army of such as are unwilling or unable to face their bills. The philanthropy of the business man as such must therefore be confined to rendering a fair equivalent for money received, there being no demand of exorbitant profits or the selling of worthless commodities. Within limits set by the balance sheet there may be kindliness and sympathy, although an ever-present tendency is to exalt profit at the expense of social considerations.

Under existing trade conditions consideration for the other person tends to remain within narrow limits. It is doubtful if a seller mindful of the buyer's actual needs would succeed best in a money sense. What would happen to the seller of automobiles if he always took into account the buyer's ability to afford the purchase? Oftentimes a family needs things more than the thing about to be purchased, but the seller may harden his heart and effect a sale of an article of luxury when necessities should be bought. It may be argued that the buyer is the one to decide which wants to gratify, but every dealer knows that it is possible to exert a pressure resulting in unwise purchasing.

2. Business Controls Views

The dealer is so closely identified with his business that convictions are often largely determined by the interests of that business. The railroad man looks upon society through the lens of his employment; he tends to pass upon writings and views by noting their bearing upon the prosperity of railroads. A change which would benefit society is likely to be condemned by the man whose own business seems to be adversely affected. The union railroad station meets with little favor with the man who owns a transfer service; the parcels post seems iniquitous to the director of an express company; the elimination of the middleman is unspeakably offensive to the middleman.

This tendency to view social problems from the occupational standpoint is one of the dominating facts of present intellectual conditions, and is a notable and dubious contribution by business to the social consciousness. The support of the individual, his physical maintenance, has not become sufficiently sure as yet to free his mind for the impartial viewing of social problems; his convictions are stuck fast to his job, and it is only in a limited number of cases that individuals detach themselves from the job point of view. Those who gain the academic point of view represent an attitude much to be desired; here the mind may move about a subject freely. The judicial mind is theoretically free in the same way to view all sides of a question irrespective of occupational advantages, social welfare being the supreme test. But both in university and judicial circles, while thought is theoretically impartial, conclusions may actually be colored by former experiences or by the present influence of trafficking occupations.

Throughout the literature of merchandising runs the thought that to be successful the salesman must believe his goods are superior. Salesmen are exhorted to have faith; they must either believe or affect to believe that the goods they sell are inferior to none. Emphasis is always laid upon the enthusiasm resulting from extreme conviction of the excellence of what one has to sell. This imperative is difficult to reconcile with well-developed thought. It is not easy to

hypnotize oneself into the belief that any special make of
article is really superior to all others. It is asking almost the
impossible to demand that each representative of perhaps a
dozen different makes of fountain pens shall be convinced, or
simulate conviction, as to the surpassing merit of the
particular pen which he has for sale. The salesmen may either
come to believe upon insufficient grounds or school himself
to appear an ardent convert. In either case mental integrity
suffers a strain.

Surely no one could be a master of selling without at least
pretending to be candid or enthusiastic. If the prospective
purchaser catches a hint of disbelief he is not so likely to
purchase. But it does not follow that the salesman may not
really have mental reservations. A highly successful tobacco
salesman, a district manager, thoroughly hated his
occupation and was made sick by his slightest use of tobacco
in any form. The higher one goes up the scale of positions
the more likely to be found a lack of harmony between the
seller's job and himself. The most intelligent salesmen are
most irritated when disposing of goods in whose merits they
cannot really believe. In their case there must be a studied
dramatic attitude and an affectation of sincerity.

3. Discreet Silence

Business may not only involve a pretense of
conviction but it may suppress the utterance of conviction.
The dealer naturally wants to attract customers and he must
not conflict with prejudices; it would be unprofitable to spoil
a sale by getting into a political argument. The seller must
often refrain from crossing swords upon the occasion of
expressions of opinion which inspire resentment and
contradiction. The public suffers from this indisposition to

jeopardize profits, for it comes about that almost any humbug may achieve considerable vogue through being licensed by the fear that comment may hurt business. There are comparatively few people, of course, in modem society who can safely say what they think. Emerson speaks of telling a missionary straight out that he begrudged him a dollar. This freedom is lacking in people engaged in business; out of prudence they give a good many dollars for the silliest of causes and against their real opinions.

An extreme case of self-effacement is represented in the principle upon which one large business house was founded, that the customer is always right. Evidently the customer is not always right, and to concede this position makes rather for profits than for truth. To act from native impulse and by straight thinking would be to deal in a much less suave manner with various patrons, who might be ejected into the street with additions to profane history. The check upon free expression imposed by trade has contributed to social timidity, over-susceptibility to example, a paralyzing prudence, and to servile attitudes.

The suppression of individuality is a severe indictment against trade. The conditions for the highest social welfare lie somewhere between extreme individual variations and too great uniformity. The tendency of business is to reduce outstanding individual traits to a common level, for it is well known that peculiarities and differences often irritate and repel as they appear in speech, clothing, and ways. In opinions and in affiliations with churches and secular organizations the salesman and the business man seek to appear regular and conventional. The pendulum has swung far toward a characterless uniformity among individuals, and at many points the dealer's attitude has contributed to bring about this result.

4. Tact Developed

But the disposition to suppress one's views, to conciliate, and even to truckle, has yielded an advantage in the development of tact. It is hard to imagine how hostile, stoical, and altogether unfinished might be our social dealings if buying and selling had not smoothed off corners. People have been disciplined into fairly agreeable habits through the relationships of commerce. We sometimes flinch at the hint of unctuousness in the salesman, but forced courtesy and abject strategy are as auspicious as the rough and stodgy relationships appearing among a non-commercialized population. Tact grows out of imagination directed upon others' conditions and needs, and this particular social asset is closely related to attempts to sell.

Tact has a near neighbor in the mental agility necessary in bargaining. The mind of the trader must meet practical tests of quickness and discernment. The sort of consciousness required in a pastoral occupation is not the same as that required in town. A different kind of ability is involved in the selling of a farm animal from that required for raising the animal for the market. Whereas the rural mind is applied to long-time projects, the city mind must be especially quick in dealing with emergency situations. This trait is also accentuated by the great multitude of stimuli constantly before attention under business and urban conditions.

Probably in the case of no other mind is there such an unremitting consciousness of the profit motive as in the case of the dealer. The artist holds before his mind the completion of his work, perhaps occasionally giving thought to the selling price; but in trade the focal object of attention is price and profit. Hence the dealer falls a prey to the habit of judging by the dollar. Now the dollar cannot express certain values; it is not a unit of measurement of the finer relationships of human life. While the dollar is a very fundamental fact and is the basis of a structure of refinements, the persistent contemplation of the dollar tends to destroy appreciations and prevent the development of idealism. The business man's intolerance of theories and speculations— philosophical ones— grows out of a consciousness of the ledger. This intolerance does not tend to the highest civilization. If there is an3rthing we need most it is to spin webs of fancy, and through speculation and liberal conversation to erect ideals of inspiring rational achievements.

The intensely practical tendencies in business are, however, not sure protection against superstitions. When not in his element the tradesman who is highly specialized is no more sure of himself than would be the most visionary philosopher as an accountant. The quantity of superstition which still thrives in close proximity to business is startlingly large. The culture of business is a special one.

One cannot help feeling that the illusory great-man theory of history is supported through business influences. The man who deals with large affairs is regarded as a large man. Men are little, average, or big according to bank accounts and the magnitude of their commercial undertakings. From the standpoint of psychology the valuation of individuals by such standards is highly unsound. The methods required to run a department store in a town of 10,000 population are presumably not radically different from those required in a metropolis. The juggler who, when revealing a trick performed with a one-dollar bill, confided to his audience that the same trick could be successfully performed with a ten-dollar bill, contributed something to the exposure of the great-man theory of business. The elements of large business are present in small business.

Principles of investment which must be observed by the man who has a thousand dollars are not of world-wide difference from those try which the financier must be guided. There are enormously wider differences in the proportions of business than in human psychology. Figures are simply symbols, and there is little difference in principle between operations with a million cents and with a million dollars.

CHAPTER X
FEAR AND THE GROUP

OUR ancestors had a great many things to be afraid of. If they had not been afraid they might not have survived to become our ancestors. They were afraid of wild beasts, high water, and clubs. We inherit a tendency to be afraid, and the caution which protects a business man from buying a gold brick had its origin perhaps in fear of bricks of a different sort.

We appreciate the service rendered by our ancestors in being afraid of things. When they sat in the tree-tops in a thunder storm and shivered with fright lest they be shaken down into the wide-open jaws of the cave bear, they were laying the foundation for suspended judgment and unwillingness to be quoted. They wrought better than they knew in equipping us with emotions which tend to save our lives in crossing streets in which pedestrians no longer have rights.

The tendency of fear is inherited as well as a tendency to be afraid of certain things, but there are certain things that we ought to be afraid of for which we do not inherit fear. What are the things which menace life and happiness? Nicotine, germs, automobiles, the sedentary life, pastry, and strong coffee. Do we fear these things? We are more likely to be afraid of ghosts, the dead, reptiles, eels, thunder, mice, and what people will say if we wear last year's hat.

We must not be too hard on our ancestors; but It looks as if we had inherited useless terrors and were but poorly equipped with useful fears. A harmless garter snake inspires more dread than a live wire which it is death to step upon. If our fears were up to the requirements of the hour we should shriek and flee from a vial containing a diphtheria or a cholera culture. But we do no such thing. We convince ourselves that certain things are dangerous and cultivate prudence, but it is reserved for clammy and creeping things to make us shriek.

The fear experiences of our ancestors reveal themselves in childhood. The child knows terrors felt by primitive man and reverts to states of mind that existed long ago. Not only do children give us an insight into the fears that prevailed, but the victim of alcoholism who sees snakes is also an unwitting witness.

1. Fear and Admiration

Ancestral fears are, strangely enough, closely related to our admirations. The liking for fur is not far removed from the fear of furry animals. The liking for the sea is the obverse of the dread of the sea. There is a fur feeling and there is a sea feeling, and whether the feeling is one of dread or admiration is relatively unimportant. The fact is that fur and the sea were stamped upon the nervous system in the ancient past. There is oftentimes a fascination in the horrible, and aversion may pass over to admiration. Perhaps there are many things our admiration for which is based upon a primitive dread. The charm of the forest may be a modem form of the anxiety which early man felt when he passed under dark boughs from which a wild animal might spring down upon him.

Our fears being but poorly adjusted to the conditions of the times, it becomes necessary to put down some and to establish others. Cautions with regard to parlor matches and gasoline would be less necessary if children were born with a tendency to keep out of risky modern situations. What inheritance has failed to endow us with in the form of

caution must be developed through appeals to the
imagination and to judgment.

2. Fear of Social Separation

Among our compelling fears are those associated with
public opinion and social relationships. The dread of the
disapproval of our fellow-men inspires us with conciliation
and makes us sensitive to being cut off from others.

The man who invented solitary imprisonment hit
upon a diabolical idea; and the history of invention is not
complete without that sinister portion dealing with
misshapen forms of creativeness which make up a dualism of
intelligence with all that genius has discovered and contrived
for the uplift of the race in art and mechanics. This invention
has exacted its toll out of the souls of men. Think of Prince
Krapotkin in the muffled horrors of the Russian fortress of
Saint Peter and Saint Paul, shut off from the human face,
tapping out for another prisoner, by means of an
inconceivably tedious code, the whole history of the French
Revolution. Not to be in communication with others is to go
mad.

The instinct of the group which is outraged thus, is
one of the deepest in nature. There are flocks, herds, schools,
coveys, packs, and tribes. In autumn one may see a flock of
sparrows— equidistant vibrating brown specks poised in the
air— whirl and volley toward a tree-top or a chimp of tall
weeds, all animated by a collectivism of mood and thrilled
with a subtle harmony. And while men, each inflated with
self, go and come with assurance, the ties of association
appear to the larger vision to govern as surely as bees are
bound by the law of the hive. We are not complete in
ourselves, and we do not like to be left alone. Our thought is

not perfected except by discussion, and many of our sentiments and views are borne in upon us from the tribe.

And yet too much social pressure is resented. There is repugnance as well as attraction. We want to have people near us, but not too near; we like others to keep their distance, but not get out of sight; such is the war between the individual and the social self. We want companionship, amusement, sympathy; we want to hear someone else talk, and we want to do a good share of the talking ourselves. We like to feel at one with others, and nothing is more acceptable than praise. Even undeserved and suspiciously strong commendation is not unwelcome; there is much charm in a friendly liar.

3. Common Ground for Sociability

To get upon a common basis it is necessary to propitiate the gods of sociability with common rites. The four hundred million dollars' worth of cigar smoke with which the heavens are blurred annually in the United States is largely in the interests of conversation. And then there are knitting needles and chewing gum. Shaking hands, which is a refined way of shaking fists, puts two nervous systems in harmony more gently than the older form; but fighting is one way of making new acquaintances. To have been at the same place establishes a common point of reference, a fact to which travelers and alumni bear witness. The social craving may be relieved without direct acquaintanceship; to be where people can be seen, as in the theater or on the street, will in part suffice.

Someone should write a history of the sociability of occupations. In popular fancy the sheep herder becomes insane from solitude, and sometimes he does. Anyone will become a trifle queer at the end of a few days apart from the world. Genius, which is profitable queerness, is said to be developed in solitude, and great religions have been born in deserts and under the mystic stars. When alone, the mind runs in free routes, little affected by pressure from without; it acquires a mild insanity of license, favorable to works of imagination. Exempt from reality self fills its world with figments of instance and unique characters often far superior to what the dry fields of the actual afford. Hence the praise of solitude. Out of regard for the hardships of farming Sir Thomas More provided in Utopia for an alternation of labor between country and city, but the arrangement would equally be warranted by the need of alternate experience in solitude and society. To be too much alone and to be too much with others is unfortunate, a condition which an ideal employment would avoid. The farmer has lived too much by himself, while the salesman sees too many people. One's mental sap oozes out as fast as it accumulates with constant meetings, which is as bad as to have one's mind stiffen about unchanging topics in solitude. Housewives have been, historically, isolated; no wonder they have been disposed to economize time in chance visits by all talking at once. They, too, belong to a sex which is not so highly individualized as are men; feeling more keenly variations from accepted forms and hungering more for assurances of common experience.

4. Sensitiveness to Public Opinion

The yearning for companionship is related to a sensitiveness as to what others are thinking about us. Of course we do not really want to know, yet our ears itch. In this responsiveness and apprehension Mrs. Grundy has her sphere of influence and conventionality its mighty seat. We are never quite sure that the herd will not hook us out to graze by ourselves. The potentialities of paragrapher, pamphleteer, or soapboxer are far from insignificant, and the critic has a power whose origin is as ancient as that of the ancestry of the clouds of winged ants whose coming casts a shadow on a summer's day.

CHAPTER XI
SLOWNESS OF ADAPTATION

THERE are few who have not had the experience when in unfamiliar surroundings of being "turned around" with regard to the points of the compass. Some live for years knowing which way is north yet feeling otherwise. An unobserved kink in the road or a temporary inattention leaves one with certain impressions as to directions, which, if incorrect, are righted only with the greatest difficulty, if at all.

1. Feeling vs. Judgment

All the arguments that may be marshaled, however convincing to thought, have but slight effect upon such stubborn obsessions. If water from a certain river was once contaminated and non-potable, but afterwards purified by methods employed in supply systems, there will be found residents who cannot bring themselves to look favorably upon the liquid in its regenerate character and who will refuse to drink it, all the chemists and bacteriologists to the contrary notwithstanding. The tyrannical inner sovereign of sentiment is not easily propitiated by appeals to the understanding.

A good share of the time one cannot fully agree with himself, for he will think and know one way and feel another. One would naturally suppose that one could get together with himself, but not always so. There is often a deadly seesaw which causes one to think of flipping a cent for decision. The root of the trouble is in the opposition of feeling and thought. There are disharmonies in the inner

218

man, a fact which has not heretofore escaped observation. Thought collides with emotions and feelings bump into other feelings.

2. Primitive Tendencies and Civilization

One of the fundamental reasons for this inner factionalism is found in the disagreement between our inherited natures and the requirements of civilization. Civilization, as much as we have of it, is comparatively new and artificial, and it frequently galls Old Adam, who may serve as a convenient symbol. For example, it is the custom in the best circles to wear shirts; but there are hot days in the summer, summer being an old institution too, when to discard this modem impertinence appeals to one. Civilization attempts very imperfectly to impress us with the ethics of turning the other cheek; but primitive feelings suggest that we hit the other fellow squarely on the nose. Business and the desk require that one work steadily and forge ahead toward wealth and office, while from within comes a seductive insinuation that the fish might bite. The collision of duty and desire is not a mere personal frailty, but a common condition which weighs heavily upon all mankind as it would rise above the reeking and selfish simplicity of the hairy ones.

The things of civilization are new and the natures which we possess are old. Prehistoric man did not have railroads and encyclopedias, course dinners and the Ph.D. degree. Law and the refinements of custom did not exist as we know them. About the only specimen of art in the cave man's gallery was a free-hand sketch of a bison or mammoth, and so far as regularity of meals and church services are concerned, there was little in the prehistoric calendar to correspond. There was no regular calling hour, and when a call was made it was possibly for the sake of braining a new acquaintance with a rough stone hammer.

No one really knows how old he is, because his mental traits run back to the very beginning of things; but we know how old the modern environment is; it is not much older than Newton, Harvey, Watt, and Edison. Civilization is new, very new; the paint is not yet dry, and the machinery creaks in every joint.

It is no wonder that we discover a discord between ourselves and our institutions and jobs and places in the world. It is not surprising that we should often feel like taking to the woods, discarding starched linen, table forks, morals, and manners; law and order, system, and industrial exactions, are a harness which chafes at nearly every point of contact

The modem system of things is one which appeals to our judgment, and the ancient order was one in which our preferences had their birth. The comparatively new reasoning nature of man, out of which modem social ideals have arisen, conflicts with deep-seated tendencies which became established long ago; thus very frequently feeling and sentiment pull one way, while judgment pulls another.

The irrepressible conflict of feeling and thought is increased, if anything, by the way we train the young. Children receive a far more extended emotional than rational training. They are taught to feel and defer long before they understand what of both good and evil custom may represent. They acquire prejudices for and against races, religions, countries, and men during their early years, prejudices which hold in spite of all they may later learn and understand. Habits of feeling certain ways soon become fixed, and many of our feelings are habits.

3. Emotional Training in Childhood

If emotions were better directed during childhood, the individual at maturity would less often find feeling and thought at variance. A good deal of energy in one's later years is lost in a conflict between reasoned conclusions and the attitudes set up during the impressionable years of childhood, a period when the young generation is susceptible to the intellectual moods of bygone ages, a period when the contagion of antiquity and tradition can scarcely be resisted.

The conflict between feeling and thought is of importance because of its relation to practical affairs. It is easy to act unwisely in business or social relations through yielding to impulse and obscure motives. Everyone has observed the erratic and whimsical conduct of children and childlike adults. Such act from primitive impulse or from captious considerations rather than from well-reasoned grounds. One has to be on his guard constantly against acting from frivolous and unsound promptings. Unfortunately one's first impressions may be completely out of keeping with true wisdom. There are those who "think" with their feelings, who feel when they ought to think. There are lives that have been wrecked by acting from a succession of prejudices, grudges, fanciful anticipations, and mysterious internal suggestions. Lines of action should be established in the white light of judgment and in clear view of the circumstances of the modem world; motives resting back upon primitive nature and the impressions of childhood must be carefully weighed.

The Control of the Social Mind

ORIGINALLY EDITED BY
Dr. Joseph Jastrow
Professor of Psychology at the University of Wisconsin

FIRST PUBLISHED IN 1923
BY D. APPLETON & CO. OF NEW YORK
AS PART OF "THE CONDUCT OF MIND
SERIES"

PART I

FUNDAMENTALS AND THEIR APPLICATIONS

CHAPTER I
CONTROL THROUGH PSYCHOLOGY

AN increasing use of psychology is being made for effecting desirable adjustments. No longer is the worker regarded as merely a mechanical unit of production, nor the first offender as an incurable instance of depravity. In industry and penology the psychological viewpoint dictates new procedures. The economist, the judge and the lawyer, through giving greater heed to mental phenomena, tend to pursue different courses than formerly. In education both discipline and instruction have been revolutionized by specific effort to understand the child. The advertiser has become an adept in commercial control through utilizing laws of habit and suggestion. Through analysis of motives the modern student of history finds fresh clues to the explanation of early events and becomes better able to interpret present trends and contemporary happenings. Such ancient practices as sacrifice and pilgrimage become intelligible under the fuller knowledge of instincts and motivation. The application of psychology in medicine is notable, whether within the medical profession or in related activities outside this profession.

More is known about the mind than formerly, and we are more given to employing concretely the available information. The point of attack on many problems has shifted from the physical to the mental. As physical science was the crowning contribution of the last century, so psychological method promises to be a signal achievement of the present. The forces with which men consciously and explicitly deal are increasingly the mental energies. Progress will be judged more in terms of mental reactions than in terms of physical creations like skyscrapers and steel ships.

Society is undergoing a transformation by a shift of emphasis from body to brain. Trade and legislation, domestic relations and municipal government will be more definitely directed with reference to the ascertained facts and promise of human behavior.

The program of physical science was announced by Francis Bacon, its great visionary, to be the amelioration of the lot of man; so and even more certainly may be announced the prospect of psychology. Great as are the contributions of physical science, there is disappointment; the world is not yet what it should be. The menace of lethal gas is sufficient warning that the continuing welfare of the race must involve a technic of control through reflection, a utilization of the undeveloped resources and of the raw materials for happier forms of intelligence.

It is a well-known fact that knowledge of a principle does not guarantee its application. One may accept or preach one thing and rather innocently practice another. A person who knows that oil will float on water— knows it as a principle— may be the first to throw water on an oil fire. One must know that water thrown on an oil fire will spread the fire. This is an additional fact a fact of application. Without the fact of application the knowledge of the principle, while interesting, is practically useless— momentarily useless. Similarly in the field of psychology. One may know the force of mental suggestion and yet not think of its application in important relations. To vitalize knowledge of psychology by extensive and ingenious application is an inviting educational ideal.

Of far-reaching importance are the applications of known laws of mental behavior to social and civic relations and problems. The gravest problems to-day are those of social and community affairs, and of national and international relations. In this field there is need of bringing the knowledge of psychology to bear on specific difficulties.

The price of failure here is not such as we should contemplate with tranquil spirits, for civilization is at stake.

Higher social welfare must be achieved with such materials as general society affords. The "intelligence quotient" of the average man may remain little changed. Indeed, the raw materials are presumably fairly adequate if resourcefully employed. It was said by Elbert Hubbard that the man who could not build up a business with the help that he could employ was not the man to build up the business. Man does not naturally fly nor remain under water; but he does both successfully by artifice. Inventors did not despair because in many respects the physical equipment of man is poor and limited. The deficiencies have been overcome by contrivance. In like manner it is possible to supply by contrivance and supplement by system the deficiencies which all men show more or less for civic functions and social progress. We shall get nowhere by deploring the limitations of the prevailing native endowment of intelligence.

Control through psychology should be dissociated from any suggestion of clever manipulation for selfish ends. Superior faculties have superior place in the very nature of things; but in the development of the technic of civic psychology there can properly be no more hint of sinister uses or exploitative purpose than can be admitted in the enlightened constitutionalism of liberal politics. Psychology can indicate the mechanisms and resources; a social-moral conscience must set the course to be followed.

CHAPTER II
THE SOCIAL MIND

IN essence all human psychology is social, in that the mental behavior is socialized. Our powers and traits have come into being under family and group conditions. The social imprint is written all over man's mind. Instincts, emotions, motives, language— all have a social reference. With no one to look on, how long could a Robinson Crusoe keep alive the motive to excel or maintain an interest in his personal appearance? What would become of language without the presence of others with whom one could communicate? If language were not, how much thought would be possible, lacking its vehicle and preservative? Even righteous indignation implies the evildoer, present or absent. One may feel the emotion of anger when dealing with inanimate objects; but when such is the case he transfers a reaction originating in association with his fellow creatures.

The field of social psychology includes as a study of processes, mental reactions in the manifold relationships of the individual to society; and as a study of products, the many outcomes of mind in social institutions, such as law, religion, fashion, custom, art, morals, and language. The formation of public opinion, the craze and fad, the public meeting and the mob demand consideration in every comprehensive treatment The social relations of the individual form the story of his life— his relations to the family, and to economic, professional, political, cultural, and educational organizations, besides the various situations of informal contact. There are as many psychological situations as there are situations; the psychological moment constantly recurs. The present purpose is to consider aspects of mind that have special significance for further social development and better ways of getting on together.

What advantage has psychology as a science over plain knowledge of human nature? There is the advantage that any organized branch of knowledge has over knowledge of the casual type; a person can command more in a shorter time. From hit-and-miss observation and experience everybody knows something about physics and mechanics; but a systematic study goes far beyond haphazard experience In a lifetime the average person would not acquire more than a small part of the knowledge of physics that he could obtain in months from physics formulated as a science.

Psychology impresses the method of science— observation, impartial interpretation, cautious generalization; above all it emphasizes that the phenomena of mind are part and parcel of the things that are amenable to study and scientific approach. For centuries man regarded himself as an exception to natural laws. This attitude through gradual change has been dispelled. Developments in psychology as well as in the social sciences indicate that the concept of cause and effect, of environment and product, has entered far into our reasoning upon social problems.

In psychology, as in other fields of science, there is an advantage in bringing familiar things into vividness by expert analysis and clearer definition. Grammar may be studied profitably if only to pass in review processes of speech that go on habitually. To face reflectively the elements of our habitual acts tends to establish a new viewpoint and encourages progress. It is worth while to view ourselves objectively in the mirror that psychology holds up to human nature.

Social change is furthered by modern psychology through its affiliations with evolutionary biology. Dynamic suggestiveness is no small asset to social welfare; much mischief has been due to the standstill frame of mind. Progress becomes the actual program of the world's affairs.

Any group of men to-day, if asked whether they look for different and better conditions twenty-five years from now, would vote *yes*. The spirit outcropping from the evolutionary view permeates society. Civilization is likely to arrive sooner in its fullness through belief in development. Even the individual to-day seems less to regard himself as capable of reaching a stage beyond which improvement is impossible.

The common expectation of change and improvement in individual and society gives point to studies of mind and results in fuller knowledge. Man lived on the earth for thousands of years without knowing as much about its size, character and position as a ten-year-old schoolboy knows to-day. Similarly the earlier observations on the mental man were deficient. Marked advance has taken place in the understanding of human endowment and of its responses to environment; and no less in generalization, point of view, and command of data. The biological point of view applied to human traits has made as wide a change in the field of psychology as was made in cosmogony by the Copernican astronomy, or in medicine by the germ theory of disease. The treatment of the child, views regarding the criminal and the insane, industrial psychology, propaganda— these suggest how large the change.

Not only does the individual need to know as much as possible of psychology for his own survival and welfare, but society in its collective aspects can thrive only by recognition of mental forces. Knowledge of psychology is required for the wise management of public and national affairs. After the late prostration of the nations it is evident that public affairs have gone forward too little illuminated by studies of social mind, analogous to those studies that have advanced the world in its material aspects.

In public affairs the relative backwardness may be ascribed to the fact that social nature has been less systematically studied than has physical nature. The social mind has yet to be studied adequately for purposes of better and happier living. Social forces and phenomena are more complex and evasive than life cycles of insects, or the principles of levers, or the mechanics of liquids. While physical science has advanced notably, knowledge of the mind in social situations is still in its early stages. Much remains to be done by way of inventory of mental assets capable of utilization for the career of civilization. A larger science of mind is possible with corresponding improvement of social relationships and administration.

Such a science contemplates a rational and constructive use of social forces. Resources of reflection are capable of more efficient and less injurious uses. In our physical civilization constructive use has oftentimes been made of unpromising materials. Flood waters have been impounded to irrigate orchards; animals and plants have been domesticated and made to serve the purposes of society; the severities of climate have been mitigated by intelligent adaptations of fuel and clothing; barriers of distance vanish with the locomotive and radio. In the psychology of human engineering there are presumably as great possibilities as have been demonstrated in the field of mechanics and physical science. An excessive amount of friction and discord appears in the social cosmos; human energy goes to waste or is diverted to the infliction of grave injury, as in mob action and war.

The better direction of the energies of consciousness presupposes point of view and data. The psychological attitude toward social problems becomes the starting point for pronounced departures in method. Even the time-honored notion that human nature never changes casts no blight upon the promise of rationalizing the social order, for it is possible with existing materials to build the social structure into a different architecture. The crux of the matter is how traits and tendencies of human nature are developed and employed. The same bricks build structures of widely contrasting effects. The best possible world will consist of people whose traits and tendencies are utilized in the best possible manner.

The variety of occasions for psychological procedure is wide indeed, for there is no reflective behavior in any field that does not present possibilities of superior method. From casual daily experience to the affairs of nations, psychologizing promises to eliminate friction and open paths of harmonious and constructive effort; the serious antagonisms of society may be resolved and finer coördinations achieved. Social disorder implies defects of method. The laws of mind, brought precisely to bear upon social difficulties, promise insight, and such insight wisely directed makes possible results comparable in perfection to those produced by the application of the laws of physics in the harmony of the artificial world of a laboratory.

CHAPTER III
RESPONSE OF MIND TO ENVIRONMENT

EARLY man, by reason of his anatomical structure, was unique in physical adaptability. He escaped the anatomical specialization which was a limiting factor in the case of lower animals. Consider what a strangely unadaptable creature is the horse or dog. The lower animals grew specialized for defense or flight or food. Man was less specialized, and adaptable; for him the door was open for progress and free life on the planet. The human hand is a wonderful anatomical tool. Man has multiplied his problems and added immeasurably to the thought-compelling character of physical environment by building huts and houses, taming wild beasts, and stirring the soil in agriculture. The lower animals in the course of the remote past became specialized in response to fixed units of environment and remained on low levels. Escaping fixedness of condition, through pioneering to new environments and ultimately creating a new world of novel appliances to react upon intelligence, man, the supreme physiological machine, became unique in cerebral resources.

Physical equipment of generalized type became supplemented by unique brain power; otherwise the limit of human development would early have been reached. Physical adaptability can go so far and no further. The body can make certain adjustments to climate; for example, the skin undergoes some change at the advent of cold weather, but the most economical and successful adaptation to cold is through the intelligence that borrows the skins of wild animals or weaves textiles or transports coal for fuel. Increasingly in the struggle to keep alive and comfortable, man has utilized intelligence; and invention has taken the place of physical modification. As an organ of adaptation the brain has demonstrated its superiority; man, replying on certain mental functionings, "bestrides the narrow earth like a colossus." He has exploited nature and fairly conquered the physical menaces and hazards that otherwise would have reduced his numbers and have made him a slave instead of a commanding force in his contact with nature.

The intelligence utilized in man's struggle with nature has been of comparatively primitive type. Indeed the prehistoric mind is the substructure of contemporary mind.

We share in the inheritance of the prehistoric mind— the mind of the cave man and the raw-meat eater, the hairy man. Back in the eons when the prairie grasses were laying down the humus that is now soil below the surface of a wheat field, and when the waves had begun to chafe the pebble that is now sand, the pattern of the mind of the university graduate was being traced. It was then that fundamental interests, aversions, raging appetites, fears, sly trickery, bellowing melodrama and "big stick" technic were characteristic responses to environmental conditions. Early man haunted the beaches and river beds in search of food— who would eat an oyster except through atavism? The cave grandmother had to pick and pry at things out of protective curiosity— and her modern descendant surreptitiously fingers linings in the cloak-room. The human instincts, general aptitudes and abilities and the characteristic behavior of attention, memory, association of ideas, reasoning and problem-solving became functions of human intelligence in the remote past. This is not to say, for example, that the fear tendency has not undergone modification or that we have to-day exactly the same coördination of faculties as prevailed at the time when the brain cavity first reached modern proportions, but that the native tendencies and capacities of the mind are referable to archaic origin, and that the primitive mind underlies the most cultivated mind of to-day.

The nature of the primitive environment can indeed be speculatively inferred from modern mind. In many ways the tendencies we see within— our fears, rages, suspicions, desire to hunt, kill and see horrible sights, our monogamy by determination, the soothing lapse to wilds of wood and water, the indecision between cooperation and murder— enable us through imagination to reconstruct the life of the sordid mire-camp and the soaked tree-dwelling with its one warm spot of attachment.

Certain it is that modern civilization has come without late change in fundamental mentality. The changes that may be wrought later in the character of civilization will need to be made with old mind, but old mind redirected. Hereditary human nature changes, of course, but slowly, even as the dog's nature is rather different from that of his wolf ancestor. But changes in fundamental mind are too slow in coming, particularly in the absence of eugenics, to be of much promise. The saving fact for social reconstruction is that, without disavowal of original tendencies, there lies within the power of education and social control the vast resource of redirecting the expression of human nature and substituting preferred activities for those condemned by experience.

As an instance of civilization by substitution, consider the fighting activity. Probably nobody ever really wants to fight; probably no person or animal ever wanted to fight but for a purpose. But it is recognized that men will fight for cause; they will at least fight incidentally. The early tribal fights of Indians were often of the nature of games— with incidental casualties, somewhat like those of football. Tournaments and wars were risky games, before the time of real efficiency in weapons. But let us admit that there is a strong susceptibility to combat for cause— a penchant for carrying on one's business by killing the other fellow. Does it follow that this human tendency must find expression in the slaughter of war? By no means. Substitute some activity that involves the enjoyable preliminary aspects of combat but is socially constructive. Indeed such civilization as we have owes no small part to the successful substitution of other objectives than those of historical warfare. One of the great wars of civilization was the "war" of the Panama Canal; another was the war against yellow fever; another, that waged by firefighting organizations. Raids into the enemy's territory have been carried on by Stefansson in the Arctic, by Dr. Schliemann in excavating the site of ancient Troy, and by Charles Evans Hughes in insurance investigations.

The evils of modern society represent misdirected energy. Social welfare depends upon the kind of response to environment and the right employment of natural tendencies and resources. To employ these aright requires some ingenuity, but not different in kind from that displayed by a skillful elementary school-teacher who takes numbers of unformed and misformed youngsters and finds acceptable vents for energies that, misdirected, would fill the juvenile courts with cases and their respective homes with confusion and despair. The playground bully is appointed the custodian of the laboratory, and this undesirable becomes the bulwark of law and order. To utilize the meanness of the individual for the good of the state, said Abraham Lincoln, is the purpose of politics. The social, industrial and economic problem is in essence merely the matter of setting up worthy aims and then securing the focusing of thought on the means to utilize constructively the abundant resources of the mental inheritance; likewise to stimulate the good will that will pursue them strenuously.

Primitive tendencies contain the makings of a high civilization. Man does not need to be re-created, to be made anew, to be something other than he is, or to be unnatural. His nature will do as it is. All that is necessary is for him to act differently, and this is comparatively easy. The farmer acts differently with tractor and gang plow than with an old-time crooked stick. But his motivation is about the same, only he is more intelligent through science; he has changed his methods, not his nature. Social organization and relationships are about where agriculture was in the crooked-stick stage. There are enough native resources, and energy, if efficiently applied, to realize the dreams of the ages. The supermen are here; every man is that potentially. Even the criminal prospect becomes a good citizen through method—what could not be done with the good citizen?

Unlike the Baltimore oriole with its inherited mechanism for building a particular type of nest and unlike all the lower animals that acquire their arts before they are born, man lacks almost wholly any precise mental specialization at birth. It is this fact that gives the measure of unique possibilities. In the sense that instinct is attributed to animals, man is almost without instincts. Instinctive tendencies he possesses, but of mechanically perfect responses to definite situations he is largely destitute. The infant sucks by instinct, but whether the adult will eat peas with a knife is a matter of education. Tendencies toward physical and mental activity are packed in the child's nervous system, but without conscious learning he would be at a disadvantage among creatures born with definite instincts. Learning is the greatest human fact. What shall be learned?

Any trait may be modified, and the instinctive tendencies may be swerved and attached to almost any objective. It is folly to assume that society is inherently committed to precise activities. Certainly there will always be marrying and giving in marriage, but whether by capture or by the squire depends. And whether woman is privileged to be beaten only with a stick "no thicker than a man's thumb," or is granted the ballot also depends. There is no social foreordination of details. The instinctive acquisitive tendency may always be expected to make its appearance. It is not necessary, however, that its form of expression shall be only in connection with privately amassed wealth. The tendency may show itself in pride of public ownership or in the accumulation of claims to public respect. Many a man indeed has transferred the ownership tendency to the storing of scientific facts or to the enlargement of his acquaintance with literature. The surgeon takes pride in the number of rare operations that he can lay claim to; this satisfies the property sense as truly as does a bank account. Many a man would rather have the largest fish to his credit than a successful angling for unearned increment on a vacant lot.

What form of expression the natural tendency and inborn capacity will take is always problematical. Under force of suggestion and formative influences the individual becomes a criminal or a saint, a nun or a mother of a family, a Quaker or a sword-flourisher, a cannibal or a vegetarian. No one is immune to the effects of his culture materials. The supreme strategy of civilization is to cut the channels through which energies may flow to acceptable ends. There is little in the raw materials of human nature that predetermines language, laws, customs and form of social practice and institution. Original nature can be readily adapted to the career of a pirate or that of an entomologist. Mankind is always in the making.

The throwing down of barriers among peoples by modern means of transportation and communication has caught the individual with a consciousness unready for fuller social relations. The tribal mind in a world made one by science is an anachronism. The individualistic viewpoint is nothing short of a nuisance under conditions that call for the psychology of the wide community. Stump-lot provincialism does not go well with radio and express trains. Legislation conceived in terms of the colonies and judicial decisions, in terms of the dissociated production of the one-man business, are evidences of the failure to acquire the requisite social mind. A bridge of sentiment and logic must be built from the insular, provincial viewpoint to cosmopolitanism. Narrow nationalism, sectarianism, and labor crafts organization alike attest the failure to reorganize thought on lines of greater inclusiveness. The balance between private and public interests, or the balance between the individual's welfare in private and public functions, is yet to be achieved.

Individualistic tendency, a response to a simple type of environment, is an impediment when society presents a complex environment of social relationships. In principle, the social problem to-day is one of the selection of responses; it invites to closer study of human resources and to a more canny and scientific procedure in utilizing these resources for civilization. Nearly everybody spends the early years of his life trying to see things less as they are than as he would like to see them. This attitude has been general during the years of our greatest scientific progress. Human nature has been idealized and seen through rose-colored lenses. The present disposition is rather toward impartial and realistic inventory. We expect fewer boys of our acquaintance to become presidents of the United States— and are less enthusiastic regarding the office itself. While the psychology of the morning after is a low-pressure affair, abasement that leads to minute self-study and practical reconstruction is really immensely hopeful. One thing is certain: Utopia, even the preservation of the existing level of welfare, will not be assured without a higher degree of planning and conscious effort. Accordingly, the scrutinizing of mental factors and resources available for social advance is of pressing importance.

Social problems to-day afford an unparalleled opportunity for further mental development. The multiform character of the demands made on the individual under modern social conditions is an outstanding fact. Here and there are individuals or groups not particularly subject to stimulating vicissitudes; but on the whole modern life is more stimulating and less settled to repose than life in former times. Too great demands thrown upon the individual overwhelm and destroy; or the mind balks in a protective stagnation like that of a horse on city streets. But the law of progress is, that only through stimulus and everchanging stimulus can mind be kept on its cosmic career of greater sweep and control.

The problems confronting modern society are unlimited. It would be unfortunate if end there were, for we keep alive by effort. Stimulus to invention and creative thought is needed. Social issues challenge and stimulate; they are what America was to Columbus. What then should be our attitude toward the problems that press upon us, even threatening to transcend power to solve? On no ground is there cause for lamentation. True, civilization is in the crucible. It always is. Mind has reached its present capabilities through analogous discipline in the past. New traits may be forced upon it— new sentiments, emotions, cautions, types of attention, new taboos. The mind of the coming social organization will differ from ours as ours differs from that of the theologians of the Middle Ages.

Custom, institutions, tradition, routine, history and precedent clamor for a definitive society, which would mean the end of adaptation and evolution. On the other hand, education, innovation, social experimentation, and the instinct of the pioneer are strong for the supreme act of adventure— the building of a society different from that ever known— and better.

Both by physical structure and brain development man has escaped fixedness of environment. New situations and problems have accompanied and affected his upward progression. Does fixedness of environment threaten his future? His substantial mastery of nature through science and invention might hint at a blind alley, but in the field of social and economic organization problems challenge. The worldwide emphasis upon education and the appearance of the concept of engineering in social relations indicate that equilibrium, static poise and incipient deterioration are not for our time. Fixedness of environment, though with it is associated arrest of development, tend to be sought as an end; but matters get out of hand and the conservative finds himself swept along by problems that will not be stayed. In the individual bosom opposed forces of progress and devolution contend. Ulysses and the Lotus-eaters are represented respectively by the ambition to achieve and the desire to leave things as they are.

CHAPTER IV
SOCIAL SIGNIFICANCE OF HABIT

ANY consideration of the social utilization of our mental resources must necessarily take into account the reaction to environment represented by our habits. Habit and custom, like the law of gravitation, exert all-pervasive power. One often feels that the grip of social habit tends to be so complete as to yield but limited possibilities for the mobile factors of intelligence. Social welfare lies somewhere between the rigidities of custom and habitual performance, on the one hand, and the too free movement of the antennae of speculation and rationalism on the other. But for the present perhaps most of us would agree that society suffers rather especially from the rigidities of old use.

Habit is a stubborn force, though its tenacity is sometimes exaggerated. Bundles of habits though we are, yet the bundles need not of necessity always contain the same sticks. The value of habits is to enable us to do things more skillfully, in shorter time and with less effort and fatigue. The right hand writes smoothly, rapidly and with little effort and fatigue. The left hand traces one's name or writes a sentence only slowly, inexpertly, fatiguingly and with a taxing of attention.

Naturally, when once a habit has been laboriously formed and has become an easy and convenient accessory, we dislike to have it disturbed. Without an accumulation of pertinent habits no one would ever be able to have his consciousness and energies freed for use in novel and difficult situations. Knowing how to use pen or typewriter, the individual can give his whole mind to his thought and composition. Indeed, in the case of thought and composition even, habit may go far. It is said of Henry Ward Beecher that so fully had thought and composition gone down into lower nerve centers as habit, that after some of his most powerful speeches he himself knew little of what he had said; he was conscious only of attitude, emotion and purpose, and his habits of vocabulary, phrasing, and sentence and paragraph structure did the rest without involving definite consciousness. In other words, his consciousness took aim and his reflexes fired.

The sway of habit extends not only over physical acts, like writing with a pen, steering a motor car, skating, or pronouncing words, but extends as well over thought trends, emotional expression, association of ideas, and attitude and response to things generally. Without saying what my views are, I find myself possessed of certain thought and emotional habits toward Ralph Waldo Emerson, General Grant, P. T. Barnum, Thomas Hardy, Mrs. Eddy, the Negro, the Jew, the Pilgrim fathers, Thomas Jefferson, the high-wheel bicycle, and the Lewis and Clark expedition. Which is to say, the mind has acquired tendencies to react toward people and things in definite ways. Many such habits are loose and easily changed, while others are sometimes proudly declared to be good for "as long as I live," and are embedded in the physical structure of the brain.

Adaptability in one's lifetime would be a myth if habits could not be modified under pressure; we find in daily experience that even long-established habits may be superseded. Necessity is the antidote for habit. When one's telephone number is changed, one can forget the old number and form the habit of using the new number with no loss of time. The necessity of making this shift in habit dominates. Under conditions of no compulsion habits remain firmly seated. Exceptional circumstances rupture habits. A habit is said to be second nature; if so, a third and still other natures may be acquired under necessity. The habits that stay in place are those that represent the mechanics of everyday life and those that do not come in conflict with new necessities.

The most efficient type of person for social change is one who has a large and stable body of useful fundamental habits and who is comparatively free from habit, or is habitually elastic, where new responses are indicated. Under sanction of consistency, or creed, or historical party-platforms, or fear of what the neighbors will say, a large number of individuals prematurely harden into fogyism. Too much admiration of a fatuous sort has been lavished on being "always the same." It is very well to be always the same in "section one" of one's habits, but it is no less a virtue to be changeful in "section two," where to be changeful is to be more useful. Mobility is not only a delightful trait in people, especially elderly people, but is a valuable social resource. And let no one say that age is wholly opposed to new habits. Every reader can recall cases of men and women in the seventies and eighties who have open minds and take up without prejudice commendable novelty. The citizen who always does things the same way, always votes the same ticket, always reacts with the same saws and tales, always hangs his hat on the same hook and the same kind of hat at that, is far from exemplary. And no more exemplary, judged from the viewpoint of social purpose, is the man or profession strong on precedent. History affords fully as many examples of how not to do things as of the reverse. The historian may propagate undue reverence for the past by keeping before us matters that should be forgotten. If the yellowing volumes that bulge the walls of law schools were to be lost to mortal view— well, the world would manage to stagger along by getting up precedents founded on modern conditions.

At all events, it can be realized how one good custom can corrupt the world. People of middle age and beyond would be much more dynamic, if more stress were placed on the wisdom of keeping oneself constantly revised— if the inherited social tendency of bulldog conviction in the face of evidence were fairly discredited. Governed as we are by ideals, the value of publicity for the ideal of adaptability can scarcely be over-estimated. Indeed, in the instruction of children, whose plasticity is at par, the ideal of open-mindedness ought itself to be made a habit.

Education in ideals of habit revision, and of challenge of custom for cause, has large possibilities. The interrogatory state of mind can be promoted even as the static mind has been fostered by educational regimes. Instead of asking a pupil only for what he has learned from a book, he might at least be stimulated to questioning. The ultimate effect would be an attitude of inquiry, investigation and reflection. The personality-freeing kindergarten, devised by Froebel, a German, was banned in Germany on account of its inherent antagonism to subserviency, on the one hand, and autocratic domination on the other. There can be education for progress as definitely as there can be coaching for compliance with the *status quo*.

Along with specific education for mobility may be considered the progress-creating quality of various occupations. There are vocations in which survival waits on adaptability. The man who stands still in business to-day is left behind. In no part of modern society are there the tearless adieus to custom to be found in trade. Legislation, the courts, the church, the schools, all change, but tardily, as compared with business. No sooner does one automobile manufacturer produce a finished model than a competitor comes out with one having points of superiority, whereupon the first manufacturer is compelled to change his model. Business competition operating over large fields has done much to set up the modern type of progressive mind. Within the limits of his occupation the business man is often highly progressive. To what extent there is a transfer of training is another story. But the business office that daily registers price changes, market fluctuations, improvements in product, new inventions and competitors' strategies is one of the least conservative disciplines in the world. The modern business man's mind cannot stay made up. Deplore as we may the litter and wreckage of business, it has the merit of creating a yeasty condition of thought that has spelled the doom of such stagnation as prevailed in the long, uninteresting centuries before Francis Bacon.

The compelled elasticity of the business man waits only to be carried over to the wider field of social engineering and human betterment. The resourcefulness, the indomitable spirit, the challenging and even pugnacious frame of mind that have built railroads and monopolized coal, refined oil and exploited the public, are invaluable assets for social evolution. There is enough dynamic power and inventiveness, generated largely in business, to stage wonderland if directed to this end.

Consider the salesman. A perfect acquired egotism needs no formal complimentation. No missionary ever went forth more sure of the merits of his product, with more faith in the goods, than is possessed by the trained salesman. The salesman has been our most determined reformer— and the best paid. He has taken as his objective the timid retailer in a musty store and made a man of him— a business man. He has argued and cajoled, almost prayed; he has wheedled and bullied, poked in the ribs, treated to cigars and theater tickets. Finally, he has changed the habit-enveloped average man into a mood for accepting new ideas. Tremendous achievement! Millions of persons of the inertness and prideful torpor to which we are all prone has he made to see the merits of new things. The spirit for which the Hellenic Greeks are credited as the first to inoculate mankind with— the spirit of mental adventure— the salesman has spread to the ends of the earth and rendered in an epic of sales slips.

Moreover, he must be regarded along with peasants'

revolts and Gracchian sacrifices as a factor in undermining despotism and freeing slaves; for he has demonstrated the brotherhood of man by recognizing the need of having pleased customers— an acid test for crowns and thrones. Not by express design nor by immediately humanitarian precept, not in sackcloth, has the salesman thus spread a religion, but he has nevertheless popularized a procedure for a happier world; for he has tried to please— serving both mammon and God. Which brings us nearer to Utopia.

One may fear that the salesman goes too far with his philosophy of "mixing" and of being a good fellow, and with his acquiescence in seeing his cherished views spurned without witnessing for them— when by witnessing he might lose a sale. There is a loss of the heroic in such restraint. But in any field the avoidance of minor collisions is often necessary to the securing of satisfactory final results.

Personal mobility and freedom from the cramp of too many and too completely fixed habits are promoted by occupations that present new problems and from day to day challenge ingenuity. The greatest progress may be expected in societies in which the daily demands of employment stimulate the mind through the presence of novel elements. A stable and unvarying employment tends to reduce life to a habit basis and therefore is inimical to social change. The choppy sea of modern business has the effect of developing versatile mariners and setting up attitudes favorable to constructive social effort. Likewise many of the professions and personally directed occupations throw the individual against emergencies and new demands, and accordingly conduce to initiative and vision as against social torpor, custom, institutionalism and tradition.

On the other hand, there are in modern industry a large number of employments that are essentially of routine character and that tend to deaden enterprise and promote timidity and dullness. In our shops, factories, and mines thousands are employed at tasks that are soon completely mastered and thereafter involve but a minimum of intelligence and conscious adaptation. Such jobs are ill devised for making inquiring, resourceful, and forward-looking citizens. One of the problems of social engineering is to provide suitable expression for persons working at mechanized tasks. Either a vent may be found in recreation and avocation, or relief may be afforded through increased use of machinery and the shifting of the worker from one job to another for the sake of a series of stimulating experiences.

Indeed, the possibilities of neutralizing the soporific quality of fixed employment by proceeding from one trade to another, from one job to another, from one position to another, from one specialization to another, deserve consideration. Personal and social welfare are threatened by the modern tendency to divide and subdivide labor, with corresponding limitation of individual experience. Vacations spent afield, cultural agencies brought to the factory door, travel and innovation in community and home life are possible for the salvaging of the worker. In many occupations the stimulating and intelligence-taxing demands are exhausted in a few years if not months. Upon such exhaustion the individual loses intensity of consciousness. His life becomes less a life and more of a mere animal-life existence. Faced with new demands, he is jarred into vivid consciousness again, and indeed may be quite rejuvenated by shock. Even calamity and death of close associates have been known to result in a new growth of personality and vigor in people quite advanced in years. Development is always compelled. A settled life seems to be a common ideal, whereas if there is anything that is deadly, it is the settled life. Many a man of forty would make much more a success of himself by "jumping his job." The peace of the tomb is prematurely achieved by such as get the problems of life tucked away and evade vicissitudes.

Any employment is stimulating for a while. A man who learns to lay shingles is distinctly being educated and made alert while in the apprentice stage. After the art has been fully acquired there is no more mental stimulus derived from laying shingles than there is for a horse in switching off flies with its tail. One of the most deadening influences is the unrelieved pursuit of an occupation. To have habits enough and not to have too many and to live in habit enough but not too much is well. It is particularly unfortunate from the social viewpoint when accredited mentors, like judges, hold their positions for life.

Analogous to the effects of too inclusive habit on the individual is the too close adherence to precedent in society. Invariableness in institutions and laws, in social procedure and community method, is no more admirable nor to be desired than ultrastability in the individual. Early civilizations deified custom and repressed innovation. There is ever a tendency to strive for social inflexibility. Such endeavor discounts intelligence and conduces to degeneration and feebleness. Custom-breaking is as much of a virtue under justifying circumstances as is the reform of a drunkard. New paths should be sought for society not less than for the individual. Social experimentation may do for society what chemical experimentation has done for the dye industry and scientific agriculture. A good reason for some pieces of legislation is that they are experimental. Aversion to social experimentation is no better founded than the medieval horror of anatomatizing the human body in the interests of health; nor should the failure of a legislative experiment be a warning to all the ages not to try out new theories. If the business man can experiment in his advertising and the publisher with titles and bindings, there should be no initial aversion to working out social projects that have not been previously experimented with. Old technics of society, like old habits, should be assessed at true value; progress without the taking of chances and without adventuring is impossible. Practically every new law is an experiment. The frank adoption of the experimental attitude, with the circumspection of science, would do much to bring legislation and court decisions up to the level of the efficiency prevailing in laboratories and business organizations.

CHAPTER V
HABIT IN IDEAS—THE CONCEPT

THE EXTENT to which social adaptation may readily occur is measured to a large degree by the ease or difficulty of securing changes not only in habits but in general ideas or concepts. Indeed, our general ideas may be regarded as of the nature of memory habits or sets of mind, and therefore as promoting or opposing ready adaptations in the same manner as habits generally.

The general idea, or concept, represents the former experience of the individual and embodies a series of impressions. If an individual has come to have an established general idea regarding the proper limits of taxation or of the functions of municipalities, it becomes a matter of breaking habits to attempt to secure a modification of his point of view. The fact that opinions often rest on a basis of habit rather than of rationality is one that cannot happily be overlooked. We are all aware of how slow is the process of overcoming physical habit; the case is similar with reference to the meanings that the individual attaches by long wont to the terms in his vocabulary and the rules and principles by which he believes the world should be governed.

It should be noted, however, that change in general ideas, in opinions and conclusions, is possible. Electorates in various states are found to vote by majority one way one year and another way subsequently; a sufficient number of persons will change their minds to affect materially the results of elections. Apart from the influence upon elections of the first voters and of the deaths of voters, there is the pronounced factor of change of mind on the part of the voter. That people will change their minds admits of no denial; the habitual way of looking at things may be unseated in many instances; the accustomed concept may be modified and enlarged; recognition of new conditions affects opinion.

In view of the social implications of the concept, interest attaches to the processes by which one comes into possession of general ideas and convictions; it is also important to give heed to the possibility of impressing upon concepts a more social character. Some consideration of how the concept is formed and preserved is suggested by its significance in social program.

The concept or general idea originates in experience with things and cases that resemble one another. Its beginnings are seen in simple form in childhood. For example, a child sees a kitten for the first time. The kitten happens to be black. Blackness becomes a mark or quality or attribute of kitten till a white kitten is seen. Then kittens become either black or white, but having other traits also. Next others of still other color are observed, and finally the child's mind is forced to a concept of kitten that includes color but no color in particular. A general idea of kitten is achieved through acquaintance with various examples. Attributes other than color are also assimilated in a general idea, such as the possession of claws, mice-catching proclivities, night-prowling tendency and general contour and size. The child soon is able to classify a cat at sight. Cats are readily distinguished from dogs and goats. Later the child sees a tiger. The concept of cat has to expand to admit the idea of tiger; the child's mind comes to rest with a concept enlarged enough to include both cat and tiger. The achieving of a concept including both cat and tiger has entailed many readjustments. Upon achieving the wider concept the child has a more useful and effective intelligence than if he had stopped with the cat in one class and the tiger in a wholly different class. The differences between cat and cat, and between house-cats and tigers are not abandoned; but there is the useful concept of a class including cats and tigers.

This process of enlarging concepts goes forward in a multitude of experiences. The original and tentative concept is invariably wrong through inadequacy. Hence the young learner is forced to yield point after point as new examples force themselves upon his attention. A time comes, however, when one feels that he has cats and animals sufficiently well concepted, and he takes a rest; there is danger that he take a rest too soon.

In the "cat" case we have assumed that the concept was formed in early childhood, that there were enough cats to keep the concept growing; that the tiger was seen before the concept of cat became violently personal; and that nobody stood by to foozle intelligence by taboos and tales having a tendency to cause the receptive mind to behold a tiger with his stripes horizontal rather than around the body vertically. As a matter of fact children naturally perceive actual appearances and resemblances that adults may fail to note, because the former are freer from the limitation and distortion of views that instruction and words often promote.

The perceptions as well as concepts are influenced by the terms of their expression. Any one who has been taught early the words raccoon, bear, Airedale, woodchuck, chipmunk, gopher, gray squirrel, and baboon, will possibly see fewer resemblances among these animals than he would had he been taught names for all these having a common term, as dog. If the baboon were named tree-dog and the chipmunk called chattering-dog, and so on, the observer would perceive similarities that otherwise might go unnoticed or even be denied. Polonius saw first as a ship and then as a camel a cloud that Hamlet pointed out as such successively. The road to understanding is singularly set with signs capable of being misread or actually giving wrong directions.

The relation of words to accurate concepts is therefore one of some delicacy. How to guard against undue domination of the word, while utilizing to the full its unique economy, is a matter for consideration. For the moment a good strong word, spellable and mouthable, is adopted and its definition attached, there develops a tendency on the part of its possessor to cling to concept long after succeeding events have sucked away its substance. It may be that the lexicographers of the future will be found issuing bulletins warning against effete meanings and declaring extensions of significance. New conditions arise which are verily ignored or seen amiss because the most relevant word is preempted by a rooted meaning.

Vocabulary has scarcely kept pace with the need of saying things. The term "assault" refers to direct bodily attack. Now bodily damage not to be successfully distinguished from that inflicted by direct attack may be inflicted by selling some one a life-preserver that will not float. There is no word to label with equal opprobrium modernized, long distance assault and the assault of direct action, which may consist of a pulling of one's nose. Sin was a word; ah, there was a word. Are there phrases that truly convince the reader that to kill at a distance through defective workmanship is in the same class with common law murder? Or that to sell a stock that is worthless is to be conceived with entering through the coal chute? Where is the language that unveils the realities of petit larceny, grand larceny, and the separation on a large scale of investors' money from themselves?

The pitfall of the established concept is that it ignores nice distinctions that are oftentimes of the very substance of issues. The popular reaction to the words "in jail" is habitual and as such is undiscriminating. Whether honor or dishonor is to be attributed depends. St. Paul was in prison. Thoreau thought his own incarceration in Concord jail was rather a better state than being outside under the circumstances. There is a merited aversion to the thought of being sent to jail, but the unrevised concept may, at times, lead astray.

Practically every word bequeathed to us from the fathers has to be watched, or our thinking goes askew. Patriotism—holy word—and yet Dr. Johnson, in his time, essayed a fresh definition. Allowing a term to drag thought after it and accepting a word as a conclusive label is liable to lead us far from the essence of things. Especially in days of much reading and of impulsive response to headlines is there danger of unwittingly thinking evil and doing evil. It is no compliment to the circumspection of the citizen that it is currently held that the label in politics counts for more than the reality. Does the word Republican mean to-day what it meant in the days of Abraham Lincoln? It does not mean the same. Does it mean what it meant in the time of the French Revolution? Surely not. Yet the spell of the word is potent. It is convenient but unjustifiable to give words stereotyped meanings when used to apply to facts and situations which call for other terms or qualifying terms. Watchfulness in the use of terms applying to social phenomena and program is one of the most needed practices. The public should not be indulged in the impression that it is safely on the way to social welfare when a great body of terms looks one way and shoots another.

Definition is tedious, it is true. Tabloid news and radio do not affiliate with definition. But it is definition that has made science. Physics is a mass of exact definitions. He who learns chemistry learns, besides technic, definitions. Until social terms are defined with approximately the same exactness with which the chemist defines a substance or a reaction, and until some such respect is acquired for exact use of terms as every scientist regards as essential in his field of effort, social welfare and public administration will fail of their possibilities.

By too mechanical and unreflecting acceptance of words in lieu of perception of fitness for purported meaning, words become not aids and tools of thought, but disguises and false signals. Thought precedes language. Where language precedes thought— is adopted without perception into underlying facts—the proper function of speech fails and falsification appears. Somebody calls somebody else a scoundrel; the word scoundrel is easily repeated and clings to memory; scoundrel has an old, well established meaning. To be sure, it may not be the meaning that ought to be attached to the person labeled with the word. But it is easier to believe that Jones is a scoundrel, thus labeled, than to probe the facts of Jones' conduct or ascertain what his denouncer had in mind when he said scoundrel. It is objected that one cannot thus guard against the fallacy of words, that one cannot wait to ascertain the circumstances. But the practice of definition is commended.

The psychology of mechanical response to familiar words, such as fatherland, Jew, flivver, crown prince, protective tariff, mother-in-law, etc., is not essentially different from that of mechanical reaction to symbols. Flags have immense potency, whether carried for God and home and native land or for conquest and loot. It has been said that the rebellion of '61 might have succeeded if the confederate states had not adopted a new flag. In case either of words or symbols the fact of importance is that of the reality of their influence.

In the early years of one's life it is needful to revise and enlarge concepts freely. Plasticity of mind favors this and the demands of environment compel it. Knowledge is gained through personal experience and the annexation of other people's experience, and is filed away as general ideas or concepts. The exigencies of adjustment to surroundings dictate a certain flexibility in concepts in one's earlier years, a flexibility, however, that tends to pass away. Increasingly the mind tends to become made up, and increasingly the ideas that are stored away resist change. Teach the child aversion to pork, and it will take dieticians a long time to persuade to favorable consideration of porkchops; for pork has become something not conceivable as wholesome food. In thousands of instances the adult carries concepts that, whether properly formed or not, are habitual and definitive. Such finality of idea is not socially hopeful. In fact so firmly does the individual tend to become encrusted and bound by comparatively primitive concepts that institutional propaganda has always reached for the child.

The preforming of the individual's social concepts through pressure and propaganda in his childhood is, however, quite indefensible. The premature impressing of political, religious, and social concepts—where such concepts are debatable—is open to grave objection. To teach a child ideas that are to him at the time dogmatic and mind-closing is one of the ways to undo civilization. Even if parents have strong convictions, it is better to trust to ultimate rationality to bring the child to like convictions than to exert pressure. The child's mind should remain in a plastic state for arriving at concepts through enlarged experience. Provide evidence and culture materials but refrain from interference with the proper development of general ideas, should be the rule. I may be a firm believer in the government ownership of railroads, but it would be inexcusable in me to impress my concept of state function upon the immature. Such teachings would tend to make a youth a bigot. If my view of government ownership is worth anything, it will stand the test of social experience; the learner will presumably be controlled in his ultimate concepts by the available evidence and come to agree with me by coincidence; but if my view of state function proves to be erroneous he will at least be free from a false start. Similarly with religious and social views on controversial matters. If one is a Socialist, or Republican, or Methodist, or an Elk, he is not justified in putting the die on childhood. A large percentage of all the tedious and dogmatic rubbish in the world is with us because childhood has erroneously been regarded as the time to rivet on concepts. Childhood is the ever-recurring opportunity to roll away burdens of historical prejudice, social and sectarian fanaticisms and convictions for which evidence is lacking. The strongest evolutionist has no business to tell his eight-year-old son that evolution is ultimate fact. He should, on the other hand, direct the boy's mind to evidence, and let him come out ten years later where he may. It would not be such a calamity, if in the family various views were held, tentatively and until the third state of opinion, which is the agreement of the wise, were reached. It is a misconception of parental function for the heads of the family to dress up the children in the dogmas of years before. And there is no time like childhood to plant the thought that to make up one's mind in advance of evidence is not exactly the thing to do.

In dealing with phenomena that have no vital character, such as mathematical, the concept is definitive. But in the case of the phenomena under development general ideas must change with change. Moreover, in the case of vital phenomena, the evidence which supports a concept to-day may be affected by fresh evidence, whereupon there must ensue a revision of ideas.

It is not an accident that mobile intelligence has synchronized with the coming of biology. The doctrine of evolution has caused a perceptible tendency not to jump to positions from which there is no retreat. Nobody knows anything to-day with as much certainty as was displayed formerly by men who knew things that were not so. Nearly everybody to-day would admit possibility of error rather than go to the stake as a martyr. This may look like moral cowardice. Not so. It is the triumph of the sense of evidence.

Elasticity of concept is particularly appropriate for social relations. The ancient Jew had a clear idea of usury. Usury was holding up a fellow Jew. But it was quite right to take usury of the stranger. Here was a palpable case of arrested concept. Came one saying that the same moral laws should include all mankind. The brotherhood of man was a stirring and unwelcome concept of larger compass. Class justice, class legislation, class rule, class economics are proper concepts, provided the idea of class is inclusive. Nationalism is a finer concept if stretched to include the one nation of man. Class spirit in college is fine, provided it includes the freshmen as fellow creatures, and rival universities as institutions of learning. It has been said that no one amounts to anything until he forgets his college yell. Cases of restricted social concepts are many. The clan spirit of the Kentucky feudist represents arrested development; the true clan spirit, the socialized idea of kindred, stops not short of embracing surviving families in the same county, and the people of the commonwealth of Kentucky and even of these United States, including negroes, for their essential rights and fair play.

The socialized person is able to see the things that bind the many together as well as the things in which differences appear. Social vision is another name for the matured social concept. There is danger lest social concepts take fixed form with too limited connotations. Catholicity of view and readiness to modify one's opinions are of the essence of good citizenship and are an indispensable element for world citizenship.

Smug, provincial, and exclusively personal, modes of thought are out of keeping in times of the airplane, railroads, steamboats, the press, and the international organization of labor and scientists. It is the provincial and limited concept that provides submarines and Lewisite. The idea of universal brotherhood applied to armament would produce guns as destructive to the man firing as to the man fired at. A war rifle with safety at one end only is one of the least fitting symbols of equity.

Progress comes with larger ideas of social

organization and of justice; and collapse occurs through failure to adjust ideas to new developments of environment. Too restricted concepts were the psychological basis of the Civil War in America. The failure of George III and his ministers to adjust their concepts of colonial relations split the English-speaking world. In the appropriate expansion of concepts lies the world's hope. Distance, which has been practically overcome by transportation systems, exerts too great influence upon our ideas, for we as yet do not conceive of neighborhood in world terms.

Economic support for wider altruism is found in the bearing of remote societies upon local welfare. Backward groups tend to drag down education, health, and economic welfare throughout a whole country. The structure of trade and commerce is so complex and so essentially unified that no longer can one safely be indifferent to wages paid to miners two thousand miles away, or to the morale of the workers who contribute toward creamery butter. The standard of living and attitude of the Japanese toward birth-control have an international bearing. Tariff walls are erected in a spirit of disregard for other peoples. The concept of local independence and of disregard for the distant neighbor does not well conform to present facts of intercommunication and of modern business necessities.

Under limitations of concept there is a tendency to make too much of petty differences and to ignore the large bonds. Sometimes man and wife make this mistake; taxpayers have the habit too; wards and parts of cities misbehave thus, also large and small nations. Institutional Christianity has a record for magnifying unimportant differences. More can be had from cooperation than gained from selfish policy in the long run.

Wide social consciousness commends itself economically. But small part of the world's productivity is realized under present concepts of business and enterprise.

There is no end of discord and waste. Under circumscribed notions in production and distribution large resources for social welfare remain but partly perceived or utilized.

Social engineering might assure a diffusion of prosperity never known before. Uncoördinated effort, staged under narrow and archaic concepts, stands in the way of rationalized and systematized social business with tenfold more power to provide goods and services. We should all be richer if, for example, the last bit of anarchy were removed from railroad construction and operation and the full possibilities of transportation were available for every hamlet in the land. Just as the concept of a highway as being four feet and eight and one-half inches wide limited the development of the railroad, so the conception of competing carriers limits railway service. The petty retailer who competes not in price but for trade would survive as a person under consolidated stores; he would survive in some capacity; he would probably share more in prosperity for there would be more to share.

The "boosting" efforts of small towns are commendable in that they represent an attitude preparatory to larger social undertakings. But community boosting is relatively helpless if narrowly conceived. The citizen's problems are in order of importance: international; national; state; and, lastly, county, city and local. But, quite naturally, influenced by the concrete, immediate and local, he thinks of them in reverse order. In a larger view, and as affecting his general interest the most important governing body for the citizen is the national congress, and the next is the state government, and so on down to the village board. Economic and legislative influences operating over wide areas deeply affect personal condition. As a self-contained organ of government, the local unit has ceased to have large significance.

CHAPTER VI
THE PSYCHOLOGY OF DEFENSE

IN THE lower range of animal economy defense is largely a matter of physical adaptation. Animals that are preyed upon are equipped with special means of protection— horns, poison-sacs, fangs, thick skin, quills, vile smell, tusks, protective masses of tissue, bony plates and shell armor. Means of flight are a means of safety, and long legs and muscles of wire enable the antelope and the rabbit to race to security. Protective coloration has marked survival value, as does also imitative structure, as in the case of the walking-stick insect, so closely resembling the twigs and needles of the pine branch to which it clings.

As mind is the organ of adaptation in man, the system of defenses is mainly mental. Tall stature and largeness of body and strength of muscle are but occasionally enlisted for defense. By use of physical auxiliaries and mental forces, the man of medium stature or less is substantially on a par with the giant or athlete. Indeed, by reason of necessity for refining his personal defenses, the small man may actually rise higher in the scale of security through his better conceived devices and improvisations. While bulk and bigness exert a perceptible social influence, the trend of defense and authority is toward control by mental forces quite apart from actual physical strength. In ordinary affairs, in the play of forces that determine the characteristic polity and adjustments in peace-time social organization, the advantage lies with those individuals and classes that are most highly specialized in mental means for getting what they want and avoiding what they do not want. Competition and defense are very generally and increasingly being moved upward to the mental plane.

The universal aspiration for education, if not for oneself then for one's children that they may be better fitted for the life struggle, is a recognition of the shifted plane of self-protection. The illiterate is in hopeless inferiority to the man who can read. The armed bandit with the strength of ten men and with ammunition for a hundred is a pigmy compared with the telegraph operator who helps put a noose of intelligence around the man killer. A man is beaten, he is conquered, he is routed, not physically but by statistics, logic, court decrees, underselling, loss of poise, ignorance, innuendo, wit, and propaganda. Defense is to-day a matter of psychology; even war has succumbed to the superior factor of mental as contrasted with physical potentiality.

The primitive mental defense is falsehood. Instinctively the child deceives; when in doubt of policy the child often turns to untruth. The tendency may indeed be superseded within limits by the attaching of penalties and rewards but of the original response there can be no doubt. Early moralists held up their hands in horror over this supposedly iniquitous phenomenon and regarded it as clinching proof of the original depravity of human nature. Little men and little women were discovered to be just naturally "little liars." Threatened by dangers from the adult world that towers physically over his low stature, the child takes to falsehood instead of flight, instead of use of teeth or claws, vicious expectoration or digging in. He instinctively utilizes— so great a step does human evolution represent above the animal— his resources of deception. Deception is nature's shock absorber. It is biologically as great an advance over the corporeal defenses of the animals as the tractor-drawn gang-plow is an improvement over the forked stick of the Egyptians.

Worthy to be mentioned along with falsehood as a cautious tendency, and like falsehood in having a certain significance for constructive social psychology, is the defense which consists of taking the back seat. If he who runs away is safe, so also is he comparatively who takes a back seat or sits with his back to the wall. When an audience assembles there will ordinarily be a drift of individuals around the fringe of the room unless the entertainment is to consist of something to be seen and familiar through repute. The lecturer must often pray that his audience will move forward and fill up the unoccupied seats near the front. The peripheral tendencies of popular audiences have not escaped notice.

Here we have the psychology of the animal that fears an inclosure; it is the fear of being trapped. A certain ex-miner from the once wild west, on visiting his eastern relatives, was observed never to take a chair that was not tight on the wall. He had contracted the habit while living under frontier conditions, and preferred to have no chance of enemy attack from the rear.

Flee from the strange, or if drawing near, draw not too near; and if fairly faced, lie, and lie abundantly— these reactions are not of yesterday's growth. Instead of the defenses of falsehood, retreat and taking the back seat, evasion is a common ruse. In the psychological sense evasion extends to the setting up of illusions and self-deception. Or evasion may take the form of a selection of interests that minimize the possibility of conflict. Thus art and music are refuges in an autocratic society. It is not surprising that these have reached high development in monarchies, in which constructive effort and philosophizing along social lines have been banned, with Siberias in the background. In times past a multitude of thinkers and men of parts have illustrated the psychology of evasion by devoting themselves to labors that had a minimum of potentiality for conflict

Not alone by restraint from possible fields for employment of energies, but also in the vision of alluring worlds does the psychology of evasion disclose itself. Hans Christian Andersen substituted a fairyland for the real world of childhood, evading the actualities for which he was so little adapted. The downtrodden classes of the Roman empire accepted Christianity the more readily for its affording an avenue of escape into a world in which the bitter struggle of living was to be forever removed. The most unsuccessful and deprived are frequently those who dream most dreams and see most visions. The minds of dwarf, cripple, hunchback and chronic invalid are rich in evasions and cushioned with illusions. With the exhaustion of ordinary and real methods of defense, the individual flees to unreality and air castles. In time of calamity and war the appeal to charms and luck, to miracle and myth, increases. The farmer who is least consistently scientific is likely to be most devoted to "moon" farming and most conscious of the luck of seasons. By attaching results to inexplicable causes he thus saves his face. The Freudians declare that insanity itself is an organic adjustment of evasion. The victim of irreparable loss flees from himself and "becomes" by the role or route of insanity, the King of Norway or the great Napoleon. Reality too terrible to be faced becomes thus unreality, and unreality becomes the seeming real.

It is evident that the psychology of evasion is at war with social progress. Whatever mires mind in illusion and upholsters it with the fanciful is directly opposed to the making of a better real world. It is not an accident that with the more forceful efforts on the part of the church to reform modern evil conditions, there has ensued a notable lessening of emphasis upon dogma and future bliss. Dynamic individuals address themselves to immediate improvements. Material success is inversely related to certain brands of theology. With prosperity invariably comes a loss of the religious fervor related to remote objectives, for there is less tendency to evade what the day and hour present.

The presence of great poverty, of war and revolution, of industrial anarchy, is fraught with danger lest life slither to illusion through despair rather than gird up its loins. There comes a time in the life of the individual when he no longer tries to swim; he submerges. The spirit of society must be that of practicality and hopefulness, or society fails. An amount of misery may prove stimulating; but increase that amount beyond a certain limit and only decay may be expected. The most energizing mood is that of confidence born of success. There is no class so valueless for social reconstruction and abiding welfare as the class that is habituated to misery. The slums of city and country afford little material for building a better society. Long continued abasement is of little promise. It is important to society that welfare be general, that the poor should not always be with us.

A refinement of defense appears in keeping one's thoughts to himself. Avoidance of telling the whole truth and nothing but the truth serves notably for survival purposes, and escapes the burden on memory of successful dispensing lies. The morality of concealment is a stage higher than that of even the "white lie." A large part of trade rests upon concealment. The buyer knows that a tract of farm land is to be sought as golf links; the farmer is permitted to remain in ignorance of this important fact until he has signed the deed. This is "good business." The goodness of business is not inconsistent with "doing" the other fellow by keeping him in the dark. The automobile dealer markets the older model, keeping discreetly silent on improvements about to appear. If trade were to see the elimination of all deceptions and concealments, some of us would scarcely know how to do business. Trade is thus vastly lower in evolution toward full veracity than is science, which is truth without fear or favor. In the social renovation, for which science is laying the foundation, trade may approximate if indeed not fully realize the same loyalty to truth to which we are accustomed in the laboratory. The big "strikes" in the business world will possibly some day be squarely bottomed on absolute candor— scientific method. As yet few have the nerve to be scientifically honest in business, but are "law honest" or are constantly being forced by law into an acceptably ethical attitude.

The evolution of defense carries over to the use of imagination and intuition for grasping what is in the other person's mind. As long as self-protection is limited to the doing of something to meet overt attack, there is obvious disadvantage. The best defense is often correct anticipation. The individual is relatively defenseless until he can see what is going on in the mind that he encounters, until he can judge motives, until he sees what is to happen before it happens. The pugilist gets a "nose" who waits to see a blow in the air, before he sees it in his opponent's mind. Under modern conditions the mind is forced to organize for penetrating into what others know and what they will do; hence the emphasis upon psychology and character analysis.

It is idle to hope that pickerel will ever cease from eating minnows, or that superior intelligence will not take some toll from inferior; this would be too much to expect. Life struggle in human society may indeed be raised above the level of competition for plain subsistence. Bread for all may come to be an accomplished fact. But advantage seeking will none the less obtain, perhaps intensify. Honors, place, repute, distinctions, immunities, and power are high substitutes for means of subsistence, but are in true biological sequence with the struggle of two dogs for sole possession of a single bone.

Superior intelligence tends to take advantage of inferior intelligence; the only abiding protection is in the development of mental tactics of defense. Though society without exploitation is unthinkable, such exploitation by superior of inferior intelligence need not be immobile and rooted in social classes. Constitutional safeguards may be provided. By more agile defenses and by specialized leadership class lines stretch and break. Fixedness of individual status, except as children are ever dominated by their elders, is not a foregone conclusion. The mistress and maid are both in turn exploiter and exploited; the wits that are sharpest on the issue determine the respective roles. In Barrie's *The Admirable Crichton* the butler was an inferior when the family he served was in its English setting, but he in turn, under different circumstances, became a master when on the sea-girt island with the patrician family that lacked practical knowledge. The war of wits never knows an armistice; and outside of one's knowledge one is helpless.

Democracy is identified with distribution of opportunities for information and intelligence. Given free play in opportunities, the individual has democracy indeed. Social contrast and oppression have been associated with the device of depriving the people of thought-materials or with that of controlling minds through fictions and class taboos. What would autocracy be without illiteracy or special cultures of prejudice? Information and catholic culture are incompatible with the existence of submerged classes. The recipe for the security of despotism is popular ignorance and moth-like tropism toward the sun of royalty. Class advantage is least possible with uncontrolled press, church and school. In England the political ministry appoints the bishops of the established church, and the landlord owns the vicar. In pre-war Germany the clergy had no thoughts that were not visaed. The liberating of the mind to truth and science is the only defensible function on the part of cultural agencies; and when any of these agencies holds a brief for the landlord class or the monarchical group or the moneyed interests, the mental energy of the people is misdirected and betrayed, and civilization hangs on by an eyelash. The full intelligence of the people, the intellectual resources of the whole people, is the greatest assurance of general welfare, including ultimately, that of those who clutch privilege and fear its loss.

While propaganda has gained recent prominence to secure warlike responses and is increasingly employed for purposes requiring mass opinion, it is no new thing in the world. Propaganda is as old as society. There was never a time when propaganda was not employed. The distinction attaching to present-day propaganda is quantitative rather than qualitative. Propaganda is twin brother to advertising, but goes beyond commercial advertising in that control of fundamental attitudes on great issues is sought, and not infrequently for no perceptible benefit to the people whose sentiments are thus commandeered and dominated.

Just as psychological salesmanship— the refined hypnotism of the market— has caught the ordinary buyer unprepared in a counter-psychology of resistance, so propaganda has developed more fully than defensive tactics on the part of the public. The psychology of resistance is in its infancy. Hence the consumer is frequently no match for the seller and the voter is a lamb before the all-the-year publicity service of the bureau of propaganda.

There is valid propaganda and objectionable propaganda, just as there is legitimate and illegitimate salesmanship. It is no small service when the salesman promotes the purchase of goods that are within the buyer's purse and effects an upward thrust on the plane of living and intelligence. But there is likewise a salesmanship that is nothing short of a psychological and economic raid. With propaganda it is likewise. Progress is associated with propaganda; but, on the other hand, there is not a shady policy or selfish project that does not hope to use propaganda as a narcotic. The extent of governmental and private use of propaganda is strong evidence of the arrival of society at a level characterized by mental rather than physical strife. From now on it is the battle of ideas; an environment has been established wherein the mobilization of ideas and psychological strategy are outstanding features.

The ordinary man, not yet armored against propaganda, succumbs like an Eskimo to measles. His actual government, never of high visibility, becomes an invisible government. He learns what he is told and he is told what others think he should be told, for their interests. Immune from physical violence through his courts and constables, he is psychologically assaulted and ravaged with impunity. Thus he will be found enthusiastically supporting campaigns aimed at his own subversion, voting against his own interest, bawling down his best defenders and worshiping the devil. He thinks, when he thinks, on the ideas and facts presented. The control of his thought materials, through selection and interpretation, is accordingly a most effectual control over his convictions and conduct. Suffering from effects of propaganda the sufferer is the last to admit that he is sick; he feels well. The sensations that the propaganda germ set up have the seeming authenticity of normalcy. The victim of propaganda is myopic without knowing it, having no idea of how lenses would improve his vision.

The primary remedy against subversive propaganda is for the citizen to know who says what in one's daily dealings it makes a difference who says a thing. A land agent will see qualities of soil and beauties of landscape that might escape the ordinary observer. The fallibility is known, and there is locally an allowance made for overstatement. It is usual to weigh words with motives in the small circle of acquaintanceship. The questioning if motives, however disparaged, is the first requisite for successful adjustment in one's own neighborhood. Not to scrutinize motives is to repudiate cause and effect.

But in the wider circle of political and economic affairs like regard for motives is less prompted and less practicable. The remote source of opinion is endowed with a disinterestedness not attributed to the man around the corner. The panegyric on war is reverently perused with no thought of the chortling of the powder manufacturer. The ukase of fashion to wear more buttons is received with a pupil-like docility that would not be extended to a suggestion of like import from the next-door neighbor. Distance not only lends enchantment— it convinces. Anonymous advice has a clear lead over that from the reputable local authority. Propaganda from invisible and seemingly impersonal sources accordingly has a peculiar prestige and sanctity. The tendency to tolerate a wonderland where all the usual laws and phenomena are transcended, falls in with the designs of propaganda.

The citizen needs to be as skeptical of sources as is the competent historian or the scientist. The "doubting Thomas" should not be the exception but the rule. The results upon journalism would be galvanic and most constructive for social well-being. One might well finish every newspaper paragraph with a question mark, not that every paragraph is unreliable, but by way of training for keeping off the rocks of occasional doctored news and inspired interpretation. "Prove all things," is peculiarly applicable to articles published in the heat of conflict and in journals top-heavy with advertising. The gross control of news and editorial by advertisers may be unusual; but who would deny that the whole glacier-like influence of the advertising is to limit the intellectual value of the press? Publications read by the most millions are often essentially advertising mediums and should be so regarded.

Anonymity contributes to the tactics of propaganda. We can have no objection to an article extolling the use of beer as a medicine if we know the writer owns a brewery. It is the mass of articles camouflaged as scientific or disinterested that perverts public intelligence most seriously. We do not regard with favor commercial products that do not carry the maker's name. Yet the thought products that go into the mental assimilation of the people are not similarly referable to the actual sources. The signing of articles is desirable and more than that, for signatures are inconclusive evidence of motive— there should be disclosure of the economic or political origin. An importer writes or hires a man to write for free trade. We may accept the argument; but the chances of being misled are reduced if we know what interest is back of the article. Here is a powder manufacturer who believes in the evoking of superior moral qualities by blowing holes through people one has not met before. Very well; some may agree with him; give him his say anyhow. But let him not hide behind a clergyman, or buy an editor by an advertising contract. The same authenticity in mental foods that we have in other foods is desirable— name of the beneficial owner and exact nature of contents of the package. The direct linking of utterance with person and interest is a desideratum. Find the man, is the idea; see how he secures his income; listen to him though he is a homicide preaching against jails; but let us no longer be in doubt as to motives, nor should we assume that the man who writes from selfish interest may not be serving the public interest too; let us be open-minded.

Correlated with the idea of reliable information and ascertained sources of thought-materials is the ideal of insuring conditions for free speech. Only belated progress has been made toward endowing the employee with the attributes of free citizenship. Every citizen has a right to vote for whom he pleases, to espouse any political or economic theory— free speech being guaranteed by federal constitution— and criticize public officials, who are legally his servants. Does the employee have the right to exercise his rights? Legally, yes; practically, not always.

Originally the economic subordinate was kept where others thought he belonged by denying him the ballot. Then he achieved the ballot; thereafter the landlord or employer's agent looked over his shoulder when he voted. So the ballot was a scrap of paper. Then came the Australian ballot— the greatest contribution to the mechanics of democracy ever devised.

This emancipated the social subordinate. Secret voting, which is contemplated by the secret ballot, is the sheet anchor of democracy. The voter who thinks the secrecy of the ballot is being violated may attack such violation successfully without revealing necessarily how he votes. He is assured of the unique freedom of being able to vote as he will without detection. Without this freedom there can be no political democracy. This is the cornerstone.

It only remains to carry the secret ballot further. It should be available for expression of preferences on a wider range of public questions, as for example, a declaration of war and major enactments of legislation before such go into effect. But perhaps the greatest remaining usefulness of the secret vote is to be found in its exercise in a multitude of quasi-public situations where the psychology of aggressive leadership threatens the sincere expression of convictions. The chairman of a meeting, in thousands of instances where public sentiment is polled, may dominate and evoke a perverted expression of views. Job fear, fear of loss of trade, and apprehension as to how an open vote for or against will be regarded, commonly have the effect of a miscarriage of intelligence. In committee meetings, clubs and local organizations, publicity of voting is a restraint. The psychology of the individual in such groups is one thing and his psychology under the secret ballot is another. Openly voting, his concern is how others will regard him, how he will be affected, as by scorn or trouble-making. Voting secretly, his freer self finds expression. In Mark Twain's *The Mysterious Stranger* only two or three of the sixty or more who stoned a woman to death were interested to have her die. All the others joined through fear to be in a minority.

The very foundation of democracy and stable popular government rests upon the secret ballot and especially in the extension of this to weekly and daily use in the frequent local and institutional meetings in every municipality, school district, and community. The secret ballot, for all matters likely to involve job fear and the like, should be a matter of course.

True, the secret ballot is a thing for the weak. Free and open expression is a much nobler concept than furtive voting. But heaven is not reached at a single bound. The right to discuss public policies and public men, the voter's agents, is assured; it is violated only in practice.

The employee has the secret ballot; what more should he want? All the historical and logical considerations which convince that the stability of society rests on free intelligence functioning for general welfare, declare for free speech— for the composite intelligence built up when all speak freely even if some utter nonsense. Now the employer and employee may think differently; they are apt to. It is hard for the employer to realize that free speech is a blessing to society, in the long run, and hard to check an impulse to dismiss the employee who differs with him on the tariff on wool. Here is the employee who has views on labor and capital. Here is a governmental employee who criticizes the governor. Shall it be permitted? Millions of men and women are now within the working forces of government and business corporations. The job web is as wide as society. In the nature of things must the loyalty of the employee to the employer take precedence over his interest in the general welfare and stop his mouth? The tradition of democratic freedom of speech grew up when the jobs were numerically insignificant. When private corporations count their employees by thousands and the federal government employs an army of men, inquiry is in point touching the civic freedom and potentialities of these great numbers of workers.

To be a good citizen implies civic activity, and such is unthinkable without freedom to discuss issues, take part in campaigns, and comment favorably or unfavorably upon the government, which derives its lawful powers from the will of the people. To the extent to which employment silences the employee, whether he be a private or a public employee, it is in conflict with the welfare of the state. The remedy lies in guaranties of tenure as against loss of place for exercising civic rights. It is no less duress to attack the citizen economically for exercise of civic rights than for him to be attacked physically for the same cause, which no government would tolerate. When the employer is the government, it is difficult to see any distinction between summary removal for exercising civic rights and such coercion when applied by the private employer. No employer can be fairly said to buy the opinion and political life of the individual when buying his labor power. The very existence of democracy depends upon the widespread cultivation of political intelligence. There is a duty resting upon every voter not only to vote but to seek by every means to enlarge his knowledge of public issues and the industrial and economic problems now so largely identified with public affairs. To be an intelligent citizen without freedom to shape public opinion and frame resolutions, or run for office or sit on the platform at a political meeting, is a contradiction in terms. There is urgent need of meeting the requirements of citizenship. Through more rigid and comprehensive corrupt practice acts and through more complete organization of employees to protect their constitutional rights as citizens, the dismissal of men for overt citizenship should be made to take its place with relics of the past.

CHAPTER VII
THE BASIS OF COÖPERATION

PICTURE a boat, far from shore, containing several men threatened with drowning. No one man can get to shore without aiding the others to land as well. Each man would be willing to be the only survivor if only one were to survive. There is discord and harmony, "private property" and community effort. The major interest is that of making a successful passage to shore, and this interest welds all muscles into one motive force. Men tend to "do" one another, but they will also cooperate on a pinch.

There can be no social advancement, no civilization, without cooperative effort. If cooperation is not possible, civilization is not possible. There will be more coöperation in the future— partly conscious and partly in fact only, as in the coöperation the ranchman and the shoe manufacturer, who have not the full consciousness and purpose of coöperation. Deliberate and planned cooperation is illustrated in municipal waterworks, state highway construction and in community effort and team work of any kind.

Cooperation works when each coöperator thinks he can get more for himself through working with others than alone; this is the basis for cooperation. A vision of advantage is pitted against the disorganizing factors of irritations and jealousies.

Envy and jealousy are largely phenomena within the class. The resentments from class to class are as nothing to those among individuals within classes—among individuals of local association. The question of who shall be first among equals is solved with greater difficulty than who shall be first when there is a higher class to pick from, or when the class embraces individuals not of intimate acquaintance.

Oftentimes local discords can be alleviated only by bringing in a stranger. It is hard to believe that a familiar acquaintance and competitor for local repute can possess the qualifications for important office. Aside from persistent wariness lest rivals succeed, there is the besetting myth that the distant is superior. Amateur stockmen send to distant points for breeding animals though the next ranch may have their superiors; and the amateur gardener rarely thinks of saving seed from his own crops, that coming by mail being naively assumed to be better.

Democracy has even attempted preposterously to level, if not by denying elevation, then by rotation of office. Surely every citizen is entitled to hold office, from which axiom arises change of personnel and the diffusion of opportunities to do things inexpertly. The craving for office, while adjusting the balance of titular equality, does indeed often rotate efficiency out and inefficiency in.

The hatreds and jealousies of democracy yield to the sense of impending calamity or the clearer vision of benefits from joint action. Bickerings in the family, in the social group, in the civic organization, vanish under threat of harm. Identify public and coöperative effort with security and survival, charge public affairs with weightier import, and the sensibilities of rivalry are quieted. The unifying effect of great distress is analogous to that revealed when private welfare is seen to be momentously related to the proper conduct of public business.

Individualistic commercialism sprouts its growth of cooperative psychology. The emphasis upon service to the buyer, an emphasis bobbing about like a cork on the competitive sea, testifies to the social vacuum yet to be filled by cooperation. The dealer cannot live to himself alone. He must even pull with others— other dealers and his customers— to get to shore. A distinct kindliness and fraternity blossoms in trade, a forerunner of more systematized and perfect cooperation. Should tradesmen stop competing in prices and take to competing in good will and amenities to customers, the change though no relief to pocketbooks, would be of great social promise. The slogan of service, heard in the market place for some years back, is auspicious. It connotes a wider social consciousness and a sense of interdependence; it bespeaks a recognition of the good of all in the good of each and the prosperity of each in the prosperity of all. The psychological basis is being laid thus for larger political, social and economic synthesis.

Modern industry has been accompanied by a tendency toward cooperative consumption of surplus private wealth. The age of industrialism has become the age of large giving. Leaving aside the ethics of accumulation and the deficiencies of philanthropic purpose and method, the fact stands clear that wealth is conceived of increasingly in terms of public welfare. Its social origin and social utilization are distinctly implied by the colossal gifts and returns of money to common and public uses. In logical sequence follow a greater formal and conscious cooperation in the production of wealth and a greater legislative or popular direction of its distribution and use. The violent individualist and the determined socialist are really not far apart except in vocabulary. The recognition that the social body is one and we are all of that body may be denied as a theory, but it is accepted as a fact generally, though with differing states of mind and varied reservations.

Coöperation succeeds in so far as it secures for the individual things that alone he could not secure. It fails to interest the individual who will lose more than he will gain by it. Few can ever be as interested in getting things for the public as for themselves. Hence any system that flouts private property completely cannot stand. The case against capitalism is that it trespasses far upon private property, for there are great numbers who are unable to possess enough private property to satisfy distinctly personal as contrasted with public needs. If capitalism ever goes upon the rocks, it will be because it has trifled too much with the private property sense. As between no private property and public ownership the voter will choose public ownership every time. But at the bottom his choice is for private property, though not with unwillingness to see others enjoy private property. The barrier between capitalism and social ownership in its most sweeping form is the popular faith in the possibility of each person's securing a good share of private property himself; let this faith waver and strange things might happen.

It remains to be seen how fully the property sense may be satisfied by an undivided share in, say, a public library as contrasted with money in the bank to buy books. It is possible that the amount of free money the citizens would be content with might be small indeed, provided public utilities abounded on every hand. It was Thoreau who found it unnecessary to buy a farm for scenery when he could look at farms without owning them. With growth of socialized utilities it is quite possible that the sense of private property would be adequately gratified with fortunes that would look small at the present time. Balzac, in *Cousin Pons*, wrote satirically of the gilding of the gas-lamps in the Place de la Concorde to console the poor man for his poverty by reminding him that he was rich as a citizen.

Close attention to immediate results is opposed to the state of mind required for successful coöperation. Many of the advantages procurable through social big business cannot be realized at once. The need of exercising some imagination for the anticipation of benefits is a check on popular interest in the larger coördinations for social program. It is hard to interest people in things they cannot see and in matters that concern the future. Consider the indifference in this country to the conservation of forests and other natural resources. Citizens rally to fight fires but tend to be indifferent in regard to fire prevention. Once an epidemic of disease appears, active measures are taken; but social coöperation for preventive medicine is less readily brought about. It is the idealistic and imaginative who see most in cooperation. The individual who has but flighty attention and whose mind is uncomfortable in tracing relations is accordingly but slightly qualified for cooperation in its many forms; and essential dividends from social effort have not the satisfying tangibility of the cash rebate.

A certain weakness of coöperation is shown in the compensation of public servants. Coöperative enterprise to be successful needs, of course, as highly qualified staffs as are employed in private business. Democracy is not privileged to get along with inferior agents. To secure highly efficient agents rewards must be offered equivalent to those afforded by private employment. Such compensation is unusual and is attended by distinct pain on the part of citizens who would secure high skill at a unique discount. Hence it is that generally public and cooperative affairs are directly administered by men of ability who give a part-time service to the public or by persons not comparing favorably in resourcefulness and technical training with persons in corresponding activities in private business. In hundreds of communities will be found men drawing salaries from private employers much larger than any paid by the same communities to their most highly compensated civic employees. In the unequal contest public business accordingly suffers. In the final analysis all salaries, whether in public or private business, are socially derived. The citizen, however, tends to be singularly alert and thrifty, in paying his own experts, singularly given to uneconomical economy in communal affairs.

If the downtrodden turn to cooperation for security, no less so may the privileged. A very large part of the work for social amelioration has been inaugurated and carried forward by persons whose immediate needs would not seem to be served by such altruism. The spirit of social adventure is no doubt far more potent in the classes than in the masses. Imagination, forcefulness, inquiry, sympathy— these are not of plebeian character. The noblest roll of history is that of names of well-placed individuals who have felt the common lot and striven to uplift. Their stake has been the clearing of their souls from injustice, and the luxury of constructive idealism.

Economic privilege has also its essential interest in popular welfare. The monopolist cannot prosper without a market. Poverty beyond limits is a menacing condition even to those who are immediately immune. The large operations of business presuppose a degree of general prosperity.

One of the reasons most frequently cited for private as contrasted with public business is that individual initiative would tend to disappear with any considerable expansion of the latter. It is likely that personal initiative will always find avenues of expression. Initiative might merely be shifted to new fields. Public and private success are not mutually exclusive; both have expanding and largely non-conflicting orbits. The resourceful individual can always do something else. Loss of initiative would be one of the most irreparable of losses. Persons urging greater social coöperation as well as those who oppose it unite in insistence upon the need of free play for initiative. The merits of social programs must be judged according to effects upon initiative. There are those who conceive a larger field for initiative under an economic system less individualistic than that at present operative.

CHAPTER VIII
THE PSYCHOLOGY OF PUBLIC BUSINESS

IT IS assumed that civic and social progress involves wider coöperative effort and a relative increase in public as contrasted with private business. The trend of modern government is toward expansion of function, which touches increasingly industrial and economic relations.

There was a time when the resident of a city, such as London, hired guards for his body and his warehouse and lighted the street in front of his premises— when he was his own police and street-lighting department. He was also his own fire department and sanitary expert. The past century has witnessed the steady augmentation of public business. An increasing number of employees are attached to government; service offices multiply, and the citizen tends ever to get more things for himself by utilizing the coöperative mechanism of the state. Governmental regulation for protective purposes obtains where forthright ownership and monopoly have not become seated in government. In the sharp contest between public and private ownership and control, the decisions fall to socialization. The tendency for peoples under modern conditions to develop the coöperative agency of the state is an outstanding phenomenon. To mention a few examples of extension of governmental function as revealed by federal legislation: the interstate commerce act; the Sherman anti-trust law; the anti-child labor law; the farm loan act; the federal trade commission law; the Clayton act; rural free delivery of mails; the parcels post; activities of the department of agriculture; the pure food and drugs act; the Smith-Hughes educational act; the Muscle Shoals project. In states; such projects as the New York barge canal, public warehouses in Louisiana, state fire insurance of public buildings in South Carolina, state mining of coal for public uses in South Dakota, state elevators and state bank in North Dakota. In foreign countries, notably in Australasia and Germany, state enterprise has shown vigorous growth. Municipalities the world over show similar enlargement of function. There are community playgrounds and parks, libraries, water systems, food inspection, vacation schools and street railway lines. Within the school are the free dental clinic, and hammers and saws in the manual training department bought with tax money and owned by the community for a community workshop.

Yet with all the tendency toward substantial socialization, and with the accumulating evidence that social welfare involves such increase of socialization, there remain states of mind in the citizen body that seem to threaten the success of public business. It is an open question whether the citizen is going to be adequate for upholding an elaborate structure of public business.

There is, first of all, the question as to whether the citizenship can be kept informed. In case the government, which is the agent of the citizen in democratic theory, becomes walled off by itself and is virtually inscrutable to the citizen, the probability of vicious bureaucracy and perversion is obvious. Every official, board, committee, staff, court and cabinet tends to magnify office and reach for power. Unchecked and unwatched officialdom undoubtedly, everywhere, and at all times, tends to grow beyond proper limits. The seeds of autocracy are present in the most hopefully constituted instrumentalities of democracy. A strict holding to account and daylight openness of procedure and purpose are needful lest the agent become principal, lest corruption creep in and privilege and profit take the place of service to the state.

Two things are needful: first, a manageable system of reporting to citizens, and, secondly, a workable system by which the civic body can instruct its agents. In both of these particulars improvement is imperative if modern government is not to prove disappointing or the prelude to collapse.

In regard to the first, what does the citizen authentically know about the official conduct of his agents in congress, in state legislatures, in municipal bodies? What are the means by which information is provided? The opacity and inadequacy of the agent's reports to his principal, the citizen, are notorious. The other side of the moon is about as visible as the official conduct of a very large number of persons employed in government. This condition goes ill with democratic theory. Perhaps the theory is wrong, then what better theory? It is, however, demonstrated beyond debate that it is possible to fool most of the people most of the time. The official in a republic may live as in the seclusion of a hidden cave, and when put on the defensive has rich resources for "passing the buck." Any business man who turned his agents loose with power to act would regret it. The voter selects his agents but has to be a detective to follow what they do. The art of reporting on public business for the benefit of the citizen-principal may fairly be said to be underdeveloped.

On the other hand, the citizen, ostensibly principal, with power to instruct his agents, the officeholders, has but singularly limited means of making his agents hear. The agents are often honestly unable to hear from their principals, who vote infrequently and in such murky form of expression that days and days are spent after elections by the newspapers in trying to see what the elections indicated by way of policy. Parties go into power mystified as to what they are expected to do. Analyzing the election returns becomes a brain-wrecking exercise in the unknowable. It often takes years to develop a tentatively right guess as to what the voters meant by this majority or that slump.

In view of the wonderful efficiency of communication

in private affairs, as illustrated, for example, in the facility by which one calls up the grocer over the telephone and is understood, the inability of electorates to make their representatives understand by ballot is passing strange. Perhaps the form of the ballot is at fault or the infrequency of balloting. But in any event the substantial insulation of voter from agent on matters of public policy is one of the marvels of administrative mischance. Here is a representative, theoretically functioning to carry out his constituents' wishes, waiting nervously for news from back home, for an emergency issue is pending; he seizes upon the newspaper from his home town. But it is an opposition paper. No relief there. The telegraph brings messages, but possibly from persons violently unrepresentative of the majority contemplated in the expression "the greatest good of the greatest number." The baffled agent accordingly has to use his own judgment and vote as he pleases, which, according to Edmund Burke's speech "to the electors at Bristol," is "his jolly good right anyhow." The news from back home is indeed scarcely expected before the next biennial or sextennial election. How democracy can be expected to work out well, how public business can be expected to be transacted in the public interest, when such impassable denseness of medium between official and principal obtains, passes understanding. The informational and instructional facilities for representative government are scarcely different from what would be prescribed for autocracy. It is no great privilege for the voter to have a few chances in his lifetime of voting for persons to hold office if he has no means of saying what he thinks when he thinks it on specific political issues, many of which do not form until after the elected representative has packed his bag after the fall elections. Some attention to the mechanics of communication is recommended for the better functioning of representative government. The voters' pamphlet, issued in several states previous to election, is a promising beginning.

The question arises as to whether the average citizen can be sufficiently interested in public business. He is interested in his private business but tends to be indifferent to public affairs. Part of the time he does not know what is going on and the rest of the time, barring sensational emergencies, he may not care. No such heedlessness attends private business.

Civic lethargy results in part from lack of knowledge, which in turn is related to lack of means of effective communication touching public business. Knowledge breeds interest. The surest way of becoming interested in a subject is to learn something about it. Interest is an emotion of familiarity— familiarity with variations. Civic torpor, the voter's apathy, is due to a large extent to lack of information. The measure of possible civic interest has never yet been taken, for the inadequacy of suitably presented information on public business has precluded.

In this connection let a word be said for public libraries, with men and women of parts in charge. It is high time in the interests of democracy to balance the program of material development with thought materials. Immensely expensive road projects are carried out through regions in which a good public library is nowhere to be found. These same good roads might well be employed to carry books to and from splendid county libraries, especially in the agricultural states. And the librarians should be among the best paid and most carefully selected of public servants.

The deepest root of interest in affairs is that of self-preservation. It requires no urging for the individual to take an interest and see his duty when his welfare is directly and obviously at stake. In private affairs the connection between conditions and welfare is so close that there is no slackening of attention or laxness of circumspection, within the range of the individual intelligence.

Transferred to the wider arena of public business, in which the individual share of responsibility and his share of the returns from social effort are alike less certain and demonstrable, one experiences an immediate loss of motive. The citizen feels that one vote will make little difference, and stays away from the polls. He fails to attend a meeting held for the consideration of a public issue, feeling that his presence is a matter, numerically, of small importance. He stands for graft in city business because he does not see clearly that he is affected or to what extent he is affected. Individuality is lost at the door of public business.

The officeholder is likewise affected with loss of sense of personal significance. He works for the whole public, and a public that may be apathetic and unappreciative. Neither loyalty nor fear is strong as a motive. The sprawling anonymity of public service is a disintegrating influence. Both the citizen and official are under conditions that differ in essential aspects from the motivation of private affairs.

A correction of this psychological deficiency on the part of the voter might be attempted through the larger employment of citizens in consultative capacity, through committees or through the opening of the columns of civic publications for the expression of views and suggestions. Government remains a neglected abstraction as long as the citizen is left with few if any tangible connections with public functions that have their analogue in the colorful bargainings, adventure, initiative and self-assertion of the citizen in his private affairs. It is a well-known fact, that for any cooperative effort to prove successful and appeal to the largest number, there must be diffused participation. Each person must feel that he matters. Every "ladies' aid" knows this, and the woman who sits at the head of a serving table and "pours" is distinctly uplifted. Democratic government, to arouse the emotions that will give it the drive and vigilance needed for permanency and expansion, will have to see to it that a great many people have active participation even in small ways. So far as known, popular government has never made any attempt to base its rule upon the system of motives and interests that, as a matter of fact, do drive in private affairs. By way of illustration, a discovery made in the conduct of successful "parent and teachers' associations" may be cited. It is found that only by participation in meetings of a number of parents and children can these meetings be held up to an active interest. Management and program from the top down do not suffice. The active participation of parents, indeed their investiture with responsibility, and the appearance of their children in an active role, are found needful for producing the glow of interest and the devotion comparable to that characteristic of private activity.

Probably such participation in public affairs, a participation beginning on the side of genuine but humble activities, would do more to ensure the permanency of representative and democratic institutions than would any other measure. True, the enlarging of the proportion of the citizen's annual expenditure on the public side and its corresponding diminution in percentage on the private side, would tend to fix his attention on public affairs. If he were to spend less on private employment of a physician and more on the publicly employed physician or state-supported health service, the citizen, thus noting the shifted point of division in his expenditures, would be expected to take a sharper interest in public affairs. If, for sake of argument, John Doe were to spend fifteen hundred dollars for utilities bought privately for private use and another fifteen hundred dollars for utilities bought governmentally for private, but not exclusively private, use, as is the case with all community purchasing, he would follow his dollars as trade follows the flag, or the flag follows trade, as the case may be. Yet in the ultimate psychology of John Doe, the superior effectiveness of motives closely corresponding to those in the private life of wont and custom is unquestionable.

As the case now stands, with but a minor part of expenditure devoted to joint or community utilities, there is small reason to be surprised at the relatively slight amount of citizen interest in public affairs. The citizen does not fully awake to the iniquity of the grafting contractor and the embezzling official. In a city of fifty thousand people, the misuse and waste of a million dollars means only twenty dollars per capita, which is perhaps the price of a ton of coal. This is a small amount in the annual family expenditure, hence a city may be "corrupt and contented." The neighbor's cow in John Doe's sweet-corn patch produces a psychological disturbance vastly more profound. If John Doe were to pursue peccant officials with the same zeal with which he seeks reparation for direct but minor injury, honesty in office would not only be the best policy but the only policy.

Let us say that citizen John Doe spends three thousand dollars a year in living expenses. Of this he spends in taxes a hundred dollars. Twenty-nine hundred dollars go thus in buying things individually and a hundred dollars go in joint purchase of utilities with other citizens. The ratio is 29 to 1. His interest is accordingly about twenty-nine times as great in private affairs as in public. Moreover, he can see and handle the things he gets for the twenty-nine hundred dollars, while the money spent in taxes secures utilities of rather intangible and non-identifiable character. He may buy sanitation with some of the tax money, but who can get enthusiastic about an immunity? He may be thoroughly convinced that what he spends in public purchase is well spent, but he is deprived of the satisfaction of personally planning the purchase and carrying out the transaction and taking home the goods. The intangibility of public purchasing deprives the time-honored art of buying of its dramatic, speculative and concrete elements. Just as the child feels defrauded of an experience when his parents do all the buying and handle the money, so the average man, while assenting to community buying as a necessary practice, nevertheless actually takes more pleasure in buying five dollars' worth of fishing tackle than in joint purchase with a mass of fellow-citizens of a municipal structure costing four million dollars.

Related to the citizen's unimaginative reaction to public expenditure, which is far and away the most economical type of expenditure for net utility, is his singularly atavistic tax psychology. Say "taxes," and the average citizen tends to look downcast. If there is anything a man, economically speaking, ought to be cheerful over it is economical buying. But does the citizen feel happy over well-spent taxes— over the tax bill? Added to reasons given above touching the psychology of public affairs, there is in the case of taxes— public taxes— the weird phobia that derives from the tea in Boston harbor. There was a time when taxation was identified with tyranny, as in the murderous and unrequited taxing by church and state in France in the heyday of monarchical humbug. When officialdom consisted of a supercargo of licentious tax-eaters, the peasant was justified in gritting his teeth. But now? Don't we want to pay for anything? Should one not rather pay a hundred dollars to the school district than pay a thousand for private tutors? Yet the tax bill throws us into berserker mood. Observe, too, the refined consideration of allowing the other fellow to report more fully his holdings, and the modesty of dodging where possible.

How far the tax emotions are askew may be judged by noting how indifferent the individual is to private taxes— by which is meant the levy of monopoly or profiteering. In a western state an enigmatical rise in the price of coal in one year represented an increase of outlay equaling a sum which would have raised the pay of every schoolteacher in that state by several hundred dollars. Was there outcry? As would have been the case if the same sum had been added to the tax bills? Possibly no government could survive like increase in the immediate compensation of its employees. But the added burden in privately contracted debts is followed by no angry reaching for the pillars of the temple. Public expenditure is the first point of attack when the citizen would protect his income.

The reforming of mind on taxation is one of the heavy problems of democratic government in a time when there is a narrowing boundary between anarchy, on the one hand, and intelligent socialization on the other. Can rational attitude and suitable emotion be engendered? When one recalls the objects to which emotion has devotedly attached itself in the years of history, is it too much to hope that with time may come a moral and intellectual readjustment with regard to public effort, public expenditure, community utilities and the economy of making the same amount of money go a longer way? The human mind has immense possibilities of education in wrong directions; why not in the right?

The remaking of mind on the subject of taxation would, however, be a more difficult undertaking than the utilizing of existing attitudes. Observing the comparatively slight objection popularly made to the exaction of profits, one might be inclined to favor raising the immense sums of public expenditure by the profit-taking of public business. Sums that now appear as dividends or profits of privately owned enterprises, especially those like mines and railroads, might thus become available in lieu of direct taxes. The revenue aspect of the tariff illustrates a comparatively painless method of raising public funds. The taxing of excess profits is still another illustration of the slight resistance offered by the consumer to paying taxes indirectly. To subrogate profit-taking public business to monopolistic private business would possibly prove the line of least resistance in the development of taxation policy for the raising of the large sums which assuredly must be raised for public uses.

A needed attitude toward public expenditure may be stimulated by ocular evidence in the form of bargain demonstration, of which an example may be cited. In western states is known the rodent exterminator. Gophers and prairie dogs invade grain fields and wallow and destroy. They eat and destroy millions of bushels of grain. Hence the rodent exterminator. With baits and poisons and knowledge of rodent psychology, the rodent man goes on his way, being paid out of the public taxes. Mathematics being an abstract science, it has been found that statistics have no particular hold on the mind of the member of the board of county commissioners. But the rodents' bodies heaped up in the tonneau of a motor car convince. For giving the eye of faith an eyeful, it has been found by rodent exterminators that nothing does so well as heaping up the bodies of the dead rodents in a car and running such car into the very presence of the county chairman and his board and pointing to the dead gophers and prairie dogs and saying: "Lo, here!" No mental picture of the slaughtered rodents has the persuasive power exercised by the actual physical carcasses, slithering and quaking with motion and drawing the vigilant fly when the engine stops and the crowd gathers. Death is impressive, especially with no process of memory or of imagination intervening. By method the rodent exterminator draws tax warrants in the blood of the slain and evokes his own pay check. He satisfies the taxpayer.

No matter whether one justly prides himself upon the clearness of his images and the definition of his principles or not, he is more firmly convinced and is refreshed in resolution by demonstration. People will not be won to their own welfare unless they see signs. One of the larger activities in popular government must be that of adequate demonstration. Not that every service can be photographed, but at least demonstration can be carried far enough to give the citizen solid ground on which to stand while forming his mind intelligently toward social program and duties.

The citizen's psychology has been explored and exploited by the politician to a nicety; it has been studied minutely. There are practical psychologists at the head in every political campaign. Some of the keenest minds in the country are engaged in political psychology as a means of carrying elections and managing campaigns. Such psychology is of a designing kind in the main, employed not rarely for voting the voters and working the workers. It has no standing with true benevolence and higher statesmanship; it smacks of the smartness of the adroit horse trader with a ringboned nag whose defects he would camouflage; it is not sincere with the fine impersonality of Abraham Lincoln and Thomas Jefferson; its symbol is the checked vest Underrate not its technic and achievements. By it the average voter is known better by others than he knows himself.

But of civic psychology in the constructive and idealistic sense how little we know. The citizen has not been analyzed so much with a view to a better state and society. We want not such study of the voter as will perpetuate his deficiencies, but rather enlarge his constructive possibilities and make him a smoothly functioning intelligent unit in the greatest adventure of mankind— self-government. From the known ground of individual and private-life psychology it should be possible to conduct motive and will, habit and conviction, over to skillful and happy cooperation.

In private life the individual finds satisfaction in playing a solo part. Any success that he may thus achieve is unmistakably his own. A fine farm, a handsome residence, a feat of professional performance, a notable business move— all these attach directly to his name. But in many of his relations to the common weal there is no such publicity of success, no such undisguised personality. The employee of the public, serving with others in anonymous cooperation, or the voting citizen, contributing his ballot with thousands or millions of others, has little of the thrill of special attention. To be sure, the prominent public official suffers less from lack of favorable comment and admiration. Indeed he may focus upon himself the glory that logically attaches to helpers and subordinates.

There is compensation for the private in the ranks in the thought that he is one of a distinguished group of workers. But pride in group achievement does not quite fulfill the ambitions of the individual to be known and admired for his efforts. In the motivating of public service, there might well be distinct provisions for appeasing the appetite for individual mention. Indeed, in organization for destruction—war —this principle is recognized by medals and mentions. But the same idea has yet to be recognized suitably for the constructive service rendered by otherwise anonymous men employed by the public for the public. It is all too common a practice in the press and elsewhere to identify a group by the name of its chief, ignoring the thousand and one individuals who severally thirst for having their existence recognized.

The motivation of the prominent official is certain. Men are not wanting to take high office at a sacrifice of income and repose. The reward here is favor in men's eyes. Fame is not only the last infirmity of noble minds but also the first; high office in peace and war attracts irresistibly. It is the motivation of the large number whose services are not particularized and who are usually only casually mentioned by class that presents a critical problem for popular government. To judge by the ordinary textbook in history the Civil War was fought as a series of duels between a handful of stubborn northern generals and a small handful of brilliant southerners. Canals and great public works are also constructed by Herculean individuals practically singlehanded.

Some may argue that the fitness or unfitness of the potential voter is measured by the extent to which he takes part in voting. The voter who is so uninformed and apathetic as not to heed election days may be regarded as thus proving that society loses nothing by his absence from the polls. Such interpretation may have a show of correctness, but it can scarcely be thought a good omen for democratic government when there is indifference to the ballot. It would be a more favorable condition if every person, man and woman, entitled to vote, were to become so conscious of the franchise as to make neglect impossible.

In this connection the possibility of finding a stimulus in publicity suggests itself. Suppose every precinct established a public roll of eligible voters, and that at the close of election day every name were crossed off except those of persons failing to vote. It is quite likely that such bad eminence of the neglectful would speedily bring out the laggards. Once thus brought to the habit of voting, there would very likely ensue a pronounced growth of intelligent interest in elections on the part of those who have lacked vision. And, on the part of educated but cynical citizens, there would be a tendency to attack those obstacles and perversions which have too often made the cultivated wash their hands of politics.

Assurance that public business can be motivated, both on the part of the voter and on that of the public employee, is afforded by the fact that big business is a reality with no convincing signs of early collapse. In big business are the phenomena of subordination, anonymity, diffused participation, remoteness of final output and intangibility of individual contribution. Yet big business thrives. Its problems are not so difficult as those of big public business. Its methods are unquestionably more psychological, especially in the past few years. Bonuses, promotions, personal mention, pensions, emulation, the personal touch, welfare, "mothering," and what not are brought into play to steady the bees as they collect the honey. These methods are an innovation in business, it is true, and obtain most in enterprises that are most advanced and freest from the older industrial traditions. But they serve as points of brilliant contrast to conditions in public service. Not until the welfare of the employee is as much esteemed in public as in private business will the psychological foundations of democracy be made secure. After all, no government that does not place the happiness of the individual above that of a mythical state consisting of no individuals in particular, deserves to prosper or to be served with enthusiasm. The wheels of government might well stop; they have no business not to stop, until, say, the future of a worn-out worker in a department of public service is assured. Such ideas as that a faithful public employee may be turned out summarily, or that one must expect to sacrifice if he is to work for others through the mechanism of state cooperation, naturally result in inferior quality in public institutions.

The control of the voter over government implies to a degree the control of the layman over the professional, the control of the unskilled over the skilled. Government increasingly tends toward specialization and expertness. The expansion of political government over the industrial and economic field carries further the principle of division of labor and technical efficiency. Apart from major policies it is difficult for the voter to instruct governmental functionaries. Recognizing the point to which we have arrived, some would say let experts govern and let there be a short and infrequent ballot.

The relation of the voter to the expert in functions of government is like that of layman to the specialist privately employed. Without taking the case out of the physician's hands, the patient exercises authority. He does so at a risk, it is true. The relations of the architect to his employer are readily established with due regard to expert knowledge and directive preferences. The citizen, like the layman employing a professional, has the advantage of a general view. The architect, the landscape engineer, the bacteriologist, the insurance man and the nasal specialist are all specialized to purpose rather than for balance. The voter is a kind of specialist in judging how things look to a layman. The human race would not be the same again if no longer might one venture an opinion rather beyond his knowledge.

The dominating aim of public business is to secure more widely diffused benefits than are hoped for under the restricted and incidental philanthropy of private enterprise. Easier access to necessities and utilities is sought through socialized agencies. This aim can be realized only by skillful employment of human factors. The success of public enterprise cannot be assured in defiance of the nature of the individual whose abilities must be enlisted. An atmosphere of freedom, rewards for high ability, quick returns for daring and resourcefulness, prizes to initiative and skill— all these considerations must be heeded in the interests of successful group enterprise; at any rate these must be heeded as much as in private enterprises. It is not to be overlooked that private enterprise has evidently come far short of perfection; it has failed to heed the larger relationships— has been local, provincial, selfish and nonsocial in spirit; its shortcomings have given rise to the powerful tendency toward the extension of governmental function as a possibly superior means of welfare.

PART II

THE SOCIAL MIND AT CLOSER RANGE

CHAPTER IX
INSTINCTIVE TENDENCY AS AFFECTING SOCIAL CONDITIONS

Civilization through planning is yet to be developed; vision and coördinated effort for social well-being are less in evidence than are muddling through in response to instinctive tendency. The planning for careers on the part of individuals is not paralleled by similar foresight on the part of social and governmental management. Trial and error methods and reliance upon naive predilection play a larger part in social procedure than in well-ordered private lives. Due to the neglect of training for citizenship, thinking socially is not so far advanced as thinking professionally and commercially. Courts for settling private differences appeared long before attempts at international organization, and the duel passed long before the idea of salving national honor rationally made its appearance. Nations and social groups rely on special providence, turns of luck, and cure without a doctor, much more than does the citizen in his private affairs.

The ways of meeting problems may be arranged in serial order. The lowest form of response is that of random, and profuse and blindly instinctive conduct. Thus, a rat in a cage will rush madly about, bumping against all parts of the cage indiscriminately, with some chance of escape through striking a loose wire, calculation playing no part.

To invoke the aid of memory represents a higher type of effort for escaping dangers and securing benefits. Thus, to find solution through recall of what oneself or others have done before in similar situations is a distinct advance over the method of frenzy and exhaustion.

But the highest kind of procedure is to analyze the

problem, conceive of alternatives, test the alternatives mentally and select the most auspicious. The reasoning method is highly economical and more satisfactory in the face of novel difficulties. Not that this method is invariably used apart from the lower methods, for the more primitive responses contribute something to the composite process. When draymen attempt to carry a couch through a narrow passageway all of these methods are liable to be represented. One helper may try the rat psychology of main strength and chance success; another may recall an experience with a similarly refractory piece of furniture; while another of the trio analyzes the stairway and visualizes a safe exit. The prosperity of the couch and stairway lies here with the visualizer.

The greatest of social needs is that for the visionary, the thinker, the idealist. He may consider alternatives that are not practicable; but the function of holding up possibilities of social program is of vital importance. And yet how society, weltering in instinct, shuns the innovator and the theorist The entomologist is a "bugologist," the anatomist and physician a "sawbones," the scholar a "bookworm," the sociologist a "red."

Yet society is in more danger from excessive expression of instinct than from philosophies. A far greater rationalization is necessary to insure social stability and develop organization and system. The function of speculation and theorizing, of proposing remedies and posing queries, of challenging tradition and reviewing customs, is an invaluable one. It is the demonstrated means of advancement in industrial and scientific fields, and is no less fitting and prolific in social program. Social scepticism and active research represent the higher form of intelligence as contrasted with instinct with its ineffectual twitchings of remedy or its frantic and costly tragedies of war and revolution. Without vision the people perish. The age of good politics and happy economics must be an age of reason, with the Merlins left isolated with their curses. The harrying of the intellectual represents disregard and waste of social resources to which proud recognition should be given. With the ban on free and accusatory intelligence, with dogma protected by officers and mobs, society risks progressive deterioration. Evil forces in modern society are those that stand against incisive and untrammeled political and economic utterance; they represent the viewpoint of the heresy hunters and hounders of scientists in the centuries when intellectual and religious life was at low ebb. That the dogging of the intellectual appeals to classes of lowest culture level makes the business uniquely impertinent. Until learning, in all fields, and the exercise of the rational faculties are exalted as social righteousness, we invite the fate that awaits vital ignorance.

Reliance upon intellectual means and forces rather than upon the impulsions of mere instinct suggests itself as eminently desirable for the adjustment of industrial problems. Industrial war reveals at every point the dominance of an unevolved system of ideas and motivation.

The strike is a notable example of an instinctive rather than a rational attempt to correct evils. In strategy for immediate results and minor ameliorations, the strike perhaps has occasional value. But as a social method it corresponds to the tactics of a rat seeking its escape violently from a trap the nature of which is not perceived. The petty revolution of the trade strike, the larger revolution of the general strike, and the major revolution of the social overthrow, besides leaving matters much as they were before, give unwholesome persistence to inept method. They signify an incapacity or lassitude in the exercise of the rational powers, which are preëminently the powers upon which ordered welfare must rely. Strikes and wars are not constructive; they cannot be lastingly constructive because they are expedients of force in place of justice. True, the technic of war and revolution and strikes may be rationalized, but the rationalizing falls short of social synthesis; these phenomena are the phenomena of primitive reaction, and there is no health in them. One tenth of the money lost to wages in strikes of the past twenty-five years would have provided the workers with culture agencies out of which might have come a rational procedure commending itself generally. The principal disadvantage of the workers is ignorance, and strikes do little to obviate this. Lasting benefits can come only with enlightenment and specific understanding. Happily labor colleges are appearing, and the employment of statisticians and advisers promises the transfer of labor problems to the arena of scientific and rational adjustment. It would doubtless, in the long run, be a blessing to labor if strikes were banned. Modern nations have hit upon the ballot as a means of securing general welfare and of liquidating the just grievances of groups. It is for labor to qualify for intelligent use of this same instrument. The instinctive and juvenile disposition to smash things and to trust in the good luck of spontaneous readjustment is distinctly out of place in a time calling for calculation. The ideal of labor should be that of rational rather than essentially instinctive method.

     Equipped with natural tendencies which took shape under the simpler conditions of precivilization, mankind ever tends to recapitulate its past when faced by newer conditions. Just as a dog may try to bury a bone on a hardwood floor or attempt to hide its milk-dish by pawing dirt into it— recapitulating primitive canine history under inappropriate circumstances— so all of us, reeking with the primitive, are prone to inconvenient atavisms in the new circumstances of the world. An example is tribal psychology in politics, reminiscent of the effectual unification of the primitive group.

Though the major parties in England and the United States are indistinguishable in principle and practice, yet the thrall of party names and of party leaders is potent. Allegiance is given willingly, nay, enthusiastically, to candidates and as forcefully withheld from other candidates not because of significant differences, but from influence of tribal deities, totem poles, war cries, paint and feathers. The tribe itself, apart from leaders and major beneficiaries, does not well perceive that unity in diversity which so often prevails beneath insignia. The true clansman goes with the plaid. The sense of familiarity of symbols satisfies. What the verities are does not always matter. It was only yesterday that the independent voter made his appearance under the derisive epithet of "Mugwump." It was nothing short of scandalous when citizens charily ventured to follow principles rather than the time-honored chieftain. The office-seeker, however, was less victimized by party. Party fealty to him oftentimes meant something else; it was the promise of things to come.

Through unwarranted survival of tribalism, the citizen is blinded and civically nonconstructive. The decline of instinctive partisanship is therefore auspicious, for the voter thus becomes mobile and free to judge for himself. Attention turns to measures and mere chieftainship diminishes in prestige. The sublimation of personal loyalty appears in devotion to causes and principles, and the utilizing of leaders or parties without being submerged in these. Organizations become convenient instrumentalities, without fixedness of individual within party regardless of realities of principle and character. The tendency for citizens to migrate from one party to another needs only to become associated with cause to be truly promising. Migration for a change of luck is not fully satisfying. Rational migration will doubtless increase, but migration from any motive is better than irrevocable status.

Arrest of development on the plane of clansmanship means indifference to the larger group and too exclusive attachment to party, sect, county (as in the South), college, city, or state. The modern community is as wide as humanity, and the program of civilization involves the passing away of the provincial point of view. The emotional states propagated by small organizations may oppose consciousness of the wide community. Secret societies, churches, and social sets that confirm in any way their memberships in emotional provincialisms thus render a social disservice. A positive culture of catholicity is implied by the closer relations of commerce and world communication. The ideal of social oneness, which the family, the village and the sect and party have stressed within narrow limits, can be made to cover this minor planet, whose circumference has been registered on the milometers of millions of automobiles.

There is a possibility that nationalistic patriotism may remain an emotional fact long after the reality supporting it becomes a skeleton. National self-sufficiency has largely passed away. What nation is not now virtually a state in an internation? Foreign wealth may finance the railroad on which one rides; capital is internationalized; foreign-owned capital is rooted wherever one turns— in farm loans, public utility plants, railroads, packing houses, insurance businesses. Foreign elements of population swarm about us. No conquered country could be inundated by aliens more completely than has happened in time of peace. Masses of people have gone from state to state in the internation in time of peace.

Such mobility of world population will continue. Legislation in recognition of different standards of living and for birth control may affect amount, but not, in the long run, the fact of migration. The laws of mating, which little heed nationality, are pitted against inelastic nationalism. We shall have to adjust our minds to the present facts of internationalism and make ready for world legislation and federation. Our emotional and intellectual preparation for community life on the planet is backward.

Whereas the sense of provincialism was an outgrowth from tribal and geographical restrictions, the spirit of adventuring operated to give primitive man a certain variety of experience. Early man led a life of adventure, ranging for food along the river beds and by the sea, where he was constantly meeting the unexpected. The stamp of vicissitude is in our nervous systems, and when life does not present us with sufficient excitement we go in search of it. Necessity, in terms of strange beasts, peering enemies and food shortage, gave a turn to consciousness in primitive life which cannot be satisfied in man to-day without resort to occasional adventure. Penned in by the apartment house and modern conveniences, man to-day takes his adventuring symbolically and by proxy to a large extent. He fights by reading of pugilistic encounters, swims by mentally following Leander across the Hellespont, skulks through the spooky darkness of night with the hero of a detective story, finds thrills in the "movies," and invests his money in wildcat stocks.

Indeed the expression of the instinct of adventure through speculation and investment is an outstanding fact and socially a significant fact. It is not too much to claim that the character of industrial and economic life is intimately related to the adventure instinct, and that proposed social reform which does not adequately recognize this fact is doomed to miscarry. It might seem that the presence of the wage system is evidence that the adventure instinct has become atrophied. Fixedness of income by wages does not appeal to the venturesome, it is true. The wagering impulse, which is a form of the instinct of adventure, is a motive which plays an important rôle in so-called independent businesses, like farming and the retail store.

The wage-earner, however, is not without recourse.

He may adventure with his savings, and it is a commonplace of observation that one may have as much fun with a venturesome 25-cent piece as with sizable sums. The strangely placid and much bedamned bourgeoisie, the immovable obstacle to reform by revolution, obtain their adventure by investment, rather than attempt it by the more spectacular methods of the expropriated. Society is above all else a psychological organism, true to the original instincts shaped and supported in primitive, natural conditions. The sense of adventure is not lacking in the class of small owners; it insists on finding satisfaction. The adventure may appear illusory, but as long as the illusion holds— it holds.

The small-business man and the farmer and the person of the middle class who has some capital, however small, invested in business or in stocks is an adventurer. He hopes, often against reasonable hope, for wealth. There is excitement in pursuit. The lucky turn of stocks, the "bumper" crop, the imagined run of brisk sales— these constitute a satisfying program of economic adventure. Capitalism can never be shaken as long as bonds and securities are widely held by the middle and lower economic classes. The Wall Street magnate is not more emotionally compromised by the spirit of speculation— not more sentimentally attached to economic individualism— than is the clerk who buys a share of stock at 35 and watches the quotations to follow its ascent above par. The dividends on widely held shares of the profiteering joint-stock companies of ancient Rome served as hush money to the voters while the orgy of exploitation was undermining the empire.[1]

The instinct of adventure, expressed as a wagering interest in employment of means, not only determines the character of the concepts and terms of business, but exposes

---

[1] Abbott, *The Common People of Ancient Rome.* Chapter on Corporations.

the people to enormously costly and consequential raids upon small capitals, with no slight results toward abnormal and society-wrecking centralization of wealth. The readiness of the average man of small means to take a chance in investment, to believe in the "pot of gold at the foot of the rainbow," to send out his savings on perilous adventure, especially to fall under the enchantment of distance when investing, is the strong foundation of the "gold-brick" industry. The earning of money is but a part of the process of securing individual and social welfare. The spirit and conditions of investment are fully as important

The petty investor who happens to be humbugged and plucked through the bait of hope of sudden wealth not only loses economically— in the aggregate such losses are of critical magnitude— but he also exemplifies and perpetuates a functioning of an instinct of singular weakness and ill omen. "Blue sky" laws recognize, if they do not cure, the malady. Social cohesion is hardly possible to economic ends when there is individual confidence in miraculous salvation and special providences of speculation. The wagering elements of the farmer's occupation have kept him full of faith, with the result that cooperation gains little foothold in the farming class. Among millions of people faith in a transforming luck and adventure makes the individual as resistant to social and economic amalgamation as a particle of zero snow is unsuited to form part of a snowball. Consciousness of a common cause and of a common lot is excluded by the disposition to bet on one's own luck. Just as monarchy is upheld by a group, each of whom counts on special favors, so top-heavy plutocracy is upheld by the non-cooperation of the many who individually hope for great rewards, apart from the calculable returns of patient labor. It is even an axiom among promoters of shady speculative ventures that every man is willing to be victimized at least once. Scars of purse, like wounds of battle, are presumptive evidence of valor.

The psychology of the "gold brick" mind is related to adventure, but it goes beyond that. It has been a fallacy of thought in America to assume that everybody is not only, by the Declaration of Independence asserted to be created equal, but that in individual consciousness everybody feels equal. Nothing could be further from the truth than the feeling of equality. The gregariousness which marks man as well as animals of lower organization implies a readiness to follow leaders and to submerge one's own personality. Within limits, abuse of authority is expected and admired. Little resentment attaches to high-handed treatment by superior individuals. Persons having the attributes of leadership are strangely indulged by the multitude. A liar and swindler who is smooth, who shows pedigree, may be voted charming rather than otherwise. The percentage of people who inherit a full code of self-respect or arrive at it by experience and reflection is small indeed. There are great blocks of people in democracies as well as in monarchies whose outstanding characteristic is embryonic self-respect and primitive servility. Mobility of modern societies has displaced the more abject prostrations, but individual assertion is habitually deflated in an endless number of cases— a fact that shows in the unreflective adoption of fashions, editorial views, propagandas, and in mute long-suffering. Millions of people have regarded a living wage as an ideal for themselves, without going so far as to claim an economically safe old age. They have been contented with little— abject. The strength of the king has lain in the craving of the common man to have a foot on his neck.

Now it is just as much to the advantage of the classes as to the masses to have a widely diffused self-respect. Industry needs the stimulus which comes from a market insistent upon plentiful and excellent production. No manufacturer likes to turn out rubbish, and no dealer likes to sell it over the counter or from his warehouses. The more wants the people develop and the more exacting and refined their demands, the higher are the possibilities of trade and wealth production. Civilization implies an increase and refinement of wants. The man who is contented with little and that of poor quality is the original enemy of industry. The worker who is satisfied with a living wage is not so good a citizen, nor in the long run so good an employee, as one who wants a saving wage. The ultimate consuming power, and therefore market demand, is increased by the larger assertion of economic interest. If one manufacturer employed workers who insisted upon a saving wage while his competitor was able to secure employees satisfied with a living wage, the former proprietor would be at a disadvantage. But if workers claimed a saving wage the net results would include larger support for taxation, less expense for charity, less sickness, and national economy.

Production is in its infancy; the recession of servile attitude is a prerequisite for its highest development A needed stimulus is withheld if the public puts up with literature of a kind that makes the novel writer blush, accepts without complaint less than the best that art can supply, or eats poor food without felt humiliation. The cult of lowly cheerfulness and sunbeam compliance does what it can to start society on the downward path. The ability of the meek and lowly to do harm incidentally is perhaps equaled by that of no other class.

CHAPTER X
CONSTRUCTIVE EXPRESSION OF MOTIVES

THE deep-seated tendencies with which we are born, and which insistently demand outlet, are capable of finding expression in a variety of forms. The specialization of instinct in man is not pronounced. Even children, in whom instinct is least overlaid with conventional habit, show slight tendency to react with the uncanny perfection of inherited movement exhibited by chickens, puppies, kittens and birds. Human instincts function as large patterns of tendency, the ultimate character of which is effectually established by training, example, suggestion, and culture. Man has been said to have more instincts than any other animal. But his instincts are the most faded, the most plastic, the most transformed.

The nervous and bodily mechanism seeks activity, for there is a reservoir of energy which thrusts the child forward into contacts and experimentation with resistless power. The little world of home is explored on its physical side. Objects are tested by the organs of sensation. Later the muscular endowment seeks gratification in the doing of things. There is ceaseless activity, at first of ill-coordinated character and vague purpose, but increasingly purposeful and skilled.

This original tendency to physical activity ultimately is harnessed to vocations and subjected to repression and direction. The forms of the individual's physical expression, his motor and bodily repertory, come to assume a definite set. Oftentimes this ultimate range of physical expression is inadequate in the light of personal and social possibilities.

The happy abandon of the child's expression of physical interests is rarely equaled in the adult stage. It is unquestionable that modern life loses immeasurably through the hardening of the physical activities to gainful pursuits and the muscular reticence of leisure. Full, free physical existence, which is the very mandate of the instinct of physical activity, encounters social barriers, from the bondage of conventional clothing to abstention from the many diverting things that a person might do if he could forget his dignity. There is much yet to be achieved in revising the list of what a grown person may do without shocking the neighbors. Neither the laborer, who becomes a veritable cart horse for mechanical fixation of movements and immobility of muscle groups, nor the person who "enjoys" a life in ruts of respectable restraint can be cited as an example of the ideal physical being.

In a large number of cases the individual's life is unbalanced as between physical and mental expression, and in many cases boredom, irritability, a sense of futility, mental stagnation, or vicious tendencies spring directly out of physical restraint and lack of motor program. The ultimate social effects of a better distribution and a better selection of ways of employing the physical powers would be transforming. This wider use of the human physical equipment could be effected through revision and extension of vocational opportunities, and especially through universal provision for avocations having stimulating physical factors. It is a fact quite uncomplimentary to civilization that there are so many who so often do not know what to do with themselves so many who do not know how much more varied their physical experiences might become. Modern life is a pent-up life. It presents plenty of examples of excessive physical strain but fewer or a rationalized physical program, rich, varied and joyfully responding to the range of natural opportunities.

Mentally there are likewise many who do not know what to do with themselves. The original tendency to mental activity is not sufficiently specific to guarantee intellectual prosperity in the adult. Direction, encouragement, reward, and freedom are essential. With all the culture materials that the world has accumulated, there is yet lack of available culture materials for millions of people. What to read, what to study, how to investigate— these are matters that cannot well be left to chance. The best natural mind is almost helpless under privations of culture. The supplying of significant culture materials for all is an important function in society. There are great gaps of illiteracy and still greater gaps of not knowing what to read when literate. A commercial pandering and timid educational effort— unambitious and time-serving rather than exultingly dominant educational effort— are ingloriously acquiesced in. Every person is potentially an intellectual in the literal and undisputed sense of the word. Trivial, misguided, and blind-alley uses of mind are not inevitable. The factor of intelligence is slowly, too slowly, approximating its proper standing as an ideal and a practical utility.

The problem of securing fuller and finer social expression of the impulses to physical and mental activity is one that may be attacked as a problem of faulty distribution of wealth. But, to judge by the effects of wealth upon the individual under conditions as they now exist, the rationalizing of distribution would not necessarily carry with it a knowledge of the best use of life. How to live is a problem that has yet to be solved and resolved. It is a question that has been answered with dogma and clouded with sentimentalism. It can scarcely be maintained that satisfactory progress has been made in laying out the procedure for the best possible life. Millions of people, doubtless, learn late in life things that would have increased their happiness greatly, if known long before. In a sense, all knowledge and science are a basis for the best life. But a more conscious attempt to find the best employments of physical and mental energies would not be incompatible in an age which attempts to find the best in minor and relative things. For want of another word the term *eubiology* may be proposed to signify the art that would give society less the aspect of the pursuit of happiness than of its attainment.

For the achievement of the best possible life, resources are available of which, possibly, too little use is made. The lives of men and women of experience abound in materials of much significance. These materials are often less accessible for popular guidance than is desirable. It is doubtful if any information imparted to the young through the usual courses of study could compare favorably with the instruction that might be gleaned from their elders of widest and best experience. The failure to draw upon such sources more fully reveals inadequacy of method rather than challenges the value of the kind of knowledge mentioned. The net result of failure to utilize more fully the riches of ripe experience is to retard the development of the young and contribute to social confusion.

The annexation of others' experience through processes of learning implies special activities of the instinct of curiosity. Scientist, economic student, social interpreter, historian, and business analyst represent the turn that instinctive curiosity may take. Curiosity, which serves as feelers of the mind, has had a checkered career as a reputable instinct. Instead of being hopefully stimulated curiosity has, not infrequently, come in for family spankings and social disapproval. Lacking proper outlet and ventilation, curiosity, the itch for knowledge, may turn to the local and the trivial.

Such progress as has not been accidental has preceded from curiosity, the inquisitive turn of mind lifted to the higher levels of consciousness. Hence it is unfortunate when curiosity is dampened, as dampened it may be by parental taboo and social purblindness. The arrest of this tendency on the plane of the poolroom and the sewing club is a social misfortune. Cultural direction of curiosity, its fostering for developments in industry, in the professions and in social achievements, has great possibilities.

Emphasis upon the amassing of information rather than upon procedure has the effect of dulling the searching instinct. The feeling that everything has been found out that can be found out, that all that is left to do is to learn what some one else has discovered, is an unpromising state of mind. The physician does not usually ask how much the patient has in his stomach but what his appetite is. The telling fact about the supposedly educated person is not his erudition, but his alertness. The number and muscularity of the questions one proliferates, their relevancy and incisiveness, is a better indication of a going mind than the memory mass of facts. Even in the professions of expert service where knowledge counts critically, it is reassuring to encounter the type of intelligence that forever plays over information, is forever scanning and curious. One cannot know what facts mean without knowing facts, but one may know facts and not know what they mean. It would be a fair test, if an unconventional one, for schools to graduate only upon the showing of evidence that the candidate has a mind full of inquiry, of problems he might hope to solve, of places he would like to visit, of books he looks forward to reading, of impressions he would like to verify, of propositions he would like to test, of personages he would like to interview; who would, in short, continue to learn.

The instinct of curiosity is genetically interwoven with the activities by which early man obtained his living. The hunting and fishing and finding stage preceded agriculture. The games of children are notably a pantomime of hunting. There is a wild primitive joy in running down game symbolically. Finding hidden articles and playing tag as well as the overt chase of small animals reveal the inheritance of the impulse that lies anciently back of the bow and arrow, the weapons of bronze and stone, and the stealthy stalking of game. Primitive man, if not eating regularly three times a day, ate no doubt a quantitative equivalent, and if he missed his aim he went hungry. Hunting and dietary were as right and left hands.

Instincts are known not only by their unabashed appearance in the simple minds of children but as well in the preferred diversions of the grown-ups. Hunting and fishing make their universal appeal. These pursuits indeed simulate "pure" science and the fine arts in putative aloofness from the money interest. For since about 1850 it is likely that every pound of fish taken in the lesser bodies of water by the angler has cost far more than it was worth, financially speaking— perhaps on the average twenty-five dollars a pound. For economic returns amateur fishing and hunting have long since passed over to pursuits not vitiated by commercialism. They testify to the downright delight of giving the cave man his innings. Moreover, when there is good luck, does the angler stop casting or the sportsman cease firing? Not so. He then fishes and hunts for the whole tribe— only the game laws stop him, and then not if he can help it. A peculiarity of instinct is, that it never knows when to quit— presenting alike the danger of overdoing, and the zest that animates persistent activity.

Modern conditions deny primitive form of expression to the hunting instinct, which more and more has diminished to recreation and stimulating outings. But the original tendency persists and finds sublimated expression in many fields, in efforts to secure employment and maintenance. It is indeed one of the principal motivations that modern life has derived from the original nature of man. We use the vocabulary of hunting and fishing. We "hunt" for lost articles and "fish" for compliments. A man "hunts" a job. People make "killing" remarks.

The hunting interest has motivated biological work and studies in natural history. Darwin hunted until he became shocked at the sight of a bird he had wounded, and thereafter refrained from gun hunting. His *Voyage of the*

Beagle is, however, a beautiful example of scientific hunting. The intentness, circumspection, perseverance and interest in wild nature that are identified with primitive hunting, are outstanding traits of his researches. Theodore Roosevelt united the original hunting interest with its sublimated expression in natural history, the latter dominating; he explained his willingness to shoot to kill on the ground that wild animals usually meet death by violence anyhow. The study of birds and their hunting with the camera take the place of destructive hunting, and there is the bag of names and particulars in place of actual trophies of capture.

There is no end to the supplementary and symbolical forms of expression of the hunting tendency. Conceived in terms of search and hunt, all sorts of social objectives make appeal. Some of the early Judean fishermen became fishers of men and made their nets thereafter of words and example. The physician may resent a suggestion as to the cause of the patient's complaint, preferring rather to hunt for it himself; besides, his marksmanship is not to be impugned. Let the garageman find out the trouble himself; he likes to hunt. Ask a man to do a particular thing and he may feel tired; ask him to help with his superior hunting ability and he will leave his dinner.

The hunting interest, in its varied phases of search, pursuit, outwitting, and capture, may be used to social ends in problems of poverty, under-consumption, unemployment and disease. Perhaps the money hunt takes precedence to-day; it need not be so indefinitely. It does not dominate over this interest in the case of the explorer and the inventor. To hunt constructively for the common good fulfills the terms of the chase similarly with the hunt merely for the acquisition of personal fortune.

The fighting tendency, the disposition to repel dangers by force, is a reaction called forth by the challenge of harm from any source. Under primitive conditions harm came often with animals and strangers, hence fighting was with weapons and in a physical setting. With civilization the dangers that beset are less and less immediately physical ones, and more and more of a kind involving for defense a mobilization of intelligence and the use of the intangible forces of argument and ideas.

Conflict is transferred to the arena of the press, the platform, and the polls. The efficient fighter is one who prevails with the weapons with which issues are ultimately settled, and issues are not settled by force— physical force applied to a thought relation is like the use of a hammer in place of a telescope. Modern heroes of combat are found in the political arena and in civic enterprise, and are engaged in overcoming prejudice and championing reforms. Combats are waged about propositions that have a physical reference, as waterways, railroads, foreign-made goods, sites of public buildings and the like, but the instrumentalities of combat are mental and without physical body. They are ideas, used for persuasion, surprise, conviction, exhaustion. Force of utterance and vigor of language propel ideas; but it is not often, except in the catastrophic reversion and panic of war and the abrogation of intelligence represented by tar and feathers, that force is anything but symbolic. The irritated legislator may rush down the aisle and collar his adversary, but the headlines show that other members of the august body immediately intervened before physical harm was done. It is indeed impressive to observe a man of large physique forcefully expounding his views with belligerent gesture, strong and provocative voice, attitude of attack and mimic violence, no adversary being present— the occasion being simply a public meeting for discussion of a gas franchise. Combat has been raised to a higher than physical plane, though the ancient mechanics of combat survive in gesture, intonation, pose of facing the enemy and mimic pounding with closed fist and biting with glistening oratorical teeth.

Let no one think that occasions for fighting, symbolically, have diminished with decrease of actual physical encounter. Life is a battle in more senses now than in the simpler ages when famine and ignorance kept down the population. More issues and more complex ones develop with us than appeared in earlier times, and general increase of intelligence has multiplied critics and potential competitors. Now, as in seemingly more heroic times, courage and will prevail, though measures instead of men invoke the combative spirit.

The protective and assertive quality of pugnacity, so often associated with destructive conflict, has possibilities for constructive enterprise. Peace has its victories no less than war; but the contests for creative achievement involve to the full the hardihood of the fighting spirit. The material and social obstacles to higher general welfare afford an ample field for exercise of the energies that formerly were associated with the doughty warrior and the quarrelsome member of the tribe. There is never a time when there is not a fight of some description— indeed many fights— for social objectives; and there is scarcely a desirable attainment, individual or social, that is not a challenge to fortitude.

Primitive contest for mates, food and advantage is echoed in mind to-day in the spirit of rivalry and emulation. The rivalry tendency thrusts itself forward as a sense of competition. This tendency is one of the most uncomfortable that we possess. It serves the purpose of stimulating to needed activities, but it also keeps us awake at night with recollections of tactical mistakes and apprehensions of competitors' coups. As far as comfort is concerned the instinct of rivalry might better be in the Red Sea.

What escape is there from the raw force and pattern of jealousy, envy, rivalry, disparagement, competition, dispraise? Can society ever be welded together without fatal laws unless this tendency be restrained and modified? The unmodified, unsublimated instinct is capable of misleading to bickerings and social disharmony and inadequacy. It is the foe to cooperation. Families, communities, schools, committees, go on the rocks through personal rivalry.

One thing that keeps rivalry going is the fear that some one else will not play fair, that he may take undue advantage. Absolute fair play assuages rivalry. Instead of trusting others as presumable friends, we watch them as enemies, and they reciprocate. If one had the courage to believe nothing but good of people, nations included, what would happen? Should we be eaten up? It is unlikely. The result would rather be that our example would be imitated.

The socially dissolving and acidlike quality of detraction suggests a treatment that Liberty Hyde Bailey proposes for dandelions in the lawn; he says, "admire them and leave them there." Blindly instinctive emulation and conceit take in too much territory. The victim of self-love and sensitive vanity joins issue with too many competitors and for too many comparisons. In a day of specialization it cannot be expected that any one person can assert equivalents of merit and achievement with a whole group. Individuals are not sufficiently comparable to make it advisable to institute personal comparison on a large scale. Whole-hearted recognition of the valuable qualities of other individuals and other races is a social cement. Indiscriminate praise or denunciation of a people, as the Jews, the Mexicans, or the English, is directly opposed to good sense and veracity; it provokes animosity rather than helps to establish a synthetic and catholic view of the many, though not necessarily identical, excellencies of different types of culture.

Cooperation is impossible as long as attention is fixed on differences. Only by focusing on common purpose and cultivating admirations without rivalry can cooperative enterprise be successfully carried forward, be it a public school in a community of Lutherans and Catholics, Swedes and Poles— or Canadian and American coöperation to keep the three thousand miles of boundary free from cannon. The political or industrial manipulator sows discord by dragging into the focus of attention the inevitable differences which exist in any group. Press the button of religious differences and economic cooperation flies out of the window; harp on differences rather than recognize merits, and no two nations, even English-speaking nations, could live in peace. The technic of harmony calls for elimination of reference to differences, and emphasis upon common interests. The world has made a great advance in method since the days when pamphleteers hurled abusive epithets at one another and political rivals exploited their opponents' personal shortcomings. What discussion has lost in coarse picturesqueness it has gained in auspicious reticence.

The instinct of personal decoration and display shows in children and governs the dress of savages, who subordinate utility to ornament. Ornamentation of self is closely related to mating and to social survival; for display not only actually attracts the eye, but implies the possession of physical or mental qualities of practical value. The savage who adorns himself with bear and elk-tooth necklaces exhibits evidence of his prowess as a hunter; his trophies are his credentials. Jewelry performs a like function to-day as evidence of success in the money hunt, the compacting of values in small space being neatly accomplished by diamond studs and pearl earrings.

Display may take many forms. Foreign words and phrases are sometimes employed for show. Some studies, said Francis Bacon, are for ornament. Latin has been affected for the purpose, and even more so, French. Titles are de luxe forms of social display. Secret societies manufacture honorific titles and distinctions which insure the possession by members of verbal, typographical, or costume prominence. It would be a denial of life itself to challenge the function of display; but the preferred forms of display measure and project social ideals. There has been progress beyond muscular and surface physical display. Increasingly clothing has taken on utility and departed from the merely ornamental. The stage and the stagelike social occasion, the holiday and the infrequent festivity, preserve the traditions of ornateness of apparel; but science and utility turn ancient pomps to a kind of levity. The acrobat and pugilist, as representatives of a physical claim to social approval, appeal less forcefully to-day than did similar performers in the days of the serious splendors of tournament and court.

The shift from physical decoration to ornaments of mind and character marks a considerable progress. This transfer of emphasis has been less pronounced in the case of woman, who must overcome the economic resistance to marriage, and, when married, often functions as an economic barometer. But the tendency among women to supplement physical with other elements of display is unmistakable. The plainly dressed woman in science or business is not a rarity. Some claim to attention is imperative, and the individual apparently neglectful of outward appearance invariably has his preferred forms of display, which may even produce weightier results for contrasting with neglect of dress and equipage. Apparently to flout customary forms of impressing observers is to imply resources out of the ordinary. The well-known and well-established may therefore safely spurn the latest cut and the newest model.

In reciprocity of admiration and display lies a possibility of raising to effective strength ideals that signify much for a better state of society— concepts of what fame and approval should attach to reveal the inwardness of popular mind. It is notorious that the quiet, constructive careers of the pioneer who makes a beautiful farm out of the wilderness and of the self-effacing woman who is the good angel of a community are less blazoned than the success of the man who simply gets rich. The useful person who does not advertise himself can be rescued from oblivion by an alert appreciation by others. The idea back of the Carnegie hero fund has the advantage of shifting to the community the detection of merit and its publicity; it is a foreshadowing of a type of admiration not vitiated by the design or vanity of the recipient. The kinds of display that have historically won popular admiration do not necessarily meet the demands of the present. There is nothing that calls for nicer discrimination than what to applaud, and nothing that is likely to do more to shape the trend of institutions. Like other instincts, fear is a general tendency whose ultimate forms of expression are governed largely by experience and training. This is not to say that certain situations do not naturally evoke fear, for such is the case. High places, wild animals, strange faces, the dark bodies of water, the forest, snakes, thunder and lightning, and the dead, have exceptional power to arouse fears. There is a gentle current of fear at almost all times, a current that is readily expanded to anxiety, dread or terror.

This susceptibility has in past ages received abhorrent culture, being played upon by design for the control of men. Savages stand in awe of evil spirits and are tied hand and foot by fearsome taboos. The early Greeks, rationalized beyond their times, were nevertheless constantly apprehensive lest they provoke the ill will of gods inconveniently numerous and resentful. Early Christendom raised terrorization to an art; and between astronomical eclipses, the expected termination of the world in the year 1000 A. D., and the undying fire, the imaginative individual had little peace. Death was clothed with terrors unknown to an age producing the philosophy of Metchnikoff, Robert Louis Stevenson, and Walt Whitman. The practical calm of biology has robbed death of much of its terror. Society has more than once had a case of nerves, with the New England sense of exaggerated responsibility achieving no mean distinction in the list.

The practical usefulness of fear is considerable, though the hypertrophied apprehensions and sickening dreads of past ages wrought nothing but havoc. Transferred to situations of actual danger and sublimated from blind panic to rational caution, the fear impulse has constructive possibilities. But it is notorious that uncultivated fear is more likely to attach to inconsequential matters rather than to those of real import. A mouse has still more power to provoke panic than a live wire, and a garter snake than a toy pistol or rusty nails. Germs are not yet feared with a vividness comparable to that experienced in the presence of small creatures of fur and feathers. Civilized man needs to know what not to fear and what to fear. Old wives' tales are in competition with science here. Instinctive fear of the dentist is too strong, while the fear of death should, even in its rationalized and attenuated form, exceed that of going to a hospital.

The teaching of safety first, begun by industrial concerns and extended by instruction in schools, is a deliberate effort to build up useful fear. The wide prevalence of accident situations in modern life amply justifies the emphasis placed upon preventive fear. One does not fear effectually, unless informed. To know what harms and what is innocuous tends to build up appropriate emotions. Vice, seen as a monster, inspires terror. Loathing, fear and horror, which medical and social science are laying the fact foundations for, in dealing with sex diseases, are capable of assuming proportions of great efficiency. Our organization of fears is much askew for maximum social welfare. There are fears that need to be reduced and extirpated and fears that are as yet inadequate for welfare. Christian Science has done well to perceive the need of using the soft pedal on fears of a kind. But there is just as much need of inspiring fear to right ends. Emotional cultivation, the most enigmatical and neglected kind of culture, has no larger problem than to appraise and regulate fears.

Fear of impending social calamity, a fear which may have inspired the virulent attempts to reduce the heretic by torture in the dark ages, may be wholly misguided. The social alarmist imparts a subtle terror that may take the shape of persecution and panicky reversion. There is such a thing as social stampede. The meaningless fright that causes herds of horses and cattle to stampede is paralleled in society. The witchcraft delusion was a human stampede. The sinister unanimity of the stampede and the fear that drives the mob are opposed by better fears— the fear of being unjust, the fear of denying rights guaranteed by law, the fear of harming society by closing avenues of invention and inspiration, the fear of being found in the booby trap.

There are few individuals who do not suffer from too much fear, and there are probably none whose fears are suitably distributed over the field of menace and are neither exaggerated nor inadequate. Possibly fear is largely a transitional phenomenon— an expedient on our way to fuller civilization.

Nature places reproduction squarely upon an instinctive basis. In sex the war between reason and social well-being on the one hand and blind impulse on the other is equaled in violence in no other department of experience. Reason is a later and higher nature, so the conflict is between slight reason and more reason, between blind instinct and instinct touched with reflection.

Instinct would fill the world with populations fighting for food and held down to low levels of squalid conflict. An interplay of increasingly regulated instinctive forces has moved mankind toward the monogamic family and adequate care of the young. With well-organized individuals in well-organized society, initial sex interest is substantially succeeded by rationalized parenthood and altruistic social enterprise. Undeveloped interests, obscene or prurient literature, underpay and poverty, which delay or prevent mating, and lack of vision, unite to arrest the evolution of the higher expressions of sex in society.

The flowering of the parental form of sex instinct in the pride and care of children signifies much in human evolution. The parental interest has entered upon a career of symbolic creativeness. No former age ever saw such sustained and devoted nurture of the young. Symbolic parenthood is exemplified in the socially creative effort of humanitarians and teachers.

The family is significant in social organization, for its ethics and regimen are types and patterns of the larger institutions and ideals of society. However, there are families and families. There is the monarchical family, found especially in monarchical countries, where the children and mother are subjects. There is the democratic family in which there is the ideal of self-government and joint obligation. Whether the state derives from the family or the family copies the prevailing governmental example may not always be clear; presumably the examples are mutually influential. In the family, however, it is possible to develop the attitudes and practice that lie at the threshold of higher social organization.

The sense of social interdependence and justice originates and finds exercise in the rationalized family. Demarcation of individual will is involved. The franchise, balloting and committee procedure are illustrated, as well as the function of law. The advantages of skill and education, of self-restraint and truth-telling, are impressed upon the mind.

The conception of society as a family and the organization of society on a family basis have characterized all societies. It was thus with the early Hebrews and with the village communities of India. Family psychology supports the Japanese throne. The last Tsar of Russia was the little father of a large number of adult children who got out of hand. Our

Red Indian wards have been wont to address the "great father" in Washington. It appears there are fathers and fathers. But at the basis of society is the family; it is the fundamental unit of government and group. Families of the most diverse character have much in common as have governments the most diverse. The more liberal, scientific and specifically democratic the family, the better adapted it is to afford to general society preformed materials for higher civilization. The democratic culture of the family needs but to be generalized to impart its character to all social institutions.

Our inherited tendencies are by no means precisely adapted to the environment of contemporary life; indeed, it is likely that at no time in the past have instincts ever functioned with great nicety and without incidental harm. At any rate, these fundamental tendencies are significant to-day as sources of motive rather than as guides to program. Constant oversight and direction are required to shape the expressions of instinct to constructive and beneficial ends.

CHAPTER XI
THE CREATIVE ASPECT OF PLAY

THE present recognition of play in the education of the young and in the activities of adults of all social classes is both in quantity and quality a unique phenomenon. When school systems affecting millions of children base procedure upon the free activity of play, and when millions of adults, representing not only the moneyed class but the industrial worker, adopt play as a part-time employment, there is reason for reflection. We still meet the man who never takes a vacation and the person who has the unquiet servile conscience; but on the whole it can safely be said that modern life takes to play with singular catholicity and a rich material equipment. The play ideal in the school is a frank innovation, and the play of adults is as frankly a departure from the approved conduct of large numbers in times past.

Play, instinctive in man and lower animals, is an impulse from within which finds expression in obviously inherited movements. Thus the kitten chases and pounces upon a spool in a manner that testifies to the mouse-catching activities of untold generations of cats and their untold generations of catlike ancestors. The kitten rehearses family history. But in rehearsing the activity the kitten prepares for the future, for it will catch mice and red squirrels as occasion offers. The animal's play is evidently pleasurable. One can be sure of play by the joy unconfined. The passing of energy along the routes established by old wont is uniquely gratifying.

The human play tendency similarly recapitulates ancestral activities and serves to develop needed skills. The child plays imitatively, yet all his play activities are readily referred to types of ancestral activity. The exact form of

331

instinctive expression is only generally predetermined. Hence the copying of the activities of older children and of the occupations of adults is pronounced.

The reversion to old types of motor activity is attended by deep emotional satisfaction. Play releases funds of emotion whose origin is remote. The use of muscles in racially old ways in the free circumstances of recreation gives vent to the inherited nature of man. Sports and games select and organize ancestral types of activity. The ball game is a substitute for many of the features of primitive combat and chase. The ball is symbolic of the hurled missile or the weapon sent to bring down game. The running and evasions, striking the ball, even the uncouth clamor from the bleachers, make an appeal to the primitive within us. Clan and tribe are symbolized in the opposing teams.

Modern life is built so athwart many of our strongest tendencies that to go back into the past through play is like taking a cool plunge on a hot day. The knotted tensions and restrained powers of the normal inheritance find soothing and delightful relief in the comparatively rude experiences of the bowling alley and the hand ball court. Absence of ultimate design, and relief from serious calculation and sustained thought, are characteristics of play. Point by point play shows contrasts to the vocations men live by. A wide range of unconventional conduct, from sports and games to the bizarre diversions of drunkenness, war, and kleptomania, is referable to tendencies that were present in the lives of our crude ancestors.

While play derives its motives and to a large extent its forms from racial reminiscence, and its gratifications are the old delights of rudimentary society, it is an experience that carries certain possibilities of future usefulness as a social factor. The spirit and attitude of play and the contacts and liberations associated with play have no small promise as affording conditions of social progress.

Play carries with it an extensive culture for the enjoyable use of leisure and thus effects a transfer of attention from production to consumption. It signalizes the passing over of society from the pain and famine basis to that of substance and plenty. Associated with rising wants and standards of happiness, play in adult society serves to stimulate more intelligent and abundant production as a means of realizing cultural needs, which are rarely satisfied without considerable attendant expense. The present industrial period is characterized by spasmodic and throttled factory production, by absurd and wasteful duplication, by disregard for regional economies of production and transportation, and in general by a social anarchy of production, shot through with singularly successful selfish effort to amass wealth. The elephantine confusion of society in regard to achieving a maximum of economic well-being, and the keen directness of the private corporation to obtain corporate enrichment stand in sharp contrast. It is possible that the widely developing play-interest will supply incentive to cause production to enter upon a more coördinated and fruitful career. Of course, as it is to-day, the constant piling up of rather permanent forms of wealth, as in improved lands, bridges, buildings, jewelry, technic and education, makes each succeeding generation richer than the last. Inheritable wealth keeps mounting to higher and higher levels. More people inherit wealth and each on the average inherits more than was formerly possible. Disorganization of money systems may give a temporary appearance of poverty, but the essentials of wealth were never so plentiful before.

Along with increase of material means of satisfying wants, there thus appears a recreational tendency which looks toward a fuller life and ultimately higher culture standards. Thus play, whether in all cases well chosen or not, stands in lieu of a kindergarten for raising the masses to an acceptable plane of consumption. By trial and error, by silly amusement and raucous violence of athletics, the people become accustomed to the problem of living in plenty and feel their way toward the arts and amenities that can appear only in an environment not dominated by gross toil and severe necessities of production. The play instinct, finding expression in whatsoever present forms, is the potential source of fine and finer arts, of the flowering of creative talents.

To the city dweller outdoor recreation is a release from the confinement of employment and the restrictions of an artificial environment; it releases tensions and restores to a normal simplicity. Country life of the unsophisticated type is, however, stimulated and socialized by recreation. In both the case of urban and rural life, play performs the function of supplementing the usual experiences of occupations and results in enlarging the personality— a contribution of great importance. So strong an appeal is made by sports and games that some vigilance is required lest excess of diversion betray both industry and the achievement to which the play experience conduces.

The mental and physical limitations imposed on the individual by most modern employments are suspended in recreation. Herein lies a special value of play. In adult life the play instinct serves peculiarly well, as it does notably in childhood, to give confidence, and release expression for latent powers. The muscle-bound farm boy feels more competent and independent for having learned tennis and dancing. The middle-aged woman who learns to swim or drive a car takes on an access of personality and self-respect. Recreation and avocation have marked power to make people think well of themselves— and when they do that, the outlook for democracy improves. By preserving through play a plasticity like that of infancy, the adult becomes more versatile and efficient in all relations. Youth is a high condition; by play, with its demand for mobility and adaptability, the adult fends off the encroaching death of habit and factitious respectability. Obsessions, dogmatisms, finality and festering memories find difficult footing in minds made inhospitable to their presence through rich experience in the free activities of play. The dwarfing of natures through being shut off in childhood from normal play is well known. The child that has not played lacks in development; not less does the adult suffer who loses the impulses that go with spontaneous and wide-ranging mental and motor activity.

Denied free expression in acceptable forms, in the child and the adult, the play instinct may find invidious outlets. A study of youthful criminal tendencies of a number of reputable citizens, by Professor Swift, brought out the fact that in nearly every case these individuals, including business men, lawyers, teachers and others, showed such tendencies in early life. The offenses reported ranged from setting fire to buildings to stealing fruit from farmers' trees, and from ineffectual attempts to kill other children to heaving stones at widows' houses. Nearly every one will plead guilty to the charge of having done irregular and incipiently criminal acts in childhood and youth. These ill-conceived acts, instinctive all, can be culturally replaced or fanned into criminal career. The whole scheme of civilization is one for the replacement of antisocial, with social, forms of expression, of substituting wholesome conduct for that which is instinctively prompted to evil results. Games, sports and avocations are prophylactic measures of outstanding value. The phenomenal influence of physical diversion and training to rectify conduct in schools and colleges is well understood by administrators of education. Problems of discipline, as they were encountered in days of preachy restraint, have practically disappeared in such institutions— thanks to the substitutional efficacy of athletics and the gymnasium.

The motivation of professions and occupations, whether from slavish compulsion or from sheer delight and interest, is closely related to personal happiness and the future of society. The excellence and quantity of product are affected by the worker's motives, but particularly is his attitude the measure of his fatigue, content or discontent. Lack of suitable motivation, lack of recognition that the state of mind of the worker is a most important fact, not only affects production in quantity but insidiously influences quality and range. With the releasing motives of play operating in the world's work, astounding advances would be made. A person who does not like a job will not give it enough thought and patience to bring out its latent possibilities. Invention and finish spring from spontaneous, playlike, appetitive devotion to one's employment. Brusque indifference to the imponderables gives modern industry and employments a crudely mechanized and art-lacking character. In the psychological conditions of vocations lies the possibility of artlike production and, indeed, the possibility of turning the industries into fine arts. Here and there is a farmer, a stock-raiser, a florist, or a teacher who is motivated for art rather than for job. But such appear to be exceptional. Neither in immediate character of employment in its associated ideas nor in features of variation and progression does the vocation ordinarily make one tenth of the appeal made by taking part in dramatics, or playing "first base" on an improvised baseball team. The arts have stood off by themselves as unique adventures in the creative mood. It would be strange if in all the diverse vocations of modern society there were not to be found ample space for analogous creativeness and devotedness. If the usual employee were to declare that he loved his work, his fellows would snort.

We could get along with even less production, if necessary, provided employment were better contrived for motive, though increase of production would doubtless ensue from cultivating the art or play motive. There is no more pregnant enterprise than that of a better motivation of industry. How retarded such enterprise is may be inferred from the amazement of novelty that greeted Carleton Parker's discovery that the complex of restiveness of the I. W. W. of the Oregon lumber camps was causally related to the wifeless state of the members of this organization.

The craving for playful change finds satisfaction in travel and vacations. By entering new environments the individual is subjected to much the same demands for mobility that are afforded by play. The developmental influence of travel— of any radius— for any purpose, affiliates with that of play, in that it entails new adjustments and breaks up conventional attitudes. The harmonizing of the socially diverse is hastened by modern means of travel. There is a close connection between the mating impulse and the interest in travel, as witness the frequency of marriage of persons of different geographical association— intertribal as it were. Fixedness of concept and avoidance of the problem situations from which reason springs are scarcely possible to the person whose horizon is widened by adequate and significant travel. Whatever comes to the world, we may be sure that our time is decisively marked off from preceding centuries by the steel rail and the ubiquitous automobile. There are no historical parallels for a civilization that witnesses the possibility of setting free the individual from the limitation of place and of stimulating through novelty and comparison.

Avenues of social welfare open along the route of more natural and spontaneous motivation in industry and of greater recognition of the interests represented by play. Industry, though highly mechanized, need not inevitably mechanize the worker. The organization of work to present continuing appeal to curiosity and adventure is possible. Recognition of the need of improving motivation in the different employments would go a long way toward inspiring the social invention necessary for bringing about its realization.

The larger use of the great natural playgrounds of the world, freer access to them through adequate and inexpensive transportation facilities, and the liberation of pent-up urban populations to contact with nature are easily possible, lacking only determination to put material assets to social uses. An emboldened spirit of play might prove to be the world's highest wisdom.

Yet there is triumph for play. Mark Twain declared that man's supreme weapon, unused, is laughter. Books have been written on laughter, and the circumstances of this type of expression have been documented to a degree. Laughter belongs only to man; it is aroused only by man or manlike animals or things; it cannot be provoked by inanimate nature; it is an expression of self-superiority in view of the blunders of inferiors; it is symbolic defiance; it originates in happy surprise— as anger comes from unhappy and sudden obstacles; it is like stepping down two steps of stairs instead of the expected single step. Physically, the expression of laughter mimics the glad and mouthful expression of a dog making toward a bone and evincing a state, translatable into the words, "It is good, I will eat it." Such are some of the explanations of laughter.

Laughter witnesses to a sense of suitability and a perception of the incongruous; therefore the mind that laughs must know alternatives. With ideas uncompared no one would laugh. When a man has only one idea, that idea is as serious as can be; when he laughs he is virtually saying that he has had another idea. By laughter one also suggests that others possess themselves of different ideas. Napoleon's soldiers apparently always took the oratory of their hero seriously. Suppose they had snickered. Men have been known to break up meetings by laughing at the wrong place. A supreme weapon of emancipation, a unique defense of defenses, an irresistible force is laughter.

The variations of experience induced and gratified by the play instinct tend to yield the net result of fitting the individual for more happily taking his part in society. Whether play be regarded as an expression of surplus energy, or as a recapitulation of race experience, or as a form of preparation for later activities, it contributes notably to ideal social qualifications.

CHAPTER XII
SOCIAL USES OF MEMORY

THE function of memory is to provide the individual with useful images of past experience. Its function in the individual's public mind is to recall former events of significance for social welfare. In common with other memories the citizen has a store of materials relating to history and social developments. What store he possesses depends upon factors of recall. These factors, subject at all times to interest as a superior selective influence, are vividness, primacy, recency, and repetition.

Vividness has reference to the definiteness and depth of original impression. If one has been in a railroad accident, he finds that the circumstances and details are vividly impressed and not to be forgotten. The fright and terror of accident serve to impress images ineffaceably. Great joy or pain stamps impressions permanently upon the nervous system. Pain is to be avoided in the future and joy is to be sought; hence the accommodation of memory. Early settlers in the lower Hudson River valley had the custom of "whipping the boundaries." Land boundaries consisted of natural objects, as a basswood tree, a large rock or a convenient stump. One farm was marked off from another in this manner. It became necessary to remember boundaries. So the boundaries were "whipped in." The children would be given sound whippings at the boundaries; the natural objects thus serving as demarcations and their significance were deeply impressed by the accompanying stimulation. This was vividness. As a compensation for this barbarity, the children, let us believe, never failed to inherit the goodly acres undiminished, though whether, as Freudians might contend, there ever after was a fear of approaching boundaries, remains a question.

First impressions are lasting; primacy of experience gives memory a firm attachment. One remembers well how a person looked when first seen, how a place appeared when first observed. Later images may be blurred, but the original experience remains in clear outline. The clear memories of childhood benefit from the tenacity of the cells of the brain for original and primary impressions. Experiences of later years have not the same strength of attachment. A prophet is without honor in his own country because his elders cannot forget his boyhood, cannot think of him except as somebody's unprophetlike son. If George Washington, to the schoolboy, had the congenital defect of being unable to summon to his aid the most inheritable of defenses, the schoolboy can scarcely ever afterwards listen to fresh evidence or revise his conviction on Washington's singular disability. Having in mind thus the peculiar effectiveness of first impressions, we should feel less indulgent toward the practice of permitting first impressions to be incorrect.

At the opposite pole from primacy is recency as a law of memory. The most recent impression is also lasting. We remember not only how John looked when we first saw him but also his last appearance before he marched away; last views cling. We are not powerless under the spell of first impressions; the last pretty face, alas, has its spell. There is much in position. Of ten candidates for office we remember the first we heard speak, remember distinctly, and we remember the last also distinctly, for he was the last. The intervening eight, other factors being disregarded in the illustration, are less definitely recalled. A candidate might, however, have a superior claim on memory for having been the beneficiary of some special factor of vividness.

There is an element of instinctive economy in this dominance of first and last impressions. The mind shirks the labor of comparison and equity. It is easier to make up one's

mind and let it stay made up on first impressions. By
mentally giving the prize to the first speaker the burden of
judicious assessment of values is avoided; and, with the last
impression, it is the easier way to give the last speaker a
preference than mentally stage a parade of all the preceding
claimants for honors. The mind seeks the path of least
resistance with the placid indolence of a stream of water
running down hill. What strategies for getting in the last
word— and with what good reason! The vote of prejudice is
easier than that of thinking.

Playing across the foregoing factors, like a thread in a
fabric, is repetition. Great is the power of the repeated word.
Repetition dominates among the factors of recall, for the
repeated idea is sure at some time to be first or last or to be
timed with moments of vividness and emotion. If a thing is
said a hundred times the chances are that at some time it will
make a strong appeal; it will find a joint in the armor. After
sleeping through a barrel of sermons, the parishioner may
wake to hear a direful prediction and straightway beg for
mercy. Repetition has an inclusiveness like the charge from a
shotgun. Advertising makes use of all factors of memory, but
use is especially made of the law of repetition. Even
falsehood wins with repetition, for vigilance can be tired out.
Deny the repeated statement, flout it, disprove it, yet with its
repetition there is beaten up a dust which settles like an
opiate over denial. With repetition as a method even dullness
becomes leadership. The keen mind may tire of reiterating
the same idea, leaving to those who are calloused to
repetition the necessary service of saying things over and over
for twenty five years, until the majority are caught awake.

Much that is experienced is not retained; a mass of
items to which we give little or no attention, or heeding, do
not remember. As attention is selective, like a bee visiting
only certain flowers, so are the preservations of memory but
fragmentary. Governed by interest we give heed mainly to

what is significant at the moment; and thus is memory as full of gaps as were our earlier attentions and interests.

But in addition to the selection by interest, we have in the operations of memory a selective ejection of what at one time was heeded and stored in memory. Disuse and aversion unite to empty the memory of incidents and details. In the main we recall things that are of use and forget the useless. The operation of the mind is not perfect in this regard, but the principle is demonstrable. Forgetting, it must be said, is not quite what it should be. We go madly about because we have forgotten the unforgettable and think of things we should not. The things actually blotted from remembrance are not always what an unbiased jury would recommend, and the things retained are oftentimes of dubious serviceableness.

Selection, retention, and forgetting have special significance in matters of social program. Society is as much a creature of social memory as is the individual responsive to his own remembered experiences and the principles derived therefrom. What is recalled of society, for society, determines in effect what kind of civilization shall ensue. Just as the individual without memories would proceed by instinct mainly and thus differ widely from cultured man, so society divested of history and precedent would approximate primitive barbarism. Present-day society is founded upon the truth and falsehood delivered to us by the fathers, and incremented by socially memorable instances of recent origin. Social memory goes back as far as history and tradition. Well may it be said that we are the true ancients; historically, we have the longest memories.

The nature of the content of social memory is determined by interest, attention, and forgetting, as in the case of the individual memory in matters of individual import. An important role is played by those who select for the social mind, and who help it to forget. The author and the historian are from this viewpoint social architects, as are likewise the lawyer, clergyman, and teacher.

Individual well-being is closely bound up with selection by memory, depending on what one remembers and what one forgets. The person who remains too conscious of past mistakes and too alive to former animosities and hatreds is limited indeed. It is necessary to forget. "Forget it" is an admonition of considerable wisdom. The mind that constantly reverts, reverts comprehensively, is not the happiest or most promising type. A convenient "forgettery" is as valuable as a good memory. We read of people who live next door to each other for years divided by a spite fence— and we recall the history of Alsace-Lorraine. There is culture that is almost wholly retrospective. One must live out of the past, it is true, but such fullness and tenacity of indiscriminate memory as make the future uninteresting and the present opaque is a downright misfortune.

The rôle played by history is therefore wholesome or the reverse according to the stressing of materials. On the whole it can safely be said that the world suffers from history. No one can be in the city of Boston without feeling that Boston suffers from history; it benefits from history, to be sure, but it also suffers from it. France and Germany suffer from history; they will suffer from it as long as they will not forget and begin again with relieved minds.

In a measure the historical past should be neglected. We treasure the details of evil precedent at our peril. The historical way becomes the easiest way. In time of crisis, the old vicious precedent being at hand, the mind effects a tragic economy of effort by reversion to practice. With less knowledge of how our forefathers behaved, we should ascend to solutions based on reason and forward-looking considerations.

But perhaps it is not the facts of history that are opposed to progress so much as it is the spirit of acceptance and deference. History is not recorded dispassionately; such a thing is impossible. Bancroft wrote history to justify the ways of God to man, and A. M. Simons writes it to demonstrate economic determinism. The earlier school histories of the United States were written to brand the redcoats and to instill gun patriotism. Dr. Beard prepares textbooks that bring to light the achievements of the plow and the dynamo, the microscope and the blowpipe. Carlyle made a god of Napoleon, and H. G. Wells shows him as a contemptible, energetic, but not incomparable devil. The traditional idolizing of Napoleon by the Frenchman could no more exist in the presence of *An Outline of History* than reverence for Cotton Mather can exist in the mind of the reader of the Massachusetts Historical Society's letter written by Mather, hopefully referring to a possible capture of William Penn at sea and his sale as a slave to the West Indies. Propaganda is implicit in the very constitution and temperament of the historian and in the necessity of selection. Find a writer who has no point of view, no sentiments and prejudices, no emotions, no cultural background, no personality and no mouths to feed, and we may then search for the historical volume free from bias.

Historians have dropped the curtain on the horrors of the Inquisition. This precedent may well be followed in other matters. There is always danger lest what is cited for warning shall be perverted to serve for imitation. Modern society may very well have its attention diverted from much in history, and where not oblivious to it, a modern interpretation should be fairly indicated. It is of the greatest promise that fresh organizations of historical materials and compilations of newly unearthed facts are undertaken, and that history is not allowed to rest under interpretations put upon it by writers of former generations. The interpretation is the thing, for it is the emotional influence of the interpretation rather than facts given without inference that determines whether history shall prove a drag or an inspiration.

The dynamic quality of new countries is due to the meeting of difficulties for which precedents do not exist, and to exemption from history. The new country is lacking in monuments, and its place names are not directly associated with historical happenings. Something is lost in richness of associations, but something is gained in sweep and freedom. A picturesque stone railroad station of early date in an eastern city inspired local residents with sentiments of regard. Reading the date, a man from a new state ejaculated: "Time they had another."

Progress comes with the breaking of old ties, with the shedding of the cast of custom, with escape from the spell of environment which in due time makes black and white rather indistinguishable. The claims of tradition come to outweigh considerations of equity and efficiency; the luxury of habit leads through conservatism to degeneration. Not a little of the world's advance has come from men who were considerably ignorant, not knowing how impossible were the achievements they set out to do and realized. The greatest social lethargy may be found among persons of endowment whose nerve has been refrigerated by the cultures of precedent— etymology, Perry's common law pleading, the novels of Sir Walter Scott, creeds and ancient commentary, and the five-foot shelf. If the ancients were alive again they would come to us in droves to learn wisdom. Marcus Aurelius would properly look upon John Burroughs as a man-child regards his father driving the car.

In recognition of the laws of memory the first learning of history should be impartial as may be and as constructive, first impressions being scrupulously guarded. The world has a chance to begin all over again with the life of every child; and unprofitable attitudes brought down by argumentative history can at least be avoided in the first impressions of childhood. What the English are to-day, and what modern conditions of trade and intercourse are, signify

far more to the Irish than the England of Cromwell's time.
An auspicious beginning can be made by emphasizing
conditions to-day, with liberal recognition of the probability
of future change. To plunge the child into ancient and
oftentimes mal forming culture materials when he is of
nascent eagerness of memory is to fix his ideas and form his
mind too much in the likeness of his progenitors.

The factor of repetition can be utilized better through
lessons embodying socially constructive ideas than through
drills that reiterate items of dynastic and presidential
chronicle. The character of China was determined by the fact
that its youth had long been restricted to the formulae of the
Confucian classics. To apply repetition in the interests of
progress requires selection of dynamic thought materials.

The force of recency as a factor in the operation of
memory— the power of the final admonition and the last
word— is recognized in a variety of situations in home and
society. But the last word, the most recent utterance, the
pursuing, inescapable utterance is from the newspaper. What
sort of last word, of ever-recurring last word is this? It would
be well if the last word were the best considered, for it is this
that often decides policy; well if the social mechanism for
repetition were to charge memory again and again with the
highest thought and purpose. Our recollection is not too
often refreshed with the world's greatest thoughts.

Vividness, as a law of memory, can be extensively
utilized for socially constructive effort. The vividness of
dramatization has large possibilities of usefulness in social
service. Much of the most vividly presented materials to-day
have slight social value. On the other hand, much of the
news and principle that is socially potent is not found in large
type or in the movies. Science, philosophy, literature, social
and economic fact, synthetic history, industrial pioneering
and dynamic psychology all might largely share in appeal to
memory through vividness of expression. Pictures, bold-faced

type, and emotional portrayal can be harnessed to social welfare as well as disproportionately employed upon trivial or diverting subjects. A circus means less to a town than does city planning, but one would not infer this from the amount of ink used. The heaviest advertising is by no means that in behalf of civilization by design.

CHAPTER XIII
THE ART OF ACCURACY

PROGRESS is largely determined by the fields of observation entered and by the fidelity of search and exactness of report upon things perceived. Less error arises from faulty functioning of the organs for receiving impressions than from faulty inference and generalization. The belated arrival of impartial and scientific interpretation of phenomena cannot be laid at the door of any deficiency of sense organs, but rather is to be ascribed to obtrusions of preconception and prejudicial theory.

Exact observation is not only the basis of physical science but it is likewise the foundation for social welfare, of which physical science is so large an element Thoroughgoing, circumspect, and untiring observation over wide fields is an essentially modern practice. Upon its still greater popularization and extension depends future progress. A list of modern sciences is a list of the fields wherein the method of circumspect and unfettered perception has made headway. The pseudo science and misinformation of early times represent taboos on scope of observation or faulty procedure. Welfare is favored especially by carrying over to the social field the ideals of perception that have brought success in the understanding of natural phenomena.

Instead of being easy, veracious observation is the most difficult of feats, and the most unusual; it amounts to genius. To shake off prepossessions, to discount previous impressions, and to look with fresh eyes of truth is a triumph of mental skill. Few achieve it; few try; few have any doubts about the self-acting and wholly satisfactory conduct of perception when left in its natural state. That the intake of impressions is a sluiceway of misunderstanding is inconceivable to those who have given the matter no thought. We see what we wish to see; we glance and then retreat to luxuriate in memories. Believing in premonitions we ignore the hundred exceptions and shout with glee of faith confirmed, when a hit appears to be scored.

No duty is so imperative, for individual or society, as that of stripping the observational process down to working efficiency. We are lost indeed if we fumble in observation. We do not try to see with the ears or smell with the kinesthetic sense; nor should we try to see with eyes blind by suggestion, prejudice, and taboo. The precise and delicate skill required to glean the truth is a culture in itself.

An encouraging wariness, with reference to hasty generalization, is an outstanding fact of the past few years. There is coming in the world a distinct tendency to evade the burden of too great assumption. This trend is observable in political, business and philosophical circles. There is much less cocksureness than prevailed formerly. It is as if the problems of society had become too intricate for hasty judgment and dogmatism. This scientist-like pose is highly auspicious. Learning to say "we do not know" marks an advance. This attitude lends itself to inquiry, and out of teachableness come social advance and prosperity. Men in administrative positions increasingly show this saving grace. High qualifications for office are plentiful culture and information, kindly democracy, a tentative constructive program and confessed ignorance. No highly desirable candidate knows twenty-four hours in advance how he can vote on all questions.

With conviction regarding possibility of error comes a greater appetite for ascertained data, statistical information of impartial character and the findings of persons better experienced than ourselves. One of the social triumphs of science has been the creation of a demand for information. To a large extent this demand is, popularly, for information upon production. In agriculture and the industries tradition is being supplanted by exact information. Taught to call upon the laboratory or research staff for facts of production that spell success in vocation, the citizen tends to move out of the field of credulity in other matters. He realizes that his political representatives cannot well act without reliable reports. The function of commissions is respected; the survey is taken for granted. We are not likely to overestimate the immensity of social change implicit in the distribution of scientific data among the masses. Rationalizing the familiar employments widens into rationalizing the social process. The time will come when birth control can be discussed.

With the growth of interest in information and inquiry, language tends to be freed of resounding but meaningless phrases, and the spell of words to fail. The word is scrutinized and realism appears in the details of literature; oratory declines. The attaching of meanings to words is attended by greater watchfulness.

Superficial and inexact ascription of meanings is correlated with hazy perceptions and slouchy method. Numbers of words that have played important roles in history have been essentially undefined— defined without exact perceptual discrimination. Hence it comes about, that, if one declares his allegiance to words his allegiance in fact may not be questioned. To probe the fitness of words is to detect reality, and this is the peculiar merit of scientific procedure. The cloaking of meanings and production of illusion through verbalism has been one of the besetting sins. The complacent use of partly understood words, while giving contentment of knowledge, is one of the effective forms of ignorance. Acceptance of literary materials in lieu of perception of the verities, which language is supposed to reflect faithfully, gives an aspect of wisdom and learning without their substance. Endless differences appear in the private definitions of words charged with social potentialities. In one person's understanding the word "wealth" may connote the possession of fifteen hundred dollars; in another's a million. To one person old age means to be thirty-five years old; old age to another means eighty. What does honor mean? Honor and dishonor may be found, in individual definition, to apply to the same reality. Agreement on meaning, or, if not this, then declaration of precise connotation of terms lies at the basis of sound popular intelligence. Legislative acts drawn up to contain definitions of special terms used are exemplary in this respect.

The ultimate definition of words is in experience. Meaning is shadowy and unreal except as it is derived from real perception. A dollar earned by the sweat of the brow is a larger coin than one of easy money. Understanding is most complete when there has been actual experience with the realities. No one can use the word "grindstone" with full authenticity without having seen a grindstone, applied the tool, and turned one by hand under pressure. To a person of easy-chair associations a grindstone is an object having dimensions and but little weight or power to tax muscle. Early advocates of trade training for all held, that, by acquainting the upper classes of society with physical toil, the indifference of wealth and leisure to the worker's lot would be diminished. As a basis for social understanding such a program has much to commend it Social sympathy and the sense of fair play can scarcely develop without a common experience of labor.

An interesting disclosure of the state of mind which is prone to adopt empty forms of words and which prevails in the absence of experience is that of the child who attempts to do things beyond his strength. Every child will propose to do things that he is unable to do. A boy of four has no hesitation in trying to run an automobile. His conceptions of weight and force, of distance and momentum, and of engine power and the resistance of obstacles are so slight that he will attempt to do the work of the skilled driver. Small boys will request permission to use sharp and heavy axes that they can barely lift. Ladders are mounted by five-year-olds in blissful ignorance of the force of gravitation. In hundreds of everyday situations the child, and the inexperienced adult too, for that matter, will reveal an almost grotesque unconsciousness of the qualities of physical objects. The person who has always ridden on rubber tires knows little of what it means to walk twenty miles in a hot sun.

The knowledge possessed by child or adult in the absence of experience is of a weak and watery kind. The limitation of a child's experience appears to be the basis for his willingness to attempt to do the impossible. He has no measure of his own powers, for he knows little of the resistance one meets in trying to do things. The psychology of the inexperienced child was that of Marie Antoinette, who could not understand why the masses starving for bread did not eat cake.

The prospects for the prosperity of truth are compromised because so few of us have any idea of the difficulty of accuracy. Equipped with good intentions we do not realize how naturally fallible are observation and report. Yet accurate observation and statement are extremely necessary for procedure in a hundred different situations where amelioration and justice are at stake. Accurate statement is a fine art. Though we may not at a bound acquire this art, we become at once more desirable citizens by facing the fact that the whole truth is laborious.

The story-telling impulse is strong. There is keener natural desire to be the ballad singer and the great boaster, the applauded wit and potential author of best sellers, than to relate with plodding fidelity. The disposition to turn facts so the silver lining reflects our own glory and distinction is practically irresistible. Moreover, we are not above winning favor, with the powers that be, by editing to placate. The truth— what is the truth? The answer is simple compared to that to the question, the truth— where is it? Who would be so rude as to disagree with others who are convinced, or drop an irritating fact in the midst of peace and unanimity?

Consider the following account from the Nation, February 15, 1922:

> Thirty-eight persons positively identified a man in Chicago the other day as an accomplice in a swindle. He was lodged in jail to await trial. There, in the usual course, fingerprints were taken, and were found to vary entirely from those of the real culprit, which fortunately for the prisoner were on file. The man was thereupon taken to court and released, the judge calling the mistake the "most startling proof of human fallibility" he had ever seen. A mistake of that sort may well startle all of us, but it is not as unique as one would like to believe. Lawyers and journalists are alike aware of the uncanny fallibility of eye-witnesses, but juries and the public are still chiefly swayed by this kind of testimony.

In an article, "Certain Defects in American Education," Charles W. Eliot, President Emeritus of Harvard University, recognizes the general tendency to error in statement and report, and suggests educational remedy:

> Since the United States went to war with Germany there has been an extraordinary exhibition of the incapacity of the American people as a whole to judge evidence, to determine facts, and even to discriminate between facts and fancies. This incapacity appears in the public press, in the prophecies of prominent administrative officials, both state and national, in the exhortations of the numerous commissions which are undertaking to guide American business and philanthropy, and in the almost universal acceptance by the people at

large, day by day, of statements which have no foundation, and of arguments the premises of which are not facts or events, but only hopes and guesses. It is a matter of everyday experience that most Americans cannot observe with accuracy, repeat correctly a conversation, describe accurately what they have themselves seen or heard, or write out on the spot a correct account of a transaction they have just witnessed. These incapacities are exhibited just as much by highly educated Americans as they are by the uneducated, especially if the defects of their education have not been remedied in part by their professional experience. The physician, the surgeon, and the public-health officer often escape these defects, because their whole professional training and experience develop in them keen powers of observation and reasoning, powers which must be generally accurate and trustworthy if professional success has been attained. Some men whose education ceased at fourteen, acquire, through experience in their trade, powers of observation and correct inference which professional men whose education was continued to their twenty-fifth year never acquire. It is the men who have learned, probably out of school, to see and hear correctly and to reason cautiously from facts observed, that carry on the great industries of the country and make possible great transportation systems and international commerce.

Eight years ago Mr. George G. Crocker, a lawyer who had been for several years chairman of the Boston Rapid Transit Commission, and in that capacity had been much interested in lawsuits which grew out of accidents in the tunnels under construction, contrived an instructive experiment on the accuracy of the testimony of bystanders. He invited twenty highly educated gentlemen, all of whom had been successful in their several callings, to witness a brief scene enacted close to them by four actors in about one minute, and to write out immediately, each for himself, a description of what he had seen and heard. Of the twenty witnesses three did not attempt to write out what they had just seen and heard at close quarters. Of the other seventeen no two agreed as to what happened before them, and no one gave a description which was even approximately correct.

The group contained one judge, one civil engineer, four business men (active), three business men (retired), and eleven lawyers. Whoever will try a few analogous experiments on groups of his acquaintances will soon learn to distrust all tales which have passed from probably inaccurate mouth to inaccurate ear and on through a series of incompetent transmitters.

The remedies for evils described have already been worked out in a few schools and in the elective courses of some colleges and universities. It remains to apply these remedies universally in all the schools of the United States. These remedies are the substitution of teaching by observation and experiment for much of the book work now almost exclusively relied on; the cultivation in the pupils of activity of body and mind during all school time— an activity which finds delight in the exercise of the senses and of the powers of expression in speech and writing; the insistence on the acquisition of personal skill of some sort; the stimulation in every pupil of interest in his work by making the object of it intelligible to him, whether that object be material or spiritual ; the inspiration in every child of tastes and sensibilities which he can use to promote actually his present enjoyment and therefore in all probability his future happiness; and finally the persistent teaching of every pupil how facts are got at in common life, how to make an accurate record of observed facts, and how to draw safe inferences from well-recorded facts. Every boy and girl in school should learn by experience how hard it is to repeat accurately one short sentence just listened to, to describe correctly the colors on a bird, the shape of a leaf, or the design on a nickel. Every child should have had during its school life innumerable lessons in mental truth-seeking and truth-telling. As things now are, comparatively few children have any direct lessons in either process.

Any one who will make the experiment of reading

aloud a sentence or paragraph to a group of people and of securing statements as to the content will probably be strongly impressed with lack of accuracy. Normal characteristics of attention and interest as well as untrained powers combine to make report unreliable. Yet the very basis of social well-being is scrupulous accuracy of observation and narration. Much harm is done by unfounded rumors and reports that are not sufficiently attested by evidence. Mob action, unbalanced public opinion, antagonisms, and miscarriages of justice in communities where talk is loose, can be traced ultimately to lack of regard for perceptual truth. As a foundation for social organization the practice of accuracy is second in importance to no other requirement.

CHAPTER XIV
THE POWER OF SUGGESTION

TO ONE brought up in cannibal society, with no opposing ideas in circulation, cannibalism would seem just and right. The kind of civilization is determined by the prevailing kinds of ideas. The most abhorrent practices, as for example, the drinking of warm blood from the cut necks of horses strung up by the heels, a Patagonian custom, would look proper to us if this were approved by our elders and we were instructed to this end from infancy. There is little that is inevitable in social evolution; a great deal is due to the ideas that chance to be presented. Man does not inherit any set idea against eating his relatives and neighbors; but a Christian civilization, which is a large body of ideas, forbids. We may not even eat small children, the tidbits of orthodox cannibalism. We may, however, employ them in factories. It is all a matter of ideas. The history of ideas is the history of mankind; modern social conditions are largely a product of suggestion. What ideas rule within the mind, and whether one idea or another pulls the trigger of behavior, is determined very largely by the agencies of suggestion.

Any presentation of ideas to consciousness constitutes suggestion. As conscious or voluntary action is in response to ideas, the determinative influence of suggestion is evident. By control of range and character of ideas presented, virtual control of behavior is ordinarily effected. The control of ideas results in the domination of decisions and actions— as may be readily observed in the conduct of children or in responses of individuals in public meetings. The idea of an act may be regarded as the onset of a force that naturally eventuates in corresponding performance.

The power of suggestion has its root in a tendency of

people to economize their efforts and follow the line of least resistance. It is often easier to act than to think; hence an idea that once gains the focus of attention tends to result in corresponding movements and to govern conduct. If a person were restricted to one idea his action could be predicted, for he would have no alternative except to carry out a single thought. Where there is a variety of ideas or suggestions in a given period of time a selection has to be made, as not all can be carried out The hypnotist controls the behavior of his subject by limiting the latter's field of ideas. Restricted to a single idea, such as that of crowing like a rooster, the subject proceeds to crow; he cannot do otherwise if his mind has only the idea of crowing.

The essential fact to note is that all behavior that is consciously directed is in response to images and ideas. If the idea of murder never entered any person's mind, homicide would cease. If no one thought war, the occupation of the warrior would be gone. The actual selection of ideas determines civilization and governs the individual.

Differences appear in the susceptibility of persons to suggestion, some responding quickly and readily, while others show greater resistance and seem relatively immune. This difference in resistance is correlated with the number and strength of inhibitory ideas, many of which have originated in painful experience. The child is highly suggestible because he has fewer ideas derived from experience to hold against the fresh suggestions. A person whose memory is meager or enfeebled as in sickness is rendered more suggestible, as his remembered stock of opposing ideas is less than normal. But all people no matter how virile and mature are suggestible. One can no more resist the bombardment of suggestions from the press, from history, and from social contact than he can resist the influence of the weather upon his skin. The greatest men of the past have been strangely like the men of their time in most of their ideas and in general outlook; if more advanced in some particulars they have been of the mass in others. The pressure of suggestion is like the pressure of atmosphere, resistless even if not recognized. Li Hung Chang, Chinese viceroy, acclaimed one of the greatest men of his generation, showed in his outlook on life but slight divergence from the prevailing set of ideas of his day and land.

A distinction may be made between positive and negative suggestion. If a person is told not to do a thing, he is given a suggestion of doing it coupled with the suggestion not to do it. In practice the constructive suggestion is better than the negative caution. It is better to say, "Sit up straight," than to say, "Do not sit bent over." The latter form presents the idea of sitting bent over; one has an image of this position, and the negative may not neutralize the improper image. So with the "movie" that shows a burglary of a railroad station, with the burglar ultimately captured and brought to justice; that the burglar is caught may not wholly neutralize the impression left by showing the commission of the crime. Depraved suggestions may be imparted under the guise of moral lessons. Safety lies in the avoidance of the expression of ideas associated with things society does not want done. It is doubtful if preaching against war on the ground of its idiocy and horror would be nearly so effective as saying nothing about war and putting emphasis upon constructive and antithetical measures of civilization.

The early Romans used biography as a source of suggestion. The Roman culture was brought down for centuries by instruction based upon the careers of former statesmen and leaders. Biography is a prolific source of ideals— and its use is capable of forming one generation very much like preceding ones. Literature and history are effective vehicles of suggestion. If literature and history are presented with scientific impartiality and fullness, bad examples as well as the good are brought to attention. Perhaps the scientific historian would oppose obliviscence for masses of historical material, informing, say, regarding the Roman arena, the exposure of infants, and human slavery; but one cannot be enthusiastic over parading suggestions which, carried into action, would plunge us back into barbarism and savagery. At any rate it is a fair inference that there is need of cultivating resistance to suggestion, and, in the case of the young, of noting closely what their reactions actually are to questionable types of culture materials.

It is not possible to know in advance what suggestions will prevail; an example may be imitated or it may provoke defiance. A suggestion that falls in with tendencies is of course much more likely to be acted out than one that goes against desires. In his essay on Liberty, John Stuart Mill maintained that the appearance of drunken men on the streets had a good moral effect as an object lesson for sobriety. There is such a thing as getting wholesome lessons from unworthy examples, but the risk is great. The reaction against the bad example may be violent at first but change later. Given examples of inebriety, the young man might come to regard getting drunk as quite the proper thing, no matter how repulsive the original example appeared. The strange practices of foreign peoples at first strike one as being beyond the possibility of imitation; but no one can be sure that in a given social environment he would not at last quite fully assimilate what at first seemed repulsive and immoral. A man challenged to fight a duel to-day in America would be amused— but not so, in the days of Alexander Hamilton, when the force of this custom and suggestion was so strong that a challenge meant anything except amusement. Up to a little more than a century ago, the suggestion of honor as related to dueling was so pervasively spread through conversation and print that youth grew up locked in a corresponding set of ideas. Then people deprecated dueling and set up a current of suggestion that destroyed the institution.

An example of the effect of suggestion is reported by a man who, as a boy in Iowa, studied one winter an elementary text in American history abounding in military descriptions. Shut in by winter, a number of the boys dramatized military campaigns. One boy would be Grant, another Sherman, another Lee. The excitement of the dramatization was great, and an intense interest in things military sprang from this exercise. The person who reported this childhood experience said that he was inspired with an ambition to become a general and made every effort to prepare for West Point examinations. Several years later he encountered the peace movement associated with the name of Andrew Carnegie and came to have an utterly different attitude toward militarism. Multiply this case by thousands, even millions, and apply the principle to social institutions and practices generally, and one has an explanation for the culture levels of different peoples and periods. The world is what it is to a very large extent on account of basic propaganda and the control of ideas, for ideas determine behavior.

The application of the law of suggestion in health and sickness is noteworthy. One can be made to feel ill by suggestion, and he can be made to feel well by suggestion. It would be attempting too much to expect that suggestion would make a man with a broken leg feel comfortable and whole, but within limits ideas have wonderful power over physical conditions. Patients accustomed to injections of morphine to allay pain are sometimes given without detection a "shot of water" instead. Physicians who have little faith in drugs have found it impossible to practice medicine successfully without some show of medicine bottles, powders, and pills; they lose practice if not sufficiently recognizing the appeal to the imagination of a display of curative agents. Cripples have been known to throw away their crutches under the powerful suggestive influence of sacred shrines and relics. The cheering presence of a well-fed and optimistic physician is often worth more than any medicines he prescribes. But tell a sick person how ill he looks, or advocate the advantages of a sandy soil for burial and the tables are turned.

Of course it will not do to blink facts and deny that evils exist. The emotional response, however, may be directed toward cheerfulness and courage. It is sometimes difficult to decide how far to go in recognizing and denouncing evils, as for example, graft exposures. Take the case of an official who, making purchases for the government, pays a top price for materials and secures an unlawful rebate by dealing with a certain company. Does the description of such a practice tend to honesty or dishonesty? In dealing with matters of this type care needs to be given to the emotional response. The offense would need to be dissected and its bearings shown. The idea that dishonesty is smart would need to be checked by fuller considerations. It is a matter of practical judgment as to how far to go in publicity in dealing with matters of this sort.

A good deal of the discretion required for getting along in society without undue friction consists of a practical recognition of suggestion, lest a casual comment arouse undesired associations. Some imagination is required to say the thing that does not give, even indirectly, an undesired suggestion.

Attitude, dress and manner give suggestions. A cringing attitude invites censure ; a confident manner carries with it the idea of success and efficiency. It is often difficult to know when to apologize and how much to apologize. Abject apology may suggest to the injured party that his injury was greater than it was. More than one person has got himself into a tangle by attempting explanations of small matters that might better have been disregarded. The advantage of saying nothing, when that is the best thing to do, appeals to one whenever he notes an example of an unexpectedly perverse association of ideas.

The individual is one person when alone and another when in the presence of others. Let any one turn his mind inward upon itself, and he will discover how changed he becomes by joining with others. Here is a man who in solitude reaches certain conclusions which he confidently expects to urge at a public meeting. He strides zealously to the forum with his convictions bristling. The murmur of the crowd reaches his ear, whereupon he hastily reviews his program of utterance and smooths out a few wrinkles. He joins his fellows and experiences a psychological influence from the antagonistic unanimity of the crowd. His individuality of conviction suffers a strange and sudden shrinkage in the face of massed difference. His ideas, which stood distinct, authentic, and reputable, in solitude, now encounter all the countervailing ideas that an assembly may represent. The invader may now hold to his convictions and declare his faith in the single tax, but he is under strain. His feelings are not what they were in his study, and his utterance will show dips and evasions and placating phrase. The influence of the many is to strip the individual of individuality and assimilate him into the group. The spell of the crowd may be resisted, but there is no man living who does not become a different person in quality of consciousness when in a group.

There is the compulsion to win the favor of the group. Deep in instinctive inheritance is the need to stand in favor with one's fellows, lest they turn and rend. Man is gregarious and always has been one of the herd— he dreads to be horned out of it and left to batten on the moor. Truer he may flout one group, having his eye on some other group for its approval. But every man is playing to a gallery and cannot live without applause.

Spurred by group admiration, the individual will dare

what would terrify him when alone. Men in crowds will face dangers and undergo discomforts that as individuals they would flee. Under the stimulus of others' eyes men choose physical hazard as the lesser of two evils, for most men would prefer to risk being killed than to live under scorn. Bathers who would not dream of going into cold water unsupported by mob psychology will affect a fine abandon when of a party of campers. The crowd acts as an anesthetic. The highest type of courage is that of flouting crowd force and opinion. So-called physical courage is as nothing compared with the courage of holding to individual conviction and conduct, with the crowd antagonistic. The crowd is the coward's refuge; the man who is brave only with the pack is the fundamental coward.

Representing a relatively primitive level of mentality and emotion, the crowd supplies ideal conditions for conflagrations of suggestion. Ideas run through compact groups with facility. Such quickness of response and unity of reaction were no doubt conditions for survival in prehistoric ages. A strangely instantaneous unity of movement may be witnessed in the flight of flocks of birds, a flock turning, rising and alighting as if the different members were held together by invisible wires. Something like this instinctive harmony and dominating oneness attaches to man in the mass, with slaughtering effect upon individuality.

Add to the primitive abasement of mob psychology the possible accompaniments of bad air, physical contact, inclosure, fatigue, hunger, and hypnotizing oneness of stimulus, as the silver-tongued, the band, the spectacle— and it becomes a miracle that the tribe has been saved from itself. Happily radio promises to make the building of large auditoriums less likely, and the extension of the ballot to nominations should reduce the number of occasions for crowd orgy in political assemblages.

Something approaching conditions of crowd

psychology is implied in the extension of modern means of communicating ideas; but there is the saving factor of interval. Nothing abates crowd psychology so much as a day for deliberation. With time the bowed branches and withered leaves of personal intelligence revive. Anything that makes for delay between suggestion and reaction is therefore a means of grace; time means time to think. Inhibitory ideas come with the dawn; herrings swim across the waters in the meantime. We can be civilized by acting from suggestion, but only from such as the best intelligence certifies.

Conditions that discourage the unanimity of mob mind are auspicious; the opposition of leaders and a diversity of group ideals contribute to the ultimate welfare through affording range for variations of opinion. Free thought came into the world in the gap between the two great branches of the church, a gap which widened into scientific development. Opportunity for social development appears in conflicts of prestige and denials of jurisdiction. It is a happy augury when complaints are heard touching the uncertainties of fashion. That one city rivals another in ultimate authority over what is correct to wear is an advantage. Happy day, when standards are "up in the air"— when no one knows what real poetry is, nor any one knows the ultimate ideals in education, or the true position of women. Inability to know one's place is not without a certain kind of promise; it has the merit at least of preserving us from blasting finality. When there is no one to tell us exactly what to think, we are perforce compelled to think for ourselves.

Convinced of the electrical equality of suggestion, its potency to make behavior and to form institutions, one is impelled toward censorship. But no censorship can prevent partial disclosure, and the surreptitious has strange power to charm. Not in censorship by legal methods can suggestion best be governed for social welfare. The free sifting of ideas, free speech and yet more freedom of speech, free discussion and yet more— these are the means of social safety, just as freedom without stint or limit has been the indispensable condition for the development of science. The scientist is only too ready to disavow a false hypothesis. Yet in the search for economic and social knowledge there is less confidence that the stream will run clear. An error in social theory is as sure of detection and disavowal as a scientific error. The major technic of science can wisely be imitated for social progress. Society can profitably use a larger supply of constructive and rational suggestions and socially salutary ideas. The best way to dispose of a perverse suggestion is to oppose to it a better one, and keep up the process until the people are competent judges of ideas.

CHAPTER XV
ATTITUDE TOWARD THE SOCIAL ORDER

IN THEORY government is derived from the people, and, in theory, is thus quite secondary to the powers from which it is derived. But there is a tendency for government to harden into a rigid institution and to aspire to social primacy. The continuity and strength of judicial precedent and legislative practice have the effect of making government an ultimate fact rather than a passing phase of social mind.

Established government tends to become too well established, too firmly intrenched through occupation of strategic position. There is rarely in governmental circles as full and free play of ideas as obtains in the more mobile world of general society. Instead of performing the function of agency, government is liable to claim logical priority. True, the right of revolution has been declared, indeed, was declared by Abraham Lincoln; and such assertion shouts the principle of subordination of government to people. But a cross section of government at any time would show that the governing mind is but imperfectly representative of the full social mind, and that often it is not in proper mood to reflect such mind. To achieve a theory and practice of government which will sensitively reflect social development, which will go as fast as the people go, and which will not become in some measure an agency of counter-civilization, is a serious problem. The best ideas, ideas that meet with approval and finally do become part of government, may batter the doors of legislative resistance for years before finding admittance. Woman suffrage, in various countries, the pure food and drugs act, and the income tax law, in the United States, may be cited as examples of the tardiness of legislative compliance.

Society's alter ego, government, may even attempt to snatch the function of forming the popular mind, thus becoming by inversion a commanding rather than a responsive instrumentality. Designing groups may penetrate into government and speak with its great authority to ends that are at odds with the general welfare. Whereas the government should have no mind but the people's mind, there is a tendency for government to declare its mind with intent that the people think the same way. "Eternal vigilance is the price of liberty," spoke the fathers from experience.

The path to welfare lies not through government as a primary agency of social control. Back of government and forms of law are the formulation of opinion and the cultivation of sentiment, of which laws are an expression. Education is a point of origin to law and government; consequently the super-governmental mission of universities and colleges, of thinkers and nonofficial philosophers, may be conceded. It is an ominous condition when it can be asserted that government, in its transient and official character, or any quasi governmental unity, as a powerful financial interest, dominates the means of social enlightenment— that the university, the press, and the pulpit are controlled. If these agencies are not nobly free, they become mere auxiliaries of government rather than contributors to the whole social mind that would employ government as a convenience. A contrast can be asserted between the whole state and the official state, the social state and the mechanized state. It is in the interests of the whole state, the common weal, that agencies of enlightenment be free to exercise the prior rights of investigation and discussion. The distinction between the people and government which was made in the case of Germany some years ago in war time, can be said to exist to some degree in any case. Institutions of learning belong peculiarly to the unofficial state and the whole people, and should be unaffected by official mood and unstirred by the comparatively ephemeral governmental organization. The educational function should be separated in control as far as may be from the vicissitudes of opportunist legislation and the fortunes of candidates for public office. It would be well indeed if the whole state, the totality of citizenship, should assimilate the spirit of a self-denying ordinance by noninterference with the processes by which truth is ascertained. There could be no more thrilling experiment than freedom of thought. Education is the most fundamental government.

If there is anything that the busy business man and the laborious laborer needs to know it is how matters stand to-day in the intellectual and scientific world. Even people of some leisure find it difficult to keep abreast of thought developments. Just to know something definite of the data and purposes of organized labor in this and other countries would require considerable effort; and there are men even in public office who do not find time to inform themselves. Nothing short of a straight drive for truth in modern terms will suffice. Similarly with cosmogony and biology. The nonscientific character of much present-day consciousness in these fields is too patent to require argument for more enlightenment. In default of fair-minded introduction to the modern cultures, the pseudo-scientific book and the patent medicine encomium have unwarrantable vogue. Physicians throw up their hands in despair over the ignorance upon vital matters shown by patients. Only the caution of commerce keeps the salesman from fatal amusement over the ignorance of customers with regard to the sources, manufacture, qualities and intrinsic values of goods. Professional men retire to guffaw in concert over revelations of naive ignorance. The minds of most of us might be better furnished.

There is need of ethical culture fairly based on modern realities; for our emotions of moral approval and disapproval are so little set to the realities of modern offenses of omission and commission, that we are like one who should habitually laugh at the wrong place and shed tears at the authentic joke. "Thou shalt not steal— small sums," says some one. Our consciences antedate big business and modern incitements. The newspapers report severe sentences to prison imposed on young men who steal used cars or forge checks for small amounts. Price jugglings on a national scale, infinitely more harm-producing, easily evade the sentinels of conscience equipped with rusty flintlocks and guttering, tallow-candle lanterns. Forgery has an ominous, common-law sound. Signing certificates of watered stock has no such horrific suggestion. We lack in modern equipment of conscience. When the full circumstances and results of conduct are brought out, when actions are interrupted in the light of all the evidence, there is little likelihood that appropriate social attitudes and revised conscience will not make their appearance.

A few decades ago British workingmen in large numbers followed the scientific instruction in popular form presented by Thomas H. Huxley, Edward Carpenter, and other able leaders. Huxley's lecture on a piece of chalk was a model of exposition on a subject of fundamental scientific import While the need of exposition in similar fields is still urgent, the greater interest to-day would lie with discussion of social and economic problems. Digestible lessons covering a wide range of unit topics, might prove singularly acceptable to-day, if presented under much the same conceptions as governed the popularization of physical science a generation ago. A wider instructional use is possible of the voluntary or involuntary leisure, always available among millions of adults and young citizens.

Change of popular attitude toward war is among the possibilities. War is waste— waste of wealth and lives. But especially does militarism devastate in the field of mental values; it is a confession of lack of vision and has never attracted men of philosophy and liberal tendencies. Militarism is sterile. The atavism of war brings into prominence and insidiously revives states of consciousness out of harmony with the higher forms of intelligence. Religious and ethical concepts go by the board in war time, and principles of conduct laboriously established among men in private dealings are discarded with the abandon of a Reservation-School Indian returned to the tepee. Theft, lying, homicide, revenge, license, violence— which in peace are outlawed— reappear in the weird relaxation of war. War is a solemn spree imperfectly hallowed by holy names and putative virtues.

It is difficult to express adequately the completeness of antithesis between orthodox militarism, as, say, developed in the Prussian war group, and social program as conceived in the nonmilitaristic mind. A history of the intellectual development of mankind could show no greater contrast than that between the military conception of values and the conceptions identified with education and social science.

Nothing is less implicit in militarism than the democratic ideal. Indeed militarism embalms and hands down as tradition the domination and servility that have characterized caste societies. Feudalism, autocracy, slavery, and the one-man show are implications. The necessity in war for the submergence of personality on the part of the soldier, for his automatization, is at loggerheads with educational theory since Pestalozzi and inverts the emphasis of individual worth asserted by Christianity and given impressive utterance in periods when human rights have been democratically defined. Whereas the aim of modern culture is to bring out personality, military practice represses and standardizes. Ties, associations, ideals, habits, interests tend to be severely erased. It was the purpose of Prussian militarism to reduce the common soldier to an automaton. Success in war would be a high price to pay for the imposition of automatized responses upon society as a whole.

In the light of social evolution the obtrusion of militarism, even when associated with unavoidable necessity on the part of defendant parties, is a deplorable interruption of progress, of the temper out of which progress springs. Any laudable program of social integration or socialization must ever present the strongest possible contrast to militarism, in point of recognition of individual worth and self-direction. It is a debasing experience for society to take on, voluntarily or perforce, temporarily or enduringly, the military mind. The dominance of military groups in society is comparable in principle to supplanting a city commission by its police force.

The fact that wide differences in native capacity exist is a stumbling block to democracy. But ultimate differences are largely due to nurture and education. The inevitable differences in individual ability are probably neither large enough nor distributed in such manner as to conflict with ideals of democracy. The potential intelligence of backward groups and peoples doubtless warrants full confidence in the theory of popular government. Large improvement comes to any mind when it is supplied with ample and suitable thought materials and stimulating opportunity. Through the general diffusion of the best knowledge, and the service of leaders obligated to satisfy a public increasingly rendered critical by education, an approximation to a classless society appears possible.

Whether rational mind shall be limited to class or developed throughout all society is a question that carries with it the issue of caste and slavery. The idea of a return to slavery of the American negro is not extinct, and attempts to destroy organization among the working class would, if successful, amount to nothing less than a step toward the vassalage and serfdom of former times.

The difficulty of abasing to slavery any considerable population would now be great indeed. The possibilities of sabotage are enormous under the conditions of modern labor. At a thousand different points industry is vulnerable to attack. Popular education can hardly be denied, though by an early imposition of narrow vocational training and neglect of quality in elementary schools, as in such rural schools as do not teach reading effectually, the status of a great number could be injuriously affected.

No society is safe that has ignorance and helplessness at its base. Rome might not have fallen had it not been for laws and strategy that undermined the welfare and checked the development of the common people. Democracy and social justice are desirable from every point of view. No social class has any assurance of continued well-being in the absence of welfare in other groups. Universal elevation of standards of living, of enlightenment, of education, and of material prosperity are much the concern of the favored minority. The employer who would break unions would harm society. The individual, unorganized, is unable to hold his own against organization. The competition of group with group is a phase of social evolution higher and more promising than that of individual with group: accordingly the attempt to disrupt and discourage organization among certain classes in society is opposed to ultimate general welfare.

Rational and less rational mind are set against each other at many points. Just as the individual is torn between impulse and reason, so is society thrust one way by reasoned conviction and evidence and turned another by instinct, unreviewed tradition, and force of custom. The welfare of society is bound up with the ascendancy of rational mind.

Every age is an age of reason, but in varying proportions and duration. The dominance of rational intelligence in material progress is an outstanding fact. Rational methods applied to manufacturing, transportation, bridge building, mining, and in all the fields in which modern materialism has made its advance, have been the formula of progress. Scientific and materialistic advance have come in the absence of repressive measures. While the early chemist was regarded with suspicion and the anatomist with horror, for a long time the scientific man has had increasing freedom from interruption by the ignorant and superstitious. Physics, astronomy, chemistry, engineering, and within limits, biology, have been allowed freedom of thought; hence the progress in corresponding fields of material civilization.

But in political, ethical, religious and economic fields, like freedom to grow has not been vouchsafed. It has not been good form to correct inadequate beliefs in these matters with the unsparing criticism that has served to advance science. Higher criticism has been the exception rather than the rule in the social consciousness. Politics and religion have been touchy subjects on which men have shown a temper that would be strangely out of place in chemical research. Experimentation and hypothesis have speeded scientific discovery, while in ethical and economic matters and in law, rational method and criticism have been less employed.

As a result we are adults in scientific knowledge and children in economic and ethical knowledge. We are adults in knowledge of skyscraper architecture, germs, internal combustion engines, thermo-dynamics, histology, long-range guns, submarines, soil physics, and plant pathology. But we are children when it comes to taxation, international concord, public utilities, poverty, unemployment, court procedure, justice and profiteering. The mind has gone ahead where few barriers have been encountered; but in other fields we are still in peevish and childish confusion. We have put away childish things in scientific agriculture and surgery, but we cling to them in relations of politics and economics. Thought is timid and restrained in the laboratory of society, though free and forging ahead in mechanical and scientific fields.

Rational intelligence must extend freely to social

problems if it is to equal here its success in the material achievements of our boasted but uncertain civilization. But of even more significance than absolute gains in knowledge is the social attitude. Viewpoint regarding fundamental matters, as war, industry, races, type of government, position of women, and the function of free intelligence, is of critical importance. Again and again must society turn to the clarification and restatement of fundamental principles. In the case of individual career, outlook and trend of thought have controlling influence; so, social attitude and assumption have ultimate importance, for these largely determine the direction of social change.

CHAPTER XVI
AVAILABLE CIVIC ENERGY

THE EARLY years of life are of little dynamic value for social organization. The child has neither the interests nor knowledge qualifying him for substantial contribution. His life is largely spent in a series of changes roughly corresponding to the early evolution of man. The lower ranges of human experience engage his activities. He is individualistic, possessing neither the motivation for social organization nor the experience on which social intelligence and vision are based. The immaturity of his faculties is a definitive barrier to contribution to social organization. Vast potentialities lie in the nurture and admonition of youth, in the formation of social mind through specific instruction, family training and the cooperative experience of school and playground and of juvenile organizations. But effective social activity is of course not for the first, fourth or fifth of the span of human life.

On the side of infancy it may be said, however, that the very ingenuousness of the child reveals clues of no small value for mature society. The happy freedom of this period knows little of class and caste distinctions. The child is the original democrat. His world is one of singularly clear values, freed from tradition and adventitious considerations. Food, relatives, actual conduct, and how things really look, are peculiarly within the child's range of veracity. The careers of St. Francis Assisi, Mark Twain, Jean Jacques Rosseau, Henry D. Thoreau and John Brown, childlike all, suggest alluring "slants" on life derived from infantile characteristics carried over to adult society.

For influence upon language the life of the child affords treasure. If the child's lead were followed, many of

377

the irregularities and monstrosities of book-controlled
English would disappear, such as the irregular verb. The
child says go, goed; not go, went. He says take and taked: not
take and took. His penchant for smoothing away the illogical
shibboleths of good grammar is unconventional. Likewise
with his unfettered phrasings and impromptu vocabulary. He
calls a spade a spade or anything else that it seems to
resemble— no small service to language. It has been
brilliantly contended by John Erskine that the greatness of
Shakespeare as a user of words was from the fact that he
spoke with the freedom of the child— thought took shape in
words with rare disregard for the dictionary, which, thus
fortunately, did not exist in his day. With the coming of the
authoritative "unabridged," modern writers are all the time
thinking of how they look from behind. Thanks be to
Hendrick Van Loon for a whiff of freedom of vocabulary in
his *Story of Mankind*. Havelock Ellis, in his *Appreciations*,
attributes virtue to Zola for enlarging literary vocabulary by
use of terms of the people. Awed by the "unabridged," we fail
to assess at their true value the naive improvisions of the
speech of childhood.

There is revisional power, too, in the child's reactions
to adults. Many a parent has perforce seen himself in a new
light through the reactions and comments of his child. The
child unwittingly acts in ways to simulate the effects of the
frontier on American mind, producing inventiveness and
versatility on the part of parents and adults in the
neighborhood.

At the other extreme of life stands the inertia of
age— its lessened motivation and completed adjustments. In
old age life loses its dynamic attributes. Interest in change
and social adventure is diminished. The big, buoyant
illusions of early manhood lose their sustaining power. The
circle of vision tends to become limited to the routine of
familiar business and a safe place for slippers. What matters

social reform when, at best, the fruits cannot be enjoyed by the laborer, when, unlike youth, with its assumption of an earthly near-eternity, age knows for a certainty the remorseless haste of the sands of the hourglass?

It is not even a certainty that old age is peculiarly fitted for counsel, if reference be had to the newer problems. For counsel touching matters of long experience old age is especially fitted, though there is the danger of misplaced precedent. The adage, "Old men for counsel, young men for war" implies no improvement on former methods of settling differences. For arbitration and international relations, the counsel of the elder statesmen is not the happiest. There is a tendency on the part of age to put new wine into old bottles, even to deny that the wine is of recent fermentation.

But a cultural extension of dynamic interests and information until very late in life is happily illustrated in the case of many individuals who have tapped the spiritual fountains of youth. The flexibility of a used and frank mind is remarkable in age, while, on the other hand, there are persons of twenty who show the fixation of habit and viewpoint commonly attributed only to advanced years.

The highest point of individual development, viewed socially, is the age, when, with maturity of powers, there is imaginative daring, scepticism of tradition, and ambition coupled with experience that makes aware of the complexity of social relationships and of the difficulty of producing lasting change by violence and revolution.

This intermediate age, in the case of women, is now made especially significant by the franchise. Their civic potentialities are the greater for their relative inexperience and therefore notably receptive attitude and undulled expectations. Their tendency to test institutions and measures by personal effects is of the utmost value to society, for the world has too long been under the spell of institutional formality and solemnity that have diverted attention from painful facts of living conditions. The civic youngness of women provides a factor of spontaneity and significant ingenuousness. The social structure of the future will differ from any before known or possible otherwise than through the presence of the feminine factor in politics.

Not only in civic childlikeness but also in a centering of interest upon child welfare does the woman citizen promise to be a powerful factor in the coming state. The question has historically never been asked in politics. What effect will this measure or that policy have upon the welfare of the child? Non-use of this touchstone has left legislation in the control of one-sided forces. To apply the principle of child welfare means nothing short of a radical reorganization of viewpoint with ultimate revolution of policies. Any public issue, from tariff to good roads, from food laws to prohibition, is viewable in the light of possible effects upon childhood. The woman legislator and the woman voter will be sure to raise the new question. It will be hard to convince mothers, for example, of the necessity of war under any circumstances. Having in mind their hazards of childbirth and their long and arduous experience in securing the physical survival and well-being of their children, they will be likely to agree with General Grant in declaring that there never was a war that could not have been avoided. The enfranchisement of women is likely to prove the turning point between the older state and a revised civilization.

Intelligence in man and woman is a resource which has its limitations as truly as there are limitations of natural resources consisting of coal, oil, or forests. The conservation of intelligence is of the utmost importance. Mind may be undeveloped, misdirected, wasted— futilely employed. The art of civilization involves to a greater degree than heretofore the conservation of mental energy. As the space surrounding a target is larger than the bull's-eye and the chances of missing are vastly more numerous than of making a hit, so the possibilities of error outnumber those of success in the attainment of social ideals. The skillful utilization of limited mental resources therefore is a challenge supreme.

The civic interest is in competition with other interests, and shares, rather than monopolizes, the mental resources of the individual. Indeed it is not of rare occurrence that the civic interest is quite overshadowed. When not overtopped by other interests it is nevertheless limited by conditions of fatigue. The amount of time and energy that the average citizen has left over from private business for the affairs of his city or the business of a board of education, to say nothing of state and federal governments, is oftentimes slight indeed; it is only a feeble fringe. Preoccupation and fatigue are allied for the neglect of civic duty. Especially is it true of factory and mine employees and manual workers in homes and on farms, that there is little energy available for public affairs.

Physical fatigue is directly opposed to interest in the commonwealth, for such fatigue is opposed to the gathering of the knowledge out of which intelligent interest grows. There is a vast amount of actual physical disqualification for intelligent citizenship. The leisured class has usually monopolized politics and managed government largely because of leisure. The makings of civic and political wisdom are not represented by farmers and mechanics who meet late in the evening after the day's work. The singular lucidity of the Athenian Greek's mind and the rare civic perfection of early Athens were not unrelated to the fact that the Athenian citizen was a man who did not know what a day's work was. Democracy will have to find time in the day's program for civic activity. It will not thrive on fragments of time purloined from sleep. In the church of democracy it will not do to have the pewholders snoring beneath the pulpit.

Like fatigue, in representing a factor of civic deprivation, is the modern tendency to give heed only to certain types of experience and information. We have come far since the pansophists of four centuries ago. Francis Bacon took all knowledge to be his province. Men of learning used to blush when forced to admit there was anything they did not know. The attempt was literally to know it all. Milton nearly accomplished the feat. We have decided that it is necessary to know it all simply in one line. The specialist is quite sensitive about revealing any ignorance in his own field, but it seems to detract from the fullness of specialization to be caught with information outside of it. Far from blushing for ignorance of general information the specialist owns up to it or even parades it.

Such contented ignorance might be simply refreshing did it not go so far as to include social science and public questions. But these are included too often; and issues which the citizen is, in democratic theory, charged with finding solutions for in his own thoughts, are lumped together for neglect with knowledge of the other man's specialty. Hence the physician may complacently disavow any interest in or knowledge of public business, and the architect look pained upon being presumed to be interested in a railroad strike except as it means an unwelcome interruption of business.

Such facts and ideals of specialization strike at the very heart of democratic organization. Every citizen should have besides his occupational specialization a civic specialization. Capable or brilliant minds should not be lost to the commonwealth through being penned up exclusively in a profession. Every professional school might properly require a knowledge of economic and social science, of world history and trends of government. The new ignorance should have no standing in modern society. No electrical engineer, dentist, accountant, trained nurse, pharmacist, should be licensed without showing the possession of the essentials of a specialization for efficiency in citizenship under present-day conditions. The candidate who disclosed a dangerous indifference could be advised to emigrate to any country still having a monarchical form of government.

The aversion to becoming an actor in civic business is partly due to the slowness of parliamentary procedure and the laboriousness of the committee. Brisk business men are tortured by the verbose indirection of the city commission or the state legislature. One enters committee meetings with feelings not wholly different from those ascribed by Dante to victims entering the nether region. It is so easy, comparatively, to get things done for oneself by oneself and so devious and irritating to do business with debating clubs. The relative futility of councils and committees is a matter of jest. Congressional method is slow and inefficient. The committee on public business reminds one of the so-called measuring worm that, with its rear body attached to a surface, arches its back and with its claw-equipped front body reaches and feels and tries in all directions for a safe contact, and perhaps makes an end by refraining from forward movement.

Yet laborious and time-consuming parliamentarianism is the only way apparently for liquidating the problems of the myriad-headed public. In private business, outside of corporations, the individual has only one will to express. In public business unreconciled groups and individuals, the community body of the state, press for consideration their conflicting interests; this gives pause. One type of mental product from deliberative assemblies is well represented in pre-election speeches of candidates, which minimize hostilities by presenting platitudes and declaring for propositions that have become extinct through unanimous consent.

The character of legislative procedure is largely due to the guessing of the minds of constituents represented by members. Given a clearer mandate from constituents congresses would fumble less. Apart from the necessary circumspection of dealing with many-sided issues, the dilatory and lethargic character of collective procedure rests on the curable defect of lack of mechanism for ascertaining majority opinion. Collective deliberation is clouded, too, it must be said, by the psychology of vanity and display. The talkative member is not infrequently more concerned with rhetorical display than with the truth of intercourse and the prosperity of projects.

The work done in parliamentary bodies in the form of analysis through discussion is work that must be done somewhere. The bringing of minds into effective agreement is of fundamental value. The process of making up one's own mind is often slow enough; then how much more deliberate must be the process of forming policy collectively? The making up of individual mind, moreover, is not only slow, but the conclusions which one reaches independently are almost certain to be found faulty in some particulars. One rarely thinks a thing out so fully that he is not compelled to modify his thought when it is subjected to criticism.

The burden which democracy throws upon its deliberative bodies might be lessened by preparatory study and discussion on the part of citizens organized in small groups. A network of clubs for civic study would lay a foundation for a more expeditious disposal of public issues through legislation. Such study of social principles would clear away much of the difficulty that now faces the legislator. In democracy citizenship is a career rather than merely a voting privilege.

A phase of effective citizenship has to do with the conservation of mental resources. Social welfare demands that the individual apportion his energy between personal and community functions. It follows that whatever economies can be effected in vital forces may contribute to socially creative energy. Avoidance of energy-wasting situations is enjoined for personal well-being and for meeting the requirements of a civilization ever becoming more complex.

Energy is conserved by reposeful attitude and the cultivation of relaxation. One occasionally sees a person who nervously rides in an automobile without touching the upholstery at the back, and others who while riding in trains support bundles and packages that could be placed on a mechanical rest without adding to the load of the locomotive. The flexing of muscles and holding them in cramped positions tire. With the arm relaxed the weight is from the shoulder; but with unnecessary rigidity of muscles or with faulty bodily positions the nervous system assumes an abnormal burden with reference to gravitation.

An application of scientific management in the use of one's endowment of energy might make a large contribution to social as well as personal welfare. A multitude of items will occur to one. Excessive talking, the energetic expression of ideas that go by implication, the head-on collisions of disorderly conduct in conversation, might be mentioned. The fatiguing character of worry and fear is everywhere recognized. Not only is fear exhaustive of energy but in many cases serves no purpose, as imagined crises often fail to make their appearance, and the final problem is not one that was anticipated.

Social contacts are of themselves fatiguing, for they are stimulating. Alert attention is provoked by the many new situations that develop when two or more are together. When one is under observation he undergoes more of a nerve strain than when off by himself. To sit or stand in a conspicuous position, to be where others can watch every move, is an exacting experience. Persons who work in offices in full view of passers-by are subjected to a certain strain from this cause. There is little relaxation with full publicity. Hence the value of partitions, screens, ground-glass panes, awnings— anything that will soften the gaze of the observer and afford a suggestion of the privacy of the caveman's cave, the cottage, and the castle.

Predominant employment of the finer muscle represents a special tax upon energy. It is less fatiguing to use the larger muscles of the body and limbs than to do things requiring nice adjustment of the smaller muscles. It is far easier to work in the garden than to write with a pen. Indeed people find their spirits restored by turning from the minute movements of eye and finger to the large movements of play and ordinary physical labor. One of the errors formerly common in dealing with the child and youth was to require an undue amount of work involving close muscular coördination. An example of this is given in *Village Life in America*, by Caroline Cowles Richards. At the age of fourteen, in 1856, she wrote thus in her diary:

> Grandmother has offered me one dollar if I will stitch a linen shirt bosom and wrist bands for Grandfather and make the sleeves. I have commenced, but, oh, my! it is an undertaking. I have to pull the threads out and then take up two threads and leave three. It is very particular work and Anna says the stitches must not be visible to the naked eye. I have to fell the sleeves with the tiniest seams and stroke all the gathers and put a stitch on each gather. Minnie Bellows is the best one in school with her needle and is a dabster at patching. She cut a piece right out of her new calico dress and matched a new piece in it and none of us could tell where it was. I am sure it would not be safe for me to try that.

Modern employments abound in kinds of labor involving finer muscular movements. Compare the occupation of the proofreader with that of the primitive hunter or shepherd. The printer's and the tailor's trades outrage a good many of the natural tendencies of man in their restraints upon free and large movements. The accountant whose work is to set down figures and make computations is singularly restricted in his mental activities and no less so in the physical activities associated with pencils, pens, and rulers. A great deal of scientific work, carried on with microscope and laboratory instruments, represents experience quite abnormal when judged from the viewpoint of man's early free state and the vast leisure of pre-civilization.

It becomes correspondingly important to mitigate the severities and nervous strains of modern employments. Change of work, the avoidance of monotony, shift of physical position and limitation of hours are all to be given consideration. Rubber heels mediate happily between the nervous system and the flinty substitutes for the yielding surface of good old mother earth over which our ancestors trod with springy step.

Considerable attention might well be given to method of attack upon pieces of work. The man who is barely under way at ten o'clock in the forenoon is more likely to accomplish a large amount of work than one who wakes early and eats breakfast with agitation. The day can be spoiled by a too early and too intense start in the morning. The time spent in leisurely approach is far from wasted. The mind can be best utilized by charging one's thoughts with a purpose and then allowing the inner resources to crystallize toward achievement. Once the purpose is in mind, subject matter will seem almost to collect itself. Items will drift into consciousness and cement themselves to the main theme. By charging the mind with the general topic, a sort of law of gravitation operates for preparation. Material that would not be noticed if the mind were not charged with the topic will be picked up casually.

Premature effort and worried diligence have little constructive value. Many of the most critical exertions rely upon habit for effective performance. It is a well-known fact that habitual acts are performed most successfully when there is a minimum of attention given to them. Hence it is that insouciance wins victories denied to the Marthas who take too much thought. The speaker probably gives more heed to the introduction of his speech than to succeeding parts, and there is no part that the audience usually would more willingly dispense with. One writes his opening paragraphs with rigid care and is often not unwisely advised to throw away the first pages. Assuming a class of individuals whose affairs tend to exceed possibility of performance, one feels that a closer scrutiny of energy-using methods is highly warranted.

Reinforcement of energy is no less a matter of concern than is the avoidance of positively spendthrift practices. One man finds that he needs to take a "snooze" after the midday meal for a successful day. Another, a university president, goes to bed a short time before appearing on the public platform. One widely known forensic performer does not, for a half day before his public addresses, take part in conversation or allow people to see him. Thus he saves up power for the special occasion.

The individual's energy is not a fixed amount like the water in a dam. The quantity of energy appears to be governed by various factors, and it is not possible by resting three hundred sixty-five days to have three hundred sixty-five times the normal amount of energy at the expiration of that period. Nevertheless there is unquestionably a "pool" formation for energy over brief periods. Ordinarily, rather brief periods of recuperation suffice to restore the energies, though in cases of extreme fatigue and exhaustion months may be insufficient.

An interesting phase of the subject of energy utilization is that illustrated in "blowing off steam." The angry person who vents his feelings soon subsides to equilibrium and forgets his troubles. Similarly with the man with a big idea who talks himself out on the subject. Refraining from much vocalization the individual would possibly compile a treatise or write a novel or develop an invention or launch a business enterprise. But by oozing interest and wasting the dynamic forces of motive by dissertations in the smoking room, John Doe remains John Doe in a state of exploded incentive. The surest way to lose interest in a new idea of one's own and to check the cerebral irritation that might issue in creation is to give the thought premature exploitation and too much sunlight. Indeed there is such a thing as conversing a subject into too great lucidity and hardening its fiber into the commonplace. The greatest and most inspiring works of literature contain an element of illusion and error. A degree of foggy-mindedness is as necessary to creative genius as dampness is to mushrooms. One reads H. G. Wells and wonders if his immensely suggestive and entertaining production might not have been frozen to the root by rigorous criticism and scrutiny.

The fatal tendency to talk off ideas has oftentimes been counteracted by personal circumstances which the world calls unfortunate. Many great achievements in the intellectual sphere have come from men and women who lacked normal expression. Sickness, deformity, timidity, unsocial disposition, imprisonment— all these interfere with the usual run of experiences and contacts and force the mind to develop unwonted ways of expression. Darwin said that if illness had not kept him out of society he would not have made his scientific researches. The person who has reached that goal of misguided endeavor, perfect correspondence with environment, empties as fast as he fills. The world would be infinitely poorer if deprived of the brain product of men who have been rubbed sore and had no one at hand to tell it to.[1]

---

[1] A valuable exposition of this thought is found in an article by Wesley Raymond Wells, "Intellectual Value of Physical and Social Maladjustment," *School and Society*, November 12, 1921.

In the strategy of civilization much depends upon what objectives enlist the mental energies, for serious loss is possible through irrelevant activities. The Middle Ages witnessed a vigorous exercise of mind. The universities were seats of learning, and scholars were diligent and jealous of repute. There were prodigies of scholarly zeal. But with all the fidelity and devotion of capable mind the intellectual output was negligible. The science of the period was insignificant and the literary output was largely the rubbish of scholasticism. The Middle Ages were the blind alley of human thought.

It is not enough that there be intellectual effort; it is important how that effort is organized and to what ends. The types of problems, the issues developed and stated, the objectives of investigations— these count for more than sheer mental ability.

The possession of fine powers of intelligence is no assurance of their profitable use. Individuals highly promising in youth may defeat the hopes of those interested in their success, because of failure to choose profitable aims and to direct energies aright. The character of one's ambitions, his interests, his perseverance, his assessment of values, are of more critical significance than mental endowment of itself alone. Often the person of mediocre parts makes the greatest contribution to professional or business development, because he judges well what ends to pursue and what to avoid. Concentration is necessary, joined with suitable objective. A young man may prepare for the law in a night school in the time taken by another of equal mental agility to learn to play a surpassing game of billiards.

Spendthrift use of mental resources, the waste of irrelevance, the taking of false trails, the exaggeration of the insignificant, the searching for gold in the air instead of in the ground, find ample illustration in the lives of men and of communities: hyper-trophied and frantic interest in sports and games, wordy, insincere battles for conquest rather than for truth, a mythlike sex romanticism, easeful and cajoling forms of religious languor, the perennial crops of over-advertised fads and salvations that serve to becloud issues, the obsession of money-making, the glut of current information, the treadmill of social conventionality, the corruption of thought to details.

Probably enough mental energy has been consumed in reading detective stories to have served to sift all theories of taxation, marshal all its facts and provide a perfection of theory and practice in this field. Baseball energy, commercially evoked to extravagant proportions, is perhaps equivalent to that required for overcoming illiteracy in a backward country. Invention would know no end if the surplus imagination of sex could be released to science. Civilization would be centuries ahead if insoluble or factitious theological questions had not engaged men's minds for so long and drained the faculties. Imagine the constructive power of a Jonathan Edwards transferred from terroristic speculation to the campaign to humanize or abolish child labor.

Social welfare rests back upon the mental energies and traits of the individual members of society. The functioning of mind is the crucial fact in social organization. Whether higher forms of social integration are possible or not is to be decided by how the individual's mind functions socially in its various aspects of instinctive tendency, habit, attention, memory, observation, conception, reasoning, and motivation. Social disintegration always impends, and no former civilization has escaped the factors of disorganization and lapse, which many have assumed are implicit in individual psychology. Destruction of civilization and even destruction of mankind through wars, the recrudescence of slavery, and a fatal fatigue of constructive effort and of invention and altruistic zeal are a continuing menace. There are not wanting those who hold that the peculiar attributes of human mind and consciousness— so different from animal intelligence and apparently so at odds with the intelligence of nature— originated in a cosmic chance— the supreme blunder of the universe, a blunder that would be canceled by social devolution. The renouncing of the intellectual life, the exaltation of habit, concessions to reflexes and instincts, and the abandonment of painfully sustained strivings would, from this point of view, be quite as natural as continuing the battle.

If mental resources are a worked-out mine, then of course the stage is set for the modern nations to follow in decline the nations that have heretofore risen only to collapse. But if our mental assets are capable of vastly richer development and more skillful employment to social ends, the obvious program is that of utilizing in the best ways our undeveloped resources. It is a fair statement that we know as yet little of the possibilities of mankind. Only the crudest methods have been employed for the conservation and the beneficial exploitation of human faculties. The most interesting of projects is that of redirecting and more fully developing the forces of consciousness. Here is the master undertaking of all the ages. Sociology and psychology are new sciences— scarcely more than new interests. The emphasis of the last two centuries has been on solving problems centering in natural science and in industrial production. The social problem is yet to be attacked with like plentitude of energy and idealism. Though our mental assets show natural and habitual limitations, there is promise that the individual is capable of acquiring an adequate social mind, a mind enlarged and rectified as contrasted with mind to-day.

The large problem of society is to provide joyous outlet for inherited tendencies and constructively to redirect such expressions of instinct as are not in harmony with rational program. Untutored human instinct may lead to as disastrous reactions under the circumstances of newly invented civilization as are witnessed in the case of the moth seeking the open flame through its instinctive tropism to light. Increasingly man finds need of revising his instinctive tendencies in the interest of safety, progress, and social stability. The guidance afforded by impromptu consciousness is and has always been costly and deficient.

In earlier and more rudimentary stages of human society, the largeness of the jurisdiction of instincts pure and simple and the narrow and timid reliance upon higher intelligence, were associated with a multitude of evils and oppressions. The individual who does not bring his impulses under analysis, and in many instances flout his instinctive promptings, is incapable of the greatest usefulness to society, and is doomed to a personal inferiority in terms of worldly success and achievements resting upon sustained attention and self-restraint. Just in proportion to the conscious regulation of natural tendency and the correlative exaltation of the higher powers of adaptation, do individuals and society achieve prosperity. The criminal class is a class with whom instinct prevails; savages live by instinct. Masses of people, in recent centuries of partial civilization, exemplify exuberant activity of the tendencies that formed the mind of prehistoric man. Here and there throughout the ages have appeared the man, the group, the school who, by sunlit lives, have shown the race the kindliness and creativeness possible when the expressions of instinct have been refined. The future belongs to the great natural motivations of instinct illuminated by logical analysis, developed attention, self-restraint verified knowledge, and disciplined imagination.

The Crisis Factor in Thinking

FIRST PUBLISHED IN 1914
IN THE *AMERICAN JOURNAL OF
SOCIOLOGY*
VOL. XIX, No. 4, January, 1914

IN VIEW of the fact that one reasons only when there are problems to be solved and that conditions of surprise provoke mental activity, and in view of the further fact that, historically, the greatest progress has been made when peoples have been plunged into new environments, as in America and Australasia, it is interesting to note current tendencies with reference to probable effects upon racial and individual initiative and reasoning.

It is no longer, if ever, necessary to understand principles and constructions to be able to use machinery. Commercial rivalry has resulted in the production of engines, watches, typewriters, and mechanisms of all sorts that require but a minimum of intelligent management. Many machines are put on the market "fool proof." Even the carton of breakfast wafers tells us where to open the box– "Cut on this line."

Along with the tendency on the part of manufacturers to minimize the need of mechanical insight on the part of the public, there is a centralizing of intelligence in managerial offices and a corresponding removal of problems from employees and agents. A dead level of almost automatic performance is forced upon factory employees, departmental workers, and quite generally upon salaried classes, not excluding even a large percentage of those employed in educational service. True, the individual of natural initiative may break through the organization and regimentation to which he is subject and achieve some measure of creative experience, but can it be doubted that the element of surprise and thought-compelling situations may diminish under modern conditions?

Contrast the regimented lives of city workers and persons whose activities are directed from central offices with the frontiersman's life, or with a single day of camping out. The improvising of utensils, the meeting of emergencies, and reactions to the unexpected, give an exhilarating taste of a life which seems of a different world. The life of the frontier has given the world many of its most valuable assets, from Lincoln and Mark Twain to the Torrens title-registration law and the Australian ballot. And one may add that to peculiarly free conditions of nurture we must attribute much of the resourcefulness of Edison and Darwin.

It is common to refer to modern life as highly complex. This should not be taken to mean that the complexity is necessarily thought-compelling. Often quite the contrary. One's relations to this complex life may be so simple as to preclude those conditions of surprise required for intellectual advancement. The question to be asked is, to what extent does the individual find himself actually burdened with the problems arising out of modem life? If he shares but slightly or not at all in the management of the enterprise with which he is associated, if he is surrounded by authoritative rules and conventions, if his work is blocked out for him, it may be that anything like initiative and resourcefulness will be virtually out of the question. More grave than the economic menace of big business is the intellectual menace of centralized intelligence, represented by the management of vast enterprises from central offices, accompanied on the part of employees by rule-following self-effacement, mechanical compliance, and automatic performance. The arid intellectual atmosphere of large regimented groups in business and industry forms a striking phenomenon in society today. Business and industrial complexity certainly creates many problems, but by a centralized solution the rank and file of employees tend to become far less thoughtful than if they were scattered about pursuing individual and precarious vocations.

In contrast with industrial conditions which present fewer new situations compelling thought on the part of the rank and file, civic and political conditions seem now, as never before, to demand reasoning of the citizen. The psychological requirements for evoking the highest mental processes are fulfilled in the many problems of the day which knock at every door for solution.

In our many political problems appear both evidence of lack of skill in reasoning and promise of gaining that skill, provided the electorate is admitted to the practical solution of political problems, especially under direct legislation, and is not ultimately displaced by the governmental expert representing highly centralized political intelligence. If questions of government are thrown out to all voters, as in the pamphlet to voters in Oregon containing 40 measures under the initiative and referendum, there will surely exist sufficient opportunity for exercising popular thinking. If on the other hand, the average voter were to feel that he had no more part in the administration of society than has the factory employee and the newspaper reporter in the administration of the enterprises with which they are connected, one of the greatest opportunities for developing resourcefulness and reasoning ever presented would be lost. The mental welfare of the race demands that political questions be increasingly forced upon the electorate, and that the electorate be expanded to include those who have minds to develop.

It is not to be inferred that situations of surprise immediately elicit reasoning of good quality or even reasoning at all. A cry of fire throws many into random and hysterical actions. Repeated experiences with fires, however, produce more intelligent reaction.

The persistence of strikes is an evidence of inability to respond to historically new situations by thinking. Strikes suggest the random, ill-coordinated actions of a horse frightened at a newspaper, or the embarrassment of a schoolboy before an unexpected question. A strike is a short-sighted method of securing economic justice. The efficient method of striking by votes and expressing demands through the established channels, through laws, implies a connectedness of thinking that has not yet been fully attained.

The election of mutually incongruous representatives by equal majorities of the same voters is an evidence to the same end. The preference for indirect rather than direct taxation and the assent to specious arguments for war are significant. To these might be added a multitude of vote-winning tricks with which the practical politician is familiar but which are a reflection upon the analytic intelligence of those influenced.

That the new situations of the day in civic affairs have found the public unprepared for their rational solution, and that even leaders who might otherwise be statesmen are found lacking in administrative ability of the highest grade is evidenced by failures of government. The object-minded man, the man trained too narrowly in the methods of money-making businesses, the man who never had any use for the intangible and the theoretical, and the man whose mind has never been subjected to the discipline of abstractions in literature and liberal science are largely responsible for the bunglings of legislation and the absence of consistent and real statesmanship. One of the most hopeful signs of the times, however, is that the people are turning instinctively for guidance to the university doctrinaire who but a few years ago would have been contemptuously retired in favor of the "practical" man.

Under the leadership of wise theorists the extent to which the general public may gain power to deal with the principles of social administration will no doubt prove remarkable. Uninstructed, the average man feels inadequate to the problems of political science. But the celerity with which considerable numbers get hold of general principles and theory in ethical and sociological fields proves the possibilities of popular thinking. The essential conditions are the imminence of new situations, the feeling of serious personal responsibility for their proper solution, and a fair amount of intellectual leadership. Too heavy problems thrown at once upon an unprepared public lead to discouragement and irrational response. Under right leadership the popular reactions to conditions of social surprises are increasingly rational, and the intellectual development of the race demands both the problem and the thoughtful reaction.

To insure the full benefits of new situations as compelling thinking there must be a willingness to attack difficulties. The presence of new situations does not mean much for thinking unless these are such as cannot be avoided or such as the individual elects to grapple with. Unwillingness to grapple with difficulties and undergo mental stress and strain, which appears especially in levels of luxury, and affects great numbers of young people unwisely brought up, is a bar to the evolution of intelligence. The spirit to find novel situations with which to grapple is, from the standpoint of mind in evolution, most admirable of all.

The part played by education in developing reasoning should be unambiguous. Nowhere should there be presented so many new situations and conditions of surprise as afforded by education. The school may provide more problems in an hour than the student would consciously meet elsewhere in months. From one point of view the schools are agencies to precipitate upon students unexpected situations and thought-compelling emergencies. The very nature of education for thinking implies that stubborn problems surprise the student at every turn. To the extent to which the student picks his way easily through a course, to that extent he is deprived of the invaluable experience of being compelled to think. A curriculum should represent a gauntlet of emergencies, each necessitating initiative, resolution, a grasp of new relations, resourcefulness, mental readjustment, and constructive thinking.

One who deals with students must observe that the higher processes seem to be largely unexercised in many cases. Whether less exercised than formerly may be a matter of debate. But there can be no doubt as to the meaning of certain facts and certain tendencies.

The essentially uneducated university graduate is not a myth. When one can tell neither by range of interests nor sureness of diction and thought whether a suspect is a university product or not, there is reason for pause. The fact stated by James Bryce recently, that the greatest advances in science have been made by men not trained as specialists, suggests a question as to the possibility of producing broad thinkers by intensive specialization. The gaining of the whip hand over the faculty by student interests, representing spectacular athletics and social diversion and social caste supported by wealth that discredits the impecunious professor, tends to make it difficult for instructors to hold students to grinding tasks. The instructor is perhaps more likely to find that he is subjected to problems by the student than that he is subjecting the student to thought-compelling conditions.

While thinking rests upon information, the proportion of information to thinking is a vital point. The educational world is emphasizing information as never before. This emphasis appears in attention paid to the kinds of knowledge regarded as most useful and in fulness of data and details in bulky departmental courses and swollen syllabi. It is even not yet a crime for a writer to take more pages than his contribution to thought actually demands. Whole volumes appear devoted to the expansion of a single proposition which an intelligent reader could grasp in a few moments. Over-elaboration of details leaves little need to fill in outlines and tax one's own inventiveness. An excessive amount of reference reading and the lecture system alike emphasize mass of material at the possible expense of thought activity.

As an example of an almost perfect educational situation the hypothetical case of the law schools suggests itself. Here the student is called upon to apply known principles to a new set of facts. He must meet an emergency with the aid of memory, but with the inevitable use of reasoning. Were the example of the hypothetical case more freely followed in general classes, instructors would less frequently encounter chambers of vacuity in the student's mind or sink through a quicksand of feeble associations, illustrated by the inability of a college student to decide whether any of her relatives were living two thousand years ago.

Society has a right to look to education to maintain standards of reasoning. If it fails here there is nothing in education to guarantee that along with the diffusion of useful data there will not ensue a dearth of inventiveness and a decline of civilization. A spurious educational activity is conceivable unattended by real intellectual improvement. Assuming the dementalizing influences of centralized industry, and cognizant of the distrust of popular ability to assume the duties logically devolving upon democratic citizenship, one realizes the importance of the question of the sufficiency of education to provide effective demands upon the higher mental powers. If our complex life is actually an increasingly simple and unexacting life for the individual, and if living is to become steadily easier in demands upon thought, the importance of assuring every individual insistent problems is not to be underrated. Railroad tickets are delivered at the door, and the exigencies of travel quite forestalled. Every care and worry are taken over by agents and experts-for a consideration. Struggle and confusion, judgment and enforced experimentation are ruled out by over-prosperous parents and coddling functionaries. It was never more easy for a simpleton to live. But let us not forget that an easy environment, with few conditions of surprise, throws the individual down to the lower reactions and swings the beam toward devolution and degeneracy.

A Conservative's View of Poverty

FIRST PUBLISHED IN 1917
IN THE *AMERICAN JOURNAL OF
SOCIOLOGY*
VOL. XXII, No. 6, May, 1917

THE ATTACK ON POVERTY

There is an institution which is as old as the world—poverty— old enough to command respect. But how goes it with poverty today? Instead of contentment and approval there is skepticism and challenge. While the poor cannot all be expected to be enthusiastic for poverty, the lessening enthusiasm of people of culture, means, and position is not encouraging. And there are those who boldly criticize existing conditions— speak ill of ways of getting rich— or fanatically propose a national conference for the abolition of poverty.

The institution of poverty is under attack. Those interested in keeping things as they are, believing in the rightness of existing conditions, need be alert. If inconsiderate comments, such as have gained currency in recent years, continue, poverty as an institution will be undermined, as was the institution of slavery by the writings of William Lloyd Garrison and the Abolitionists, and as exclusive male suffrage has been by Susan B. Anthony and Dr. Anna Howard Shaw.

Those attacking poverty are having everything too much their own way. Believers in things as they are must be numerous; but arguments in rebuttal are few, while those who oppose poverty are vociferous. Those who have great wealth hang on to it; they do not argue.

Hence the importance of defense at this critical time. There is need to review the whole social system and to point out where poverty-abolitionists would do harm if their views went into effect. There is need of saying, "Look here, look there"; need of pointing out how conditions would be changed for the worse under a different distribution of wealth. To maintain the *status quo* will require active effort. Otherwise the peculiar advantages enjoyed under the existing

economic system are not likely to be fully appreciated by
the general public.

POVERTY AND PRECEDENT

One who comes to the defense of the present order
finds himself fairly choked with arguments. Thoughts come
to mind with such impetuosity that the vocal organs are
jammed and overcome if speech is attempted, and the pen
devoted to setting down the ideas tends to plunge through
the paper and to contaminate with ink those parts of the
unwritten sheet immediately surrounding the puncture; while
if a typewriter be used, the authorship of confutation heeds
not the ringing of the bell and the stoppage of the carriage at
the end of the line, whereby there results the piling up of
impressions in one place, with corresponding lack of
progression.

There is composition that halts for lack of ideas.
There is that which clogs from having too many. The latter is
that of one who lays himself to our subject. Where begin? is
the question—there is so much to be said. One powerful
concept does, however, free itself from the mass and claims
first chance of record—the argument from precedent.

The poor will be always with us. They always have
been; why change? They have always been uncomfortable;
why experiment? Time has sanctified poverty, made it sacred.
It has always been. Let it always be. Would we do irreverence
to the fathers by introducing novelty? No, let us be guided by
the lamp of experience—nay, candle. Whenever the world
departs from precedent there is trouble. Ignoring precedent
results in doing something new; but if precedent is followed
changes do not occur. Precedent gives a feeling of peace. It is
better to be content under bad conditions than to change, for
change is change. Let those who have not, be content with
conditions—let them imitate the rich, who are reconciled to

theirs. The lack of respect for precedent is one of the saddest blows today's conservative has to suffer. Actually, some propose change for the sake of improvement. While change of some kinds is proper, as change of clothes, social change is a different matter. Conservatives tend to regard social change as distinctly and conclusively unwelcome. There is no use of saying more upon precedent; other arguments are ahead, and they seem to be jealous of every syllable that postpones. The claims of precedent must be felt rather than reasoned about. One just feels that poverty must always be.

CHARITY

Little do we realize what a catastrophe it would be for charity workers if poverty were abolished. The special field of these workers is the slums. Without slums there would be no charity organizations and spirit of social service and benevolence. Many of the charity workers have made special preparation for their work, have taken courses in universities, and have invested money in their vocation. To change conditions so that charity would be unnecessary would throw many out of work and deprive them of a means of livelihood. The machinery for distributing money to the poor is complex, and a good many people are required to operate it; and, while the poor themselves may not receive much of what is donated for charity, if there were no poor nothing would be donated. Hence the poor are indispensable.

The spirit of charity is singularly sweet. Who would see it pass away? Our laws have already trespassed upon the realm of benevolence, for conditions are not as they were in the Middle Ages, when beggars were allowed to be seen and alms-giving was a heavenly virtue. Charity cannot exist without objects of charity. If justice ever takes the place of benevolence, there will be such a decline of charity as the world never saw. Conditions will not be the same. The person who now buys a ticket at a generous figure for a charity ball might have to give up something beforehand, and would feel less inclined to go. Much as one might like to see poverty abolished, one should think twice about it if with the passing of poverty the pleasure and privilege of giving away worn garments also is to disappear.

SPECIALIZATION

This is an age of specialization; everybody sees that. But nobody seems to connect the idea of specialization with the need of having the poor always with us in society. Yet specialization, for its fullest application, requires economic grades, classes, and stratifications.

Some are to specialize as producers and some as consumers. Thus the highest development in these respective fields may be reached. No one can do all things equally well. If the producer should try to be a really proficient consumer, he would likely fall short of the highest standards; and, on the other hand, if the expert consumer attempted to make himself over into a producer, he might similarly achieve but mediocre results. It is best that producer and consumer each practice his forte, and thereby reach some perfection.

The awkward attempts of people who become suddenly rich to live up to their consumptional opportunities should be sufficient proof of the place of specialization in standards of living and of the imperative need of keeping producers where they belong. The hive furnishes a neat illustration. There are queens, drones, and workers. Each class is specialized, each plays its appointed part, and each has a different standard of living.

Little do the poverty-abolitionists appreciate the peculiar biological advantages of a state of poverty. If reformers will keep their hands off long enough, people will come to differ physically and otherwise like bees. But with a more uniform and monotonous distribution of wealth such differences cannot develop. The diet of the very poor results in a class of people who can almost eat nails. The babies of the destitute take milk from unsterilized bottles with big flies clustering about, drink it sour, and live—some of them. This tends to give us a class who do not require pampering. Hardships that would be most unwelcome and injurious to people on a higher plane can be borne by the lower classes. For the sake of developing a class that can bear hardships severe conditions must be provided, and poverty includes all the necessary conditions.

Ill-disposed critics of things as they are do not suitably value a certain extensive and increasing specialization laboriously undertaken by the extremely rich. It is no small matter to find new ways of spending money. It racks the constitution to maintain discontent with everything that savors of the ordinary. Many a man of great wealth would be glad to put on old clothes and go out and roll, but he keeps up appearances for the sake of his wife. The strain of keeping up strenuous consumption often wrecks the nervous system, though in time, by the law of specialization, the favored classes get used to it. How absurd, then, to underestimate the services of those who carry the burden of great wealth and pave the way, often through dutiful dissipation, to new methods of expenditures. Somebody has to face the problem of spending the huge surplus left after the wages are paid, a problem becoming greater every year. Specialization is the solution.

THE VICARIOUS RICH

All sorts of misunderstandings abound in the literature—if one can call it such—of the critics of the established order. And everywhere there is failure to appreciate the services rendered by great spenders. The rich are vicarious. Let us see.

By holding wealth back from the poor the very rich take upon their own shoulders the risk of moral degeneracy associated with luxury and pampered indulgence. Imagine what would happen if everybody could put up at the best hotels. The rich fall grandly into line and assume the risks and burdens associated with luxury and its dangers. When a man with a large roll representing what some would call "withheld wages," or perhaps the profits of a child-labor cotton factory, walks into a princely hostelry or boards a private yacht, the envious poor do not realize the sublime moral daring and spirit of sacrifice displayed. Just as stallions among bands of wild horses on the plains prance majestically back and forth, keeping off wolves from the more defenseless equines, so there are superb champions in society who go where the menace of luxury is greatest and fend the multitude from the demoralization which would result from living wages. Those who think they suffer from not having enough to live on do not appreciate such service. But if a doctor risked his life by exposing himself to smallpox out of regard for the general welfare, he would be heralded as brave and vicarious.

Centralized and monopolized wealth conduces, also, to a non-materialistic—shall I say *spiritual?*—viewpoint. The possession of property attaches the mind to property. But if one has no property his mind cannot be thus attached, surely not to his own property. Hence centralized ownership, though materializing and grave for the plutocrat, frees others from any temptation to be unduly engrossed in things owned. Thus a lofty, anticipational frame of mind which shades over into refined and etherialized longing and sweetness is established among the expropriated. Bold, crass materialism would cloud society were it not for the spiritualizing effects of the vicarious function of those who risk the inability to get through the eye of the needle on account of the camel's hump, enlarged by bales of worldly goods and securities. It is evident that one carrying little baggage can get through a smaller passageway than a party with loads of stuff. Bear in mind that the straight and narrow way is just what it is said to be— narrow. The poor, therefore, are better prepared for going to a Far Land.

VARIETY

To do away with extremes of wealth would result in sameness. As it is now, there is variety. There are editions *de luxe* and paperbound copies on cheap paper, the "movies"? and grand opera. Palatial residences and sumptuous living add not a little to the spectacular, which the poor enjoy so much to witness. What would our cities be without show places to contrast with the tenements? One has a distinct feeling of relief in leaving the squalid sections of a city and returning to the residence district. The emotions are aroused and sensations are possible where contrasts exist. A food riot is picturesque. Would you have every automobile a Ford? There is much of the theatrical where money is flush, and people not favored with this world's goods benefit by being enabled to catch glimpses of high life. Even a cat may look at a king. If the poor were confronted with a charge for every observation of splendor, they would realize hew much they are now getting for nothing.

Our industrial or manufacturing system and the whole fabric of commercial practice rest upon economic differences, with poverty as a basis. For example, there would be waste if discarded woolens were not ground up into shoddy and made into cheaper kinds of clothing. How could there be a market for shoddy if everybody could buy good cloth? There are grades of flour. Poor people use up the poor flour—or it is sent to the Japanese, but the Japs are getting wise. Every factory turns out different grades of goods, and of course there must be grades of buyers or the goods would not sell.

Even nature itself seems to behave as if there would always be poor people. Growing things differ in quality. Think of the natural differences in wool, beef, potatoes, lumber, and in the flavors of fruits and vegetables. Carp is not so good to eat as lake trout, and the fur of a rabbit cannot be compared to that from a seal. Apples have to be graded; and the good ones are sold to people who can pay for them, while other people take the culls or go without. That is nature's way.

In fact, there would be no way of using up some of the things on the market if need did not actually compel their use. Moldy foods would go begging and rents for dwellings on land subject to river overflow would drop to nothing. And, on the other hand, with the reduction of superior incomes a good many places could not be kept up, and servants would be dismissed by the thousand. It is clear that conditions are right as they are.

INDEPENDENCE

The anti-poverty propaganda will do well if it can defend itself from having increased a lack of respect for authority and social position—a lack which may be seen all about us. We are supposed to know how a beggar on horseback would act; well, if a beggar thinks he is going to have a chance to ride, he does not act the same as before. And that is just it—all sorts of people are being encouraged to expect things, and respectfulness is at a discount. Think of the insolence of the I.W.W. in daring to organize the unskilled laborers in the face of all the commercial and manufacturing and farmers' organizations. Social unrest results from talking about improving conditions. True, it also results from not talking about improving conditions, but is it not better to have the unrest from not talking? Those who talk and write simply stir up more unrest than would probably exist if no encouragement to those in poverty were held out. Anyhow there has been a decline in respect for position. Of course, the good old days are gone. Even the peasant could scarcely be expected any longer to apologize to the knight if the knight's horse stepped on the son of the soil. But the change from old-time deference to those higher up is going on too fast as it is, let alone the change threatened by the elevation of the lower classes.

How are persons kept in their places anyhow? By looking into this matter carefully we may see the dangers in abolishing economic restrictions. It is by wages and salaries paid by economic superiors that impertinence is prevented. The employee who objects may be fired, and he knows it. The corporation has the employee dangling at the end of a thread, with the shears near enough to inspire respect. Talk with any of the representatives of the great industrial concerns and hear them stand up for the system. Unless you get them into a corner where nobody can overhear, you may think they no longer think as they used to in college. They show a marked respect—marked with the dollar sign.

Free speech and a free press would be terrible if really free. It is well enough to play they are free, but who would want to live in a place where editors were not on a salary and ordinary persons were not kept in restraint by job fear? There would be an upheaval in society the like of which has never occurred. Enough radicalism has been let loose by the secret ballot, which is not to be compared, from a conservative standpoint, to the system which allows the employer to look over the shoulder of the employee when he marks a ballot, as is done in Germany. They know better how to do things in Europe.

The advantages of a salary brake on freedom of expression are seen in university circles. If professors were economically independent, they would secure academic freedom and stir up discussion and become agitators; thus many wealthy men would be less inclined to give buildings, libraries, stadia, etc., to universities and colleges, and the cause of higher education would languish.

A charming example of real graciousness and deference, such as could appear only under the usual economic conditions, was afforded in a western state. An elderly millionaire, deaf as a post and as uninteresting as yesterday's newspaper, was invited to college after college to give talks and to become acquainted with the college presidents. They made a great to-do over him, and it was not surprising after such distinction that he left sums to several institutions.

PRIVACY OF INCOMES

To do away with poverty would involve some sort of attack on people who have a great deal of money. It would be impossible to raise all to the income level of those enjoying the highest incomes, so the piling up of wealth would invite attack. The poor would be made to share in the accumulation of the rich, the poor coming to have more and the rich and privileged being allowed less.

Aside from the unpleasant impression which such procedure would produce in some quarters, there is the insuperable objection of a violation of privacy, for agents would be prying into incomes and knowing about them. The delicate consideration now allowed under the law, the secrecy which now shields income-tax payers, who are persecuted for the support of public institutions, would no longer be guaranteed, and people generally would know how one gets his money and how much he has. This would be unconstitutional. Everyone would have to tell how much he had and where he got it. Now, while this would be permissible in some cases, it would not in all. It is proper enough to know how much people of small means have, and how much salary one receives who is employed by the government. But people of large means often like real privacy in their affairs. If an employer had to tell how much his profits were, his employees might revolt and make trouble. There surely would not be very much peace in society if the facts about incomes were freely brought to light.

It is far better that things should remain as they are— poverty and all—than that the privacy of those who happen to have interesting sources of income should be disturbed. Such intrusion could not be popular with all classes. It would be wrong.

PRODUCTION NOT A BASIS OF REWARD

Boil down the views of social critics and you find the idea of compensation according to labor. Production, they say, should be the basis for the size of income received. The answer to this kind of talk is easy. How much anyone actually produces today cannot exactly be determined, and so incomes cannot be based on labor. It is like trying to prove which is more necessary, the spark plugs or the wheels of a touring car. As a matter of fact, all these parts are necessary, and the car stops if any one of a good many different parts goes wrong. Which is more necessary, a lamp or a match with which to light it? One cannot apportion the importance of such things.

A factory employs hundreds of men, all of whom are

necessary, and turns out a single product, say linoleum, which sells at so much a yard. How can one tell how much each person has done to produce the output? The work of all is necessary to produce the linoleum. No one can state in dollars just how much each has contributed. So how could people be paid according to what they produce?

The people of the whole country go about their work, and the result is an aggregate social production, from a real, if not formal, co-operation. The rancher raises sheep, and the wool goes to the mills and pelts to the factory—where "'shammy'" is manufactured, perhaps—and mutton goes to the packing-house. Everybody who has anything to do with sheep has contributed to the value of woolen goods or anything made of sheepskin. The woman in a calico dress who cooked breakfast for the men who sheared the sheep is a factor in the final selling price of the finest suit that ever went out of a fashionable shop. But how can each contribution of labor be weighed and each person remunerated according to what he does? Impossible.

The practical way to divide up is for each person to take all he can get. The woman in calico may not get a penny where the jobber gets hundreds of dollars, but that is the way of the world, and it must be so. While all the parties concerned co-operate to produce the suit of clothes, there seems to be no way of co-operating for the division of the wealth produced; they just have to fight for it, and those who do not fight, who are perhaps too busy producing to fight, simply have to have less. Suppose one person seems to get a hundred times as much as he produces, and another gets one one-hundredth of what he produces, what are you going to do about it? As was said before, it is not the ability to produce, but the ability to acquire, that counts.

A fault in common speech has much to do with wrong ideas on distribution. We say that this man or that man has made so much money. Someone, we say, has made a million. This use of language causes people to think of production and income as related, and furnishes an argument for cranks who want individual production to be the basis of individual income. How much better it would be if we would only get into the habit of saying take instead of make? We should say this man or that man has taken so much money— not say made it. Perhaps the operatives or the miners or the farmers made the money, but another gets it. So why do we not say so? A fisherman takes a fish, he does not make a fish. Nature, the working people, the salaried managers, and public demand make value, but a stockholder may take 300 per cent a year. There is a difference between making money and taking it, and the advantage is all with the man who takes. With a slight improvement in our use of words the facts would be brought out more clearly, and the ill-advised notion of distribution according to labor or services would meet with less favor.

UNEARNED INCREMENT

One cannot look into the origin of great fortunes, or of small ones either, for that matter, without being impressed with the importance of being an early bird. Promptness and punctuality are virtues that have always been held up for imitation. Nowhere can be found better arguments for these qualities than in the case of unearned increment. The importance of being born at the right time and place is unmistakable when one sees how the ownership of mines, forests, lands, rights of way, and of the sites of great cities has been determined by priority.

There was a time when water-power sites, oil lands, and corner lots could be had for a song. With the growth of population these natural monopolies become more and more valuable. There are spots of land in New York City, none too large for a chicken coop of colonial times, that now afford a rental income sufficient to support many families in idleness and luxury, and unless the followers of Henry George have their way, such tracts will continue to give their owners, without effort, income as long as the world stands. It is the same with coal mines. Those who are fortunate enough to get hold of the coal mines find their output becoming more valuable every year. People must keep warm, and they have to come to the mine-owner.

The attempt to discredit the income derived from unearned increment is not likely to succeed. In the first place, this way of acquiring wealth is ancient and people are used to it. Those who might have their attention called to how unearned increment lowers the flow of income to those not its beneficiaries are sure to be impressed with the antiquity of the process. Families in possession of great estates of land, and railroads with their land grants, alike are known to have long profited by this economic advantage.

The economic principle of basing income upon what one owns instead of service rendered is as fully upheld by unearned increment as by interest. Do away with unearned increment and you would destroy a strong barrier now standing in the way of an out-and-out labor basis for incomes. Indeed, without unearned increment to throw up fortunes for the few, it is possible that interest would tend to disappear, for the interest-taking system rests upon the disproportionate possession of wealth. If everybody had money and tried to live upon interest without labor, everybody would starve. The interest system cannot be maintained unless some have money and others do not.

There are surely enough reasons to oppose the taking over of unearned increment by the state on the theory that it is a form of wealth produced by society and not by the individual. It would be an experiment to take this over for the state. Perhaps the strongest argument, however, for leaving things as they are, is that not one of us would have been the person to refuse the ownership that later would have afforded unearned increment. We would have been first if we could, and if not ourselves but someone else bought Manhattan Island of the Indians for $24, whose fault is it but our own?

INTEREST

Interest plays a part in the distribution of wealth—a very large part. Long ago the acceptance of interest was thought to be morally wrong. Money could not breed more money, it was said, so it was regarded as wrong to take interest. The Jews thought the receipt of interest a sin—this was in Bible times. People now have made up with interest, and money-lenders take as high rates as they can get. Nobody, except the doctrinaire, questions interest as an institution, and its relation to poverty scarcely attracts any attention.

The real reason for paying interest is that one cannot borrow money unless he does pay interest. If a farmer needs a plow and does not have the money to buy one, he has to borrow it and pay interest. When he works with the plow and gets a crop, part of the crop belongs to the man who lent the money with which to buy the plow. The money-lender and the farmer unite to raise a crop; the farmer does the work and the other man lends the money.

Interest, says an authority, is a reward paid to ownership. If a man owns a dollar, he gets six cents reward for ownership. The reward is for the ownership, not for the way the dollar was gained. A man who had stolen a dollar or a million would get just as much interest as anyone else, for it is not practicable to place the reward upon how ownership came to be. So the reward goes to ownership.

Another way to understand interest is to think of it as a reward of abstinence. Some economists say this is so. The owner of a million dollars might, if not abstemious, use up all his money. If he abstains from spending, he gets his reward in the form of a certain percentage. But another man who does not inherit money or get it in some way, so he can become abstemious too, is made to pay the reward of the man who has wealth. The justice of this will be seen only after reflection.

People who think that labor only rather than ownership should be rewarded often take it upon themselves to say things against interest. They can be answered very briefly. Indeed, the best way to answer is briefly.

Tools are necessary with which to labor. One cannot produce things with his bare hands. There has to be capital to furnish a condition of production. Now, either there must be private capitalists, who for interest furnish tools to labor, or the state would have to be the capitalist. Interest could be abolished only by making the state the capitalist. There is one important objection to having the state the capitalist: people who live upon interest could no longer do so. Labor would be the only basis of income. This would be a condition that not all would look upon with pleasure.

SOCIAL OWNERSHIP

Those who propose social ownership surely do so in the full light of the fact that it means an undermining of the opportunities for accumulating great private fortunes. There is scarcely a business that has such possibilities of income as the transportation system. It is no small privilege—that of owning and operating for private profit the railroads of the grandest and one of the largest nations on earth. Whether such opportunities for private wealth should be taken away from those who now enjoy them is indeed a serious question. Certainly the owners of the roads and their attorneys are not likely to favor government, ownership. It is the same with "public" utilities of other kinds, that is, those businesses that are public in extent and private in results. Municipal ownership is just as objectionable as state or federal ownership, and for like reasons.

There is danger in attempting social ownership, for where it is attempted it succeeds. Up to 1900 only one city out of thirteen that took over public utilities, such as electric-lighting systems, returned to private ownership, and where municipal ownership was a failure it was because the city government was a failure, owing usually to the ward system. With efficient city administration municipal ownership is permanent. If inefficient city government could with certainty be counted on, there would be less occasion to view with alarm the social ownership movement. But city government is becoming efficient. So it is unwise to rely upon the inefficiency of city government as the best argument for opposing municipal ownership.

The arguments against social ownership must be of a different kind. Its advocates must be made to know how strongly some feel upon the subject. If social ownership had been entered upon long ago, when the owners of public utilities managed them themselves, the evils would have been fewer. But today there are heavy stockholders who do not know the difference between a coupling pin and the Morse code, who are entirely out of touch with the work, which is left to people on salaries. Employees and superintendents do the work in connection with public utilities, while the real owners are often far removed from the scene of operations and would be out of their element doing the actual work.

It would thus be a great hardship to deprive of ownership a class of people who have long since become rusty as producers. They have come to rely upon profits, and the idea that public utilities should be run solely in the interest of the public is about as distasteful as it well could be. Deprived of an assured income from public utilities—as assured as taxes are to the government—the present owners of our telegraph lines, express companies, railroads, mines, electric and gas plants, and street-car lines might be lost in the mass of those who work for pay. Our most distinguished leisure class would have the props knocked out from beneath it. Europe would notice the difference at once, for, except in war time, one of our largest exports is leisure.

Social ownership would give the state or city great funds to be spent for public welfare. At first glance this might seem desirable. Think again. With private ownership great funds are accumulated, and to some extent disbursed by public utility multimillionaires for the public good. Gifts to universities are an example of the way the public gets back some of what monopolists take in the form of profits. There is scarcely a university or college in the country without a library, auditorium, chemistry laboratory, swimming-pool, girls' dormitory, or Y.M.C.A. building given by a generous patron. One feels the influence of these benefactions the moment one sets foot on a campus, for it almost makes one think of a child with an empty cup and a spoon, and its mouth open. Besides universities, all sorts of projects, from hero medals to the eradication of the boll weevil, are financed by donors. Does anyone think that if the government, under social ownership, gained possession of funds comparable to those now going to public-utility owners, there would be such excellent taste in spending the people's money?

PROFITS AND LIVING WAGE

The chief reason why the men who run the business should receive the total production of wealth except wages to the workers is that the former are at a risk. But the laborer, says an eminent professor, contracts himself out of risk and accepts a definite rate of wages. Having contracted for a definite rate of wages, which wages, however, may stop any time—for he does run the risk of being fired—the laborer has no longer a claim upon what he produces.

The risk of the investor is so much greater than the risk of the worker that even if a concern makes a profit of several hundred per cent a year on investment, this profit is justified under the well-known economic doctrine of risk. The worker does not risk any capital, so he has no right to more than a living wage, regardless of production of values. Risk of a kind the worker does undergo, but it is not the right kind. In fact, a good many lives are lost in the various hazardous callings and in callings that are allowed to be hazardous because capital would hardly dare risk itself to change conditions. But, in mining, railroading, dynamite manufacture, and the building of tunnels under rivers the risk of life and limb can scarcely be regarded as so grave as the peril to dollars, so in the final division of values the workman is sufficiently rewarded by a living wage. Even a steeple jack employed to fix up the smokestack of a flour mill does not run any risk comparable to that which the owners run in undergoing the possibility that the steeple jack may fall two hundred feet and damage a shed.

The statement of the doctrine of economic risk found in the works of the most consistent conservatives will prove interesting both to those who approve and to those who disapprove the theory.

One will get a clearer view of the riskless nature of the wage-earner's relation to the business in which he is employed if one will dissociate the worker from his family. It merely confuses the issue and tends to discredit traditional economics to bring the worker's family into the account. It may be that his family does run some risk of being thrown into the street if the wages stop, but what has that to do with economics? That is a side issue, just as the risk of starvation or the bread line for the unmarried workman when thrown out of employment is a side issue. The contract is the thing, and the workman contracts himself out of risk when he bargains for a definite rate of wages. One should try to look upon the workman, then, as having reached enviable freedom from risk.

We do not need to go further to find why the employer should take the surplus of production above the living wage. Risk is the explanation. A living wage is all that the workingman should expect, for he risks no capital, only himself and family.

UNEMPLOYMENT

Usually there are numbers unemployed. About a_ million workers were out of employment in this country prior to the present war. After the war—if it ends—it is expected that many will be unemployed. The late Mr. J. J. Hill said that after the war the question for the workingman would not be one of wages, but of securing work at any wages; and Senator Borah of Idaho predicts the greatest amount of unemployment ever known, when the war closes. Whether these predictions come true or not, we know that always a great many people are supposed to be looking for work, with applicants outnumbering jobs. This is the condition in normal times—and there are those who object to it.

Before jumping to the conclusion that unemployment is an evil and before joining the social reformers, we may well investigate the advantages of the present system.

Unemployment causes one to look with great respect upon a chance to work; of course, it is to be understood that only those out of work and out of money are meant. If a man has enough to live on without work, he does not look upon work with more respect, rather less. But, out of money, the only way to get more money, usually, is to work for it; thus the job looks attractive, and the masses come to identify work with existence and to respect it and to eulogize it accordingly.

Then, too, when the job becomes thus attractive to

the moneyless, there is not so likely to be quibbling about doing more than one is paid for. One of the oldest maxims of service is that the laborer should do more than he is paid for—throw in something beyond exact measure, just as a grocer might add two or three eggs to a dozen or a bank cashier slip out a few coins in addition to what a check calls for. The worker is not to watch the clock, but is to let the hands go past the hour, and think nothing of it. The ethics of good service calls for this sort of thing, and employers have always pressed the point, and it is universally known. But if there were only two men for three jobs instead of three men for two jobs, how could this ideal of good measure be held up as it ought to be?

This is only one evil that would come from not having a crowd around the entrance whenever a man is advertised for. Consider how wages would be affected without a surplus in the labor market. Wages would go up. Then prices on articles bought by laborers would have to be put up too or workingmen would be saving money, which would result in overthrowing the present order. To be sure, prices could be put up at equal pace with wages, but what a bother. The present way is better—let unemployment serve as a check on wages.

There is still another way in which to look at unemployment— it distributes leisure. The upper classes cannot consistently be reproached with being the only people of leisure so long as unemployment is common. Unemployment makes sure of leisure for the working people; they become, in effect, a leisure class and therefore should not feel quite the same upon the subject of the leisure of the upper classes.

EXPORTS

In times of peace a billion dollars worth or more of goods is exported every year in excess of the value of imports. How does this happen? This surplus is what we produce and do not use up. If wages paid to the workers were so large that they could buy a billion dollars worth more of goods, they would do it. Then there would be no surplus to export. All the ships would do then would be to exchange goods of the same value produced in different climates or made differently. Our immense trade balance would vanish, destroyed by higher wages. Is it not better to pay low wages and have millions and billions of wealth to export than to pay wages that would enable the home market to consume goods equal in value to all produced in this country? How should we feel as a nation if our trade balance went down? The wage-earners, too, ought to be satisfied with this arrangement—if they are patriotic. They surely would rather have our exports exceed imports than have higher wages. We do them an injustice in dreaming that they prefer income to patriotism. Everybody is supposed to sacrifice for his country, and by keeping the consuming power of factory hands down by means of low wages there is something left for export, the wage-earners thereby being patriotic.

Of course money comes back for the exports, and one might think that the home market would be correspondingly increased. Yes, but the money comes back to a limited class who either keep it or travel abroad and spend it there. The spending of immense sums abroad by tourists and families who draw their support from this country takes up much of the wealth produced by wage-earners in excess of their wages. Thus the system balances nicely.

THE TARIFF

Some look upon the tariff as a bad habit, but there must be something to be said for it or it would be discarded, although not every bad habit is thrown off.

The tariff is a political invention ranking in importance with great mechanical inventions. The tariff is no less a work of inventive genius than the steam engine. It is an invention which enables the government to raise money painlessly. Tell a man of small income that he must pay a hundred dollars to the government, and he becomes an anarchist; take it out of his pockets by indirect taxation, and none is more patriotic.

The wonderful nature of the tariff is not fully realized by viewing it simply as a means of raising money painlessly for the government. It is in another connection that the tariff shows evidence of the inspiration of true genius. The greatest service of the tariff is, not to raise money for the government, but to raise prices all around. If there is a duty of 50 per cent on something, imports of that something are discouraged, and the government may receive little income or none from this source, but the price received by the home manufacturer will be about 50 per cent higher. For the millions of dollars received by the government from the tariff, manufacturers and dealers within the country—behind the tariff wall— receive billions and billions more. Professor Summer of Yale estimated that the tariff raised prices all around from 30 to 40 per cent. This would mean that a man with an income of $1,400 would have to pay it all or nearly all for goods that without a tariff he could buy for $1,000. Such a man would pay about $400 a year to the tariff—a considerable tax—but as he does not know that he is paying it, unless he stops to think, he does not object.

The worker is not likely to object because he is told that he receives higher wages on account of the protection which his employer has at the hands of the government, and it is true that the worker must receive wages high enough to enable him to pay the higher prices caused by the tariff and to keep alive—when employed. The worker is not supposed to receive wages high enough to enable him to save, so he is on the same basis as workmen in other countries. They all get a little less than enough to live on, but there is a satisfaction felt by the worker under the tariff; he handles larger sums of money.

Aside from the advantages of the tariff to ordinary people, as indicated, there are strong advantages to the wealthy. Many great fortunes have been built on the tariff. The government really lends its taxing power to manufacturers, and they are therefore appreciative and patriotic. No class is more loyal to the government under a high tariff than the manufacturing class. One could not consistently oppose the tariff without joining forces with those who object to swollen fortunes and the persistence of poverty. Attack the tariff, and be counted among those who do not favor inequalities in economic status.

Let us go back to the man of the 1,400-dollar income. If tariff prices did not sweep away the difference between $1,000 and $1,400, he would perhaps save $400 and gradually become "independent," and what that would mean is explained elsewhere in these pages.

The government, too, would be much handicapped without the tariff to raise revenue. A tax would have to be called a tax, and how unpopular that is may be judged by the way the best people have always side-stepped taxes and left the small fry to pay them. The Supreme Court has felt strongly about taxes on incomes. The government would be put to it to get money if the tariff were abolished. There would be no way left but to go after wealth or to have government ownership and use the profits; and it is against the rules for the government to own and operate anything that makes money. Private enterprise always does the things that make money, and the government does the other things.

TENANCY

The alleged facts about the increase of tenancy in this country are no doubt correct enough. Let us agree that the census is right and that tenancy is increasing at a rapid rate—that farms are being worked more and more by families who do not own the farms. Agree that the tenants are a poor class, in debt up to their ears for mules, groceries, seed, implements, fence wire, and the doctor, and that the children often do not know what a schoolhouse is.

There are deplorable facts about tenancy. But it is not fair to look merely at one side of the matter. There is another way to look at it. There surely must be some way of looking at tenancy so that the non-resident landowner will feel justified and politicians be untroubled in conscience. Nothing is more uncomfortable than to have a feeling that one is taking advantage of another. This is especially true if little children and their mothers are involved. It would pain the conscience to realize that one was reaping where one had not sowed and was gathering what belonged to another. People may pooh at ethical considerations and may ridicule psychology, but what good is an investment if one does not sleep? One must try to see how justifiable the tenancy system is, together with the loan system associated with rural poverty.

The best approach is to see the resemblance between what is happening to the small farm owner and what has happened to the small shop owner. Years and years ago such people as now work in factories were often independent producers. Then came organized industry, with capital, and swept them out of ownership and into jobs. It was uncomfortable, no doubt, for men who had been engaged in manufacturing in a small way at home or in little shops, to be put out of business, with the children and grandchildren taking such employment as could be had in factory towns. But it had to be, and we now have our industrial system.

The modern industrial system has been a moneymaker and there is coming to be a great surplus for investment. Some of this surplus is being invested in farms and lands, great private estates and heavily financed farming projects appearing. After a while a great many farmers, first becoming tenants, and later—they or their descendants—employees, will be in the same economic class with present factory employees. The farm workman, like the factory workman, will not own the business, and he will take orders. There will always be a fringe of farmers who work their own farms, but the factory type of estate will dominate in agricultural production, unless signs fail. Such being the case, why be concerned about tenancy? The country population will correspond in status with the factory population, in proportion of employees to owners, living conditions, etc.

It follows that no one can consistently oppose the coming of a system of centralized ownership of land and of tenancy unless he is prepared to attack its analogue, the factory system, which has magnates and employees. We must expect a large part of the present farming class to become employees and be under superintendents. Thus agriculture and manufacturing will be on the same basis, and agriculture will no longer be out of harmony with our industrial labor system, so much identified with our type of civilization.

Will There Be An Age of Social Invention?

FIRST PUBLISHED IN 1932
IN *THE SCIENTIFIC MONTHLY*
VOL. XXXV, No. 4, October, 1932

TWO HUNDRED years ago the question might have been asked if there was a future for mechanical invention; then probably no one saw a great field ahead for new mechanisms. At one time, even, in the history of the United States patent office its director proposed its closing on the ground that all the inventions possible had been made. But the field for mechanical invention proved wide, and for that matter probably is still boundless. Edison took out over 1,300 patents, which means that he saw at least over 1,300 mechanical situations that might be improved. The field of mechanical invention has been and will remain wide, for imagination plus irritability goes far. Scarcely a physical situation exists anywhere that is not a challenge to ingenuity for improvement. As people become discriminating, the number of mechanical situations that get on their nerves increases. The response is— better cars, better heating, better highways, better elevators, better footwear, better typewriters.

Just as there has been a field for mechanical invention, so is there a field for social invention? Just as invention flowed out of perception of mechanical deficiency, so will invention flow from perception of deficiency in social relations? Just as a mechanical way was invented by which the farmer escaped the discomfort of cutting grain by hand, so, for example, will a social way be invented to dispose of the operation of cars by drunken drivers? Just as a way has been found for keeping the physical bodies of flies from getting into our soup, so some day shall a social invention, analogous to a fly screen, protect us from "drives"? No end of social invention, perhaps, once the attitude of attack on long-suffered nuisances and unpleasant time-honored ways is avowed.

But in contrast with social invention, mechanical invention has achieved prestige. People who clung to antiquated social concepts loosened up in favor of, say, fly screens. The astonishing assertiveness of the early steam engine somehow captivated the crude senses of the times and won for Watt a hearing that Mrs. Sanger has not yet secured. Many mechanical inventions, such as windmills, tractors and wrist watches, have psychologically been toys for adults and as such have had an entrée denied to Clarence Darrow in Tennessee. Eventually the public was won over to the idea of mechanical progress, having reformed entirely of its throwing of its Roger Bacons into prison or of guffawing crudely at its Fords and Langleys. Resistance to mechanical improvements as such has reached the vanishing point. The descendants of a stock that fought the use of umbrellas as impious and resisted the use of steel plows as poisonous to the soil now stand in line to see the new models of sixes and eights, and tell the hardware clerk where this tool and that device might be improved.

The mechanical progress concept was "sold" relatively early to the general public. The "talking point" in mechanical contrivances is now that of a new feature; while the "talking point" of a social relation is that of an old feature. Actual social invention is miles behind mechanical advance.

With social invention miles in the rear, what chance is there that it will ever catch up? May we look for two centuries of social invention as striking as the mechanical progress of the two centuries next last past? Are we reaching a stage where we shall no longer, as has been done within living memory, throw into jail persons of socially inventive type? Shall we soon cease to line the fences, after a manner of speaking, to roar and simianize over the faults of new mechanisms of the social grain field and highway? Shall we soon see the day when the social inventor is not hurried towards the Siberia of disgraced joblessness, or breathless from flight from the guardians of free speech in our cities? In fine, shall we soon reach the state of tolerance for social invention that was reached for mechanical invention as the industrial revolution proceeded?

Some there may be who would deny the possibility that in number and utility social inventions can ever parallel the mechanical inventions of the past two centuries. With any such I would disagree. I believe that for every one of the great mechanical inventions of the past two centuries. With any such I would disagree. I believe that for every one of the great mechanical inventions there is the possibility of an equally ingenious and great social invention, and that for every one of Mr. Edison's 1,300 inventions there is possible an invention of the social type for the betterment of social relations and affairs. Bear in mind that social invention is still penalized, and that to cultivate a sense of conquest rather than to submit in patience is still unorthodox and revolutionary. With the shackles off social invention there would be no good reason to suppose that inventiveness would be less fertile for social progress than mechanical invention has been for mechanical advance. We have never yet hit our stride in social invention; never fulfilled the conditions, which are: a cultivated perception of undesirable conditions— a problem consciousness— and a sanctioned attach by logical imagination.

A writer[1] gives this list of some of the great inventions of the industrial revolution:

Reverberatory furnace
Galvanic batter
Paper-making machine
Screw propeller
First commercially
    successful steamboat
Stethoscope
Milling-machine
Water turbine
Electromagnet
Locomotive perfected
Dynamo
Reaper
Electric telegraph
Revolver
Electric motor
Revolver
Electrotype photography
Steam hammer
Turret-lathe
Sewing machine
Rotary press
Electric locomotive
Machine gun
Bessemer steel
Dynamite

Telephone
Gas engine (four cycle)
Phonograph
Incandescent lamp
Steam turbine
Linotype
First safety bicycle
Aluminum process
Kodak
Trolley car
Recording adding
    machine
Motion picture machine
By-product coke oven
X-rays
Radioactivity
Wireless telegraphy
    (high frequency)
Airplane
Diesel engine
High-speed steel
Airship
Tungsten filament light
Television
Electric steel furnace

Good wine needs no bush, and these great invention

---

[1] Stuart Chase, in "Men and Machines."

need no broadcast. They with a host of others have made over the mechanical aspects of human existence. They are part of the record of human affairs. Can any such list be essentially duplicated by social inventions of the future?

Social invention will affect law, regulations, constitutions, government, the distribution of wealth, administrative facilities, education, mental hygiene, economics, finance, penology, employment, international relations, courts. It will develop better techniques and connote vastly more intelligent operations on the social plane.

To state coming social inventions were to invent out of a hand. Not much more can be attempted than to point to social disharmonies which in the nature of things should inspire the social inventor; and as to discover need is the beginning of invention it must be that none of us to-day can be capable even of indicating adequately the range of the objectives that will engage the energies of the Edisons of social invention of the future. The spell of custom is so strong that we but faintly perceive the rectifications that might be made. We little dream of the gamut of laudable change possible in human relations. To-day we are in social outlook like the child born with a visual defect who assumes that distorted vision is normal. Thus there are those who say that war is inevitable because of the nature of human nature, and who in saying this are like those who knew that a boat could not be made to buck the current of the Hudson. In fact, the whole outlook toward social change and betterment strongly resembles the stodgy defiance of mechanical science centuries ago. Hence we know little of what lies in the sphere of social invention. But even with the low visibility of the field it is possible to point out a few objectives of social inventions which should compare not insignificantly with the major inventions of the industrial revolution.

Below are given some catchwords of social invention,

these terms serving merely to focus attention on aspects of current affairs from which ingenuity might make a running start with prospect of superseding older practice, introducing refinements of design, or of projecting the larger engines and leverages of social reconstitution. The terms given will mean much or little according to the imagination of the reader. Thus, rotation of occupation might be conceived as alternating the roles of sedentary bookkeeper and of traveling salesman month by month, or of scheduling rotations that would involve recurrent geographical change on the part of whole sections of population. The term is given, bare, and its connotation, reader, is left to you.

Over against, then, the mechanical inventions of the galvanic battery, paper-making machine, screw propeller, stethoscope, steam hammer, Diesel engine, etcetera, are social inventions relative to:

Tax system
Jury trial
Wearing apparel
League of Nations
Traveling libraries
Accident prevention
Capitalistic system
Medicine
Graft
Legal service
Weights and measures
Value of the dollar
War
Minorities
International language
Distribution of wealth
Noise
Health

Fundamentalism
Law schools
New wants
International trade
Alumni
Crime prevention
Poverty
Political platforms
Racial accord
Court procedure
The work of assessors
Investment
Waste of metals
Overcrowded
    professions
The "funnies"
Rackets
Simple life

Motivation of production
Disarmament
Idle time
Worry
Personal insulation
Duplication
Advertising
Tariff
Cities
Wild life
Jobs
Discovery of law breakers
Regulation of production
    to need
Moral code

Pedestrianism
Liquor control
Form of government
Red tape
Automatic referenda
Judgment test for voters
Education
Rumor damper and lie
    sterilizer
Conservatism
Rotation of occupation
Travel
Community buying and
    use
History

Along with inventions of which the above tangential terms are but obscurely suggestive, there should be a social invention to prevent interference with the work of social invention, interference by which the uninformed may harass and bedevil the man of original mind. In mechanical invention we have reached a stage where it would simply be malicious mischief to break up the model or smash the shop of a man working on a new mechanical device. And while the trick of buying mechanical inventions and burying them is not unknown, it is not regarded with favor by impartial critics. But on the whole the mechanical inventor goes ahead freely whether in Tennessee or elsewhere, with no legislature to bother him, no pulpit to rail, no policeman as mentor. Such freedom should the social inventor have, or be cramped in style. Unfortunately, the person with socially inventive ideas may now find himself as the early scientists and mechanical inventors found themselves-much disliked. All that needs to be changed, and with change would issue a flood of ingenuity from which, by a selective process, would come the big and little machines of social advance. The social inventor, otherwise thinker, or "radical," should be given a chance comparable to that enjoyed by the esteemed James Watt but denied the estimable Roger Bacon. We are now old in mechanics but primitives in social invention.

By this time the reader is perhaps experiencing a growing sense of difference between mechanical and social invention, and is becoming disposed to question the whole analogy. He sees that mechanical inventions concern things, while social invention involves people; but at a stage the two are alike— the stage of subjective creation. It is true that as soon as a mechanical invention is put to work, people are immediately and surely affected, and perhaps in large numbers. It will furthermore be observed that whereas the mechanical inventor has freedom of experimentation, the social inventor has no such freedom; he even finds that to style a political step experimental is to stigmatize it; experimentation has a status for mechanical invention, and quite another for social invention. Social invention is moreover denied an immediacy of fruition, unlike the mechanical, in that so many, especially voters, must be won over to the new thing before it can be set in motion under the laws. Inertia and ignorance in tracts of the public mind have to be overcome by the social innovation, while it is no bar to the initiation of mechanical improvements that the far-flung electorate is unready for change. The few who are at first interested in a new machine may choose to use it, which they are at liberty to do, and without taking a popular vote on the principles of its construction.

Admitting, even parading, the differences between mechanical and social invention, yet one may insist on certain likenesses. The act of invention is the same in either case; the man who thinks out an economy of municipal administration or a basic plan like that of Henry George is an inventor, in class with "inventor." He has envisaged a difficulty and mentally surmounted it, through creative imagination.

As to need of social inventions— new ways, techniques, procedures, laws, arrangements, provisions and planning in education, justice, professions, economics, trade and world affairs, the social inventor is exigently required. The mechanical inventor has given us Chicago, and the lack of the social inventor has given Chicago its city government. The mechanical inventor gave New York City the Empire State Building, and the lack of social ingenuity leaves the city to Tammany. The mechanical inventors give us bombing planes, while Cro-Magnon politicians still chip flints.

Objection may still be raised that the perfection of social and political institutions will involve a degree of social intelligences beyond the possible. If political and social development require any material change in the level of native intelligence, then of course Utopianism is a dream. But does it? It might as well have been argued, prior to the many inventions of the machine age, that human intelligence would fail under the new burden. What happened was that millions learned about machines, which carried the machine age forward some distance, and that the foolproofing of machines carried the machine age forward yet farther. The machine has educated millions in the ways of machines; the automobile age has educated incredible millions to drive at locomotive speed to the tune of seconds and inches on railless roads.

Social inventions will educate their users, as the secret ballot has educated voters. A degree of foolproofing will also be necessary-the making of techniques easy for those who are always simple and for others who are simple in streaks, as able people usually are.

The egregious waste, hostility, vain running about and febrile pantomime, characteristic of the existing world disorder and economic anarchism are comparable to the supine helplessness of man in his physical world but a few centuries ago, which has given way to confidence, sureness, conquest and research staffs associated with manufacturing establishments. The possibilities of social invention are as great as were the mechanical possibilities that lay before the early inventors of machines. The same vaulting intelligence is required for social invention as for invention in any field. Merely adaptation is required to effect on the social plane as large a transformation as was effected on the mechanical level by the science and invention of the past two hundred years.

A Strange Ailment

FIRST PUBLISHED IN 1936
IN *EDUCATION*
VOL. LVI, No. 6, February, 1936

A HINT of a strange affliction lay in a remark early in the year of 1975, by a scientist, Dr. Edison Snyder, addressing a university class. Certain influences, he said, were found to have dire effects upon the language connections of the brain; evidence existed of a factor capable of producing alexia or inability to react to and interpret printed words; the power to read might be undone, and, conceivably, perfect and universal illiteracy might befall. The generation and propagation of this factor were obscure, whether cosmic, psychogenic, or bacterial. To the class the whole thing sounded remote.

But a day came. Sitting on a backless campus slab, presented by misguided alumni, two male seniors, later in the year, conversed. As they arose and reached for their books they became confused, picking up and laying down the volumes.

"I had a blue one," said one of the students, "but my eyes have gone off, I can't read the title."

"That's my situation too," remarked his companion. "Maybe it's too many cigarets, or fumes from wood alcohol; anyhow I can't read the title, nor," he added, "a single word inside. But aside from that I feel all right. Oh, well, I can bluff to commencement."

On another seat, in the shade of lilacs in bloom, a co-ed surreptitiously produced a letter to be read for the third time. To her it was now white paper bearing meaningless markings. "Oh, well, I know what he wrote—and I'll have my eyes examined this very day."

The co-ed stood flipping her Oxford glasses as two elderly professors came by, each deaf in the right ear. They walked, stopped, jockeyed each for a hearing position, gyrated, adroitly pausing and tripping forwards, each trying for the side of the walk which gave ear-advantage; the one who was balked now turned his face well around whenever his companion spoke. Amusing. They talked glasses—"Came

on suddenly—lenses—wrong correction—couldn't get words
in focus. . . ."

At the campus gate, waiting for a taxi, a young man
stood with a suitcase stuck over with labels of foreign
travel—Genoa, Athens, Cairo, Brindisi, Berlin, Addis
Ababa. The case, as it stood, he had bought in a luggage
shop, there disposed of by a returned minister (Methodist).
As the young man gazed, furtively, at his prize, the
glamorous words turned to hieroglyphics on red
backgrounds. He could not read a word.

On a passing bus were two young men, in black
derbies and black sack suits, students for the priesthood with
a touch of the attained exotic, of self-conscious compliance
with a way of life. Evidences of literary burrowings were
about. Suddenly they stared at each other, then whispered
about overstudy, gathering up and putting aside devout essays
and catalogs of church publishing houses, which suddenly
they could not read.

Through bank windows, after hours, were indications
of surprise and disarray; clerks and accountants, stricken with
alexia, would have to call it a day.

On a porch a mother was showing her little daughter
the letters on alphabet blocks. But she stopped, seeing no
longer the letters as letters.

On the street, newsboys shouted the latest edition,
which nobody was buying; they had no idea that everybody
was now blind to print.

Cars broke traffic rules, while officers vainly tried to
take down license numbers they could not make out.
Shamefaced lads made their way back to telegraph offices
with messages undelivered for the sudden illiteracy. Lines
formed at the offices of opticians, oculists, and physicians,
seeking relief from the strange ailment that made print but
marks of no meaning.

That evening families gathered about the radio, only

to find that script readers at the microphone were as if they held only white paper before them.

Whatever else happens, time goes on, and the twenty-first century nears; the year 2000 arrives. An old gentleman, without a watch, is boiling potatoes in a rusty can over a fire among the weeds at the corner of the abandoned campus of a former world-famous university, feeding the blaze with leaves torn from a volume, library shelves supplying neatly piled combustibles. Dr. Snyder—it was he—was kept busy with stirring the potatoes to keep them from sticking and burning on the dented and corroded bottom of the can. Untagged dogs howled from the direction of the ruinous liberal arts building, where the professor slept on shavings. His favorite walk was down the railroad track, now grassed over, lack of timetables having had a quieting effect on transportation. His companion on walks was an unkempt individual who wore the tatters of his uniform of twenty-five years before, that of a postman. The clocklike regularity of the turns of this companion was so grateful to the former scientist that he would throw in an extra potato for the erstwhile letter-carrier, while the two, to break the tedium, of illiteracy, resorted to Chinese chess or arranged beetle races.

On sagged rails, crushing rotten ties, stood the mighty bulk of a rusty, oil-burning locomotive, over which at times curious and unkempt children clambered in ignorance of its history and significance and untouched by the rudiments of the ordered science which had directed its construction and operation and measured its vast efficiency in the era of great railroads. Broken copper wires dangled overhead, while the wreck of a compound microscope, which served as a toy, lay half concealed in the rubbish of old filing cases from a jobbing house. A typewriter key protruded from the sand of the right-of-way like the helpless hand of a soldier buried by the explosion of a mine. The reign of ignorance was supreme.

The university city showed a rundown condition, with banks vacant, law offices deserted, and newsstand shelves gaping and weathered; with measurements, values, debts, titles, ordinances, communications and the symbol base of light, power, trade and government lacking. No prescription had been written nor a bill rendered in twenty-five years. How the rest of the world fared no one knew; society had fallen apart and all but the most primitive relations had vanished.

The younger generation, raucous and wild, regarded the oldsters, all of them, as crazy. Aging men and women tried to tell their descendants of the world prior to the dread year of 1975, of the golden age of print, but could make no headway. Indeed, the young barbarians might be excused for being sceptical, inasmuch as their elders could not illustrate what they were talking about when speaking of word symbols. It was easier to call the old folks crazy than to try to follow their obscure efforts to explain. To be sure, relic locomotives and copper wire, bat-infested bank vaults and junk printing presses, all gave evidence that times had been different, but the conclusion was that in the old days people lived in an eccentric manner not to be compared with the advantages of the later time. Apoplexy carried off some over fifty who tried to describe the rich mod-section of the twentieth century, but as life insurance policies could not be read, being scraps of paper, no insurance was collectible by beneficiaries not sure of their rights.

Stragglers came by from other points, Chicago and New York. As there was no way of indicating office address, the Empire State Building and Rockefeller Center lost tenants; in fact, survivors scurried into the country, back to subsistence farming, for cities are built on the alphabet.

However, oratory flourished. With Congress in permanent recess, due in part to the lapsing of the Congressional Record and the frank, former representatives toured the country making speeches, which, in the absence of written report, could be repeated hundreds of times with whatever liberties gave finish. Only the old could know how scandalously some of the orators lied, but with documentary evidence out, nothing could be done about it. Dr. Snyder did, however, use up a dozen of his oldest eggs firing them at a mountebank who declared the world had never progressed so rapidly as since 1975.

But at all events the ailment cleared away, along with the classics, through their use as fuel, vast accumulations of printed matter,— stale magazines tied up and awaiting Salvation Army trucks, old stocks of books in the warehouses of publishers, great perishable mountains of pulp periodicals, arid acreages of government bulletins, Mt. Everests of law court reports, and bales of income tax instructions. This material kept the home fires burning, and, besides, mice ate and leaky roofs did their bit. Paper disappeared with surprising rapidity and completeness, wrapping paper being spared longest, as it was free from markings and defacement. But literature, fatefully, in all its forms vanished, the only reason for the preservation of printed material was the content, and now, subjectively, there was no content. The literary accumulations of man vanished because of paper-destroying agencies and the convenience of libraries for heating purposes.

With books and volumes of proceedings gone, no one "looked at the record"; there was none. If anyone quoted from memory he was not likely to refer to the author or say he was quoting. As many as fifty different orators were giving Hamlet's Soliloquy and claiming it was original with them. The difficulty of proving a man a liar became insurmountable; pitch black intellectual darkness was just around the corner.

And speaking of corners; the end of the period of universal illiteracy and the beginning of a slow, painful, primitive pick-up of knowledge, a world's infancy begun all over again, the gradual passing off of the strange and appalling alexia, dated from the challenge of an inscription on a cornerstone. To be specific, the name of Andrew Mellon as secretary of treasury, carved in the granite of the cornerstone of a federal post-office building, served by chance as a sort of ferment in the process of retrieving the alphabet. This block of granite in a building in which a letter had not been posted for twenty-five years, witnessed the first vague and faintly successful attempts to grapple anew with word symbols, the start of the human race on its second trek toward science and literature.

Here leave we the mankind of this period, reduced in numbers, ignorant and quarrelsome, vagrants in a decayed environment, poor devils, about to try again the ascent to Parnassus. Recovering from its pathological illiteracy, mankind must begin rediscovery of the lost arts, and most were lost; begin the ten thousand quests for fact and principle whose former but vanished success had characterized the centuries of progress. In one respect man was fortunate— every book on economics was lost. But what a heartbreaking outlook; it would take thousands of years to get back to the world of 1975, which was not the best of all possible worlds but the best of the series; and unless men comparable to former inventors were born at the right time, man might not again roll on rubber tires or speed through the stratosphere. But back in the arms of the alphabet man had a chance, though not a bright one, to reattain the world that existed before alexia wiped out the cultural heritage. Incredible labors and sore fatigue lay ahead, and then—perhaps failure.

Thought of failure, ultimate and sickening, woke the sleeper, who was none other than a retired Chicago school teacher, by payless paydays left with a tendency to nightmare. Just a dream, but one of the worst. It is reported here as possibly being of interest to others of nightmarish tendency, and also as a spiritual pick-me-up for teachers, particularly for those who teach children how to read.

INDEX

THE PSYCHOLOGY OF CITIZENSHIP, p. 11

455

SOCIAL ANTAGONISMS, p. 123

Arland Deyett Weeks (December 13, 1871 - November 13, 1936) was a professor of education, and later dean of education at North Dakota Agricultural College (today North Dakota State University). Though he identified himself as a conservative in some works, he was expressly a believer in all progress being tied to proper public education, and that civic conscience must be shaped by such education. In 1910 he co-founded Fargo's "Commons Club", to discuss current events of public interest. Throughout his career he wrote numerous books and articles on education, fire safety, and most prominently on social psychology and its influence on civics.

Ken Lefebvre is a researcher and historian from Massachusetts. He primarily studies the cultural history of New England, particularly that of the Springfield-Holyoke region, as well as the oft-obscure history of social engineering.

www.ingramcontent.com/pod-product-compliance
Lightning Source LLC
Chambersburg PA
CBHW070858030426
42336CB00014BA/2248